BE ANXIOUS FOR NOTHING

THE ART OF CASTING YOUR CARES AND RESTING IN GOD

Joyce Meyer

NEW YORK   NASHVILLE

FaithWords
Hachette Book Group
1290 Avenue of the Americas, New York, NY 10104
faithwords.com
twitter.com/faithwords
First published in October 2016
This edition: May 2017

FaithWords is a division of Hachette Book Group, Inc. The FaithWords name and logo are trademarks of Hachette Book Group, Inc.

The publisher is not responsible for websites (or their content) that are not owned by the publisher.

The Hachette Speakers Bureau provides a wide range of authors for speaking events. To find out more, go to www.hachettespeakersbureau.com or call (866) 376-6591.

ISBN: 978-1-4555-4247-5

Printed in the United States of America

LSC-C

10   9   8   7   6   5   4   3   2

BE ANXIOUS FOR NOTHING

CONTENTS

Introduction

Be anxious for nothing, but in everything
by prayer and supplication with thanksgiving
let your requests be made known to God.
And the peace of God, which surpasses all
comprehension, shall guard your hearts
and your minds in Christ Jesus.

Philippians 4:6,7 nasb

Humble yourselves, therefore, under the
mighty hand of God; that He may exalt you
at the proper time, casting all your anxiety
upon Him, because He cares for you.

1 Peter 5:6,7 nasb

Peace is to be the normal condition for us as believers in Jesus Christ. But very few of God's people are enjoying that peace as a part of their daily lives.

In His Word, God tells us to be anxious for nothing and to cast our care on Him. Many people are familiar with these Scriptures but don't know how to do what these Scriptures instruct. Sometimes we are so accustomed to responding in a natural way to the circumstances we experience in life as unbelievers around us do, we spend much of our time muddling along in worry or confusion. Instead we could be enjoying the abundant life and peace God has for us!

In my own case I lived in a state of such turmoil for so many years, I didn't realize how abnormal I really was. It was only when I began to study the Word of God and apply it to my life that I began to experience the peace of God.

For a while, when I first began experiencing the peace of God, as strange as it may seem: I was bored! I was used to always being involved in some horrible mess — some big uproar. But now I can't stand to be upset. I don't even like to hurry, I so love, enjoy and appreciate the peace of God that has filled every area of my life. I have peace in my mind, in my emotions — about my family, my ministry — about everything.

In this book we examine the Scriptures which show us how to cast our care, and we look at practical ways of applying these Scriptures to our lives. We also identify specific areas, responses, or habits which allow anxiety to enter our lives, and God-directed, God-empowered actions we can take to stop some unpleasant situations from developing which easily lead to anxiety!

If you are not living in the peace of God, you can live in His peace as a normal condition.

Part 1

Be Anxious for Nothing

1

JESUS AND PEACE

*Peace I leave with you; My [own] peace I now
give and bequeath to you. Not as the world
gives do I give to you....*

JOHN 14:27

Jesus' statement above is worded as though He *willed* us His peace. Jesus left us His peace. This means that living in turmoil, worry, anxiety, fear, and frustration for a believer is abnormal. God doesn't want us to live that way. The Bible shows us how to receive and live in the peace Jesus left for us.

As believers, we have a tremendous amount of God's protection on and around us. (Psalm 91.) God wants to bless us abundantly and is always looking for ways to bless and reach us with His love so that we will be more open to receiving His blessings. (John 10:10, Ephesians 3:20, 2 Chronicles 16:9.)

But our salvation as Christians doesn't guarantee a trouble-free life. We will still encounter problems. Every one of us at different times in our life go through seasons when things don't work out the way we would like. But Jesus, the Prince of Peace (Isaiah 9:6), has overcome the world.

I have told you these things, so that in Me you may have [perfect] peace and confidence. In the world you have tribulation and trials and distress and frustration; but be of good cheer [take courage; be confident, certain, undaunted]! For I have overcome the world. [I have deprived it of power to harm you and have conquered it for you.]

JOHN 16:33

In John 14:1 just before His return to His Father in heaven, Jesus left us with these words:

Do not let your hearts be troubled (distressed, agitated). You believe in and adhere to and trust in and rely on God; believe in and adhere to and trust in and rely also on Me.

The remaining part of John 14:27, partially quoted previously, says:

...Do not let your hearts be troubled, neither let them be afraid. [Stop allowing yourselves to be agitated and disturbed; and do not permit yourselves to be fearful and intimidated and cowardly and unsettled.]

Romans 14:17 tells us that Kingdom living is righteousness, peace, and joy in the Holy Spirit. Luke 17:21 tells us the kingdom of God is within us. We were made righteous, or made in rightstanding with God, when we entered into a personal relationship with Jesus. (2 Corinthians 5:21.) Joy and peace are two of the fruit of the Holy Spirit (Galatians 5:22,23) and are inside those of us who believe in Jesus. They are ready to be released. We enter into the joy and peace of God's kingdom through believing.

JUST BELIEVE

In the passage below we are told the God of hope will fill us with all joy and peace as we believe, so that we may abound and be overflowing — bubbling over — with hope.

May the God of your hope so fill you with all joy and peace in believing [through the experience of your faith] that by the power of the Holy Spirit you may abound and be overflowing (bubbling over) with hope.

ROMANS 15:13

According to the writer of Hebrews, we who truly *believe* may enter into the blessed Sabbath rest of the Lord.

So then, there is still awaiting a full and complete Sabbath-rest reserved for the [true] people of God;

For he who has once entered [God's] rest also has ceased from [the weariness and pain] of human labors, just as God rested from those labors peculiarly His own.

Let us therefore be zealous and exert ourselves and strive diligently to enter that rest [of God, to know and experience it for ourselves], that no one may fall or perish by the same kind of unbelief and disobedience [into which those in the wilderness fell].

HEBREWS 4:9-11

In the Sabbath rest of the Lord we can cease from weariness and the pain of human labor. What is required to enter this rest? A childlike attitude of faith.

We read in Mark 10:15 that Jesus told His disciples: *Truly I tell you, whoever does not receive and accept and welcome the kingdom of God like a little child [does] positively shall not enter it at all.*

A child's faith is simple. A child doesn't try to figure everything out and make a detailed blueprint plan of exactly how his deliverance will come. He simply believes because the parents said they would take care of the problem.

If members of the church have lost the joy of their salvation, sometimes the reason is the basis of their joy has been misplaced.

When Jesus sent out the seventy to minister to the needs of others in His name, they came back rejoicing in their power over demons. But Jesus said to them, ...*do not rejoice at this, that the spirits are subject to you, but rejoice that your names are enrolled in heaven* (Luke 10:20).

Jesus tells us we should rejoice, not because we have power over the demons or circumstances of this life, but because our *names are enrolled in heaven.* Habakkuk 3:18 KJV says, *Yet I will rejoice in the LORD, I will joy in the God of my salvation.* The joy of our salvation comes from the joy of the initial and greatest gift of all — God's love for us as expressed in His Son Christ Jesus.

As believers, our joy and peace are not based in *doing* and *achieving,* but in *believing.* Joy and peace come as a result of building our relationship with the Lord. Psalm 16:11 tells us in His presence is fullness of joy. If we have received Jesus as our Savior and Lord, He, the Prince of Peace lives inside us. (1 John 4:12-15, John 14:23.) We experience peace in the Lord's presence, receiving from Him and acting in response to His direction. Joy and peace come from knowing, believing — trusting in the Lord with simple childlike faith.

2

❦

IT'S OK TO LIGHTEN UP!

Anxiety in a man's heart weighs it down,
but an encouraging word makes it glad.

PROVERBS 12:25

The Bible teaches that anxiety brings a heaviness to a person's life. The dictionary defines *anxiety* as "...a state of uneasiness: worry... Abnormal fear that lacks a specific cause."[1] Sometimes this uneasiness is vague, something that cannot be easily identified. It is fear or dread that has no specific cause or source. I used to be bothered by this kind of anxiety without knowing what it was.

THE "LITTLE FOXES" THAT STEAL YOUR JOY

❦

All the days of the desponding and afflicted are made *evil* [by anxious thoughts and *forebodings*], but he who has a glad heart has a continual feast [regardless of circumstances].

PROVERBS 15:15

I once went through a period in my life when I was plagued by anxiety. I was filled with fear and dread for no particular reason. I kept feeling something terrible was going to happen. Finally I went to the Lord and asked Him what was troubling me. He told me it was "evil forebodings." At the time I didn't even know what that phrase meant or where it came from.

13

Sometime later I came across Proverbs 15:15 in *The Amplified Bible*. I immediately recognized the term the Lord had used when He told me what was bothering me — "evil forebodings."

In those days I was like so many other people. I was looking for some "monster problem" that was keeping me from enjoying life. I was so intense about everything, I was creating problems for myself where none really existed.

Once in a meeting, the Lord told me to speak out something. Apparently someone needed to hear this: "Stop making a big deal out of nothing."

I used to be the type of person who needed to hear direction like that. I could make mountains out of molehills. I had to learn to just let some things go — forget them and go on. Some of us become upset over things that just are not worth becoming upset over — those *little foxes, that spoil the vines* (Song of Solomon 2:15 KJV). If our life consists of becoming upset over one little thing that really doesn't matter after another, we won't have much peace or joy.

As we saw before, Jesus said, *Do not let your hearts be troubled (distressed, agitated)* (John 14:1). *...Do not let your hearts be troubled, neither let them be afraid. [Stop allowing yourselves to be agitated and disturbed; and do not permit yourselves to be fearful and intimidated and cowardly and unsettled.]* (John 14:27).

In other words Jesus was saying, "Stop it!" We can see from this verse that we can control the way we respond to something that might trouble us. We can choose peace or trouble. We can choose to stay calm or *to* calm down if we start becoming agitated.

Jesus also said, *...In the world you have tribulation and trials and distress and frustration; but be of good cheer...For I have overcome the world...* (John 16:33).

We will have persecution for the Word's sake (Mark 4:17), and things won't go exactly as we would like in our daily lives as we discussed before. Jesus said in the world there will be tribulation, but He had an answer for it: ...*be of good cheer*. In today's language, we could paraphrase that statement as, "Cheer up!"

Jesus, Who lives inside those of us who believe in Him, has overcome the world. That gives us plenty of reason to calm down and cheer up!

Once I began understanding this principle, when I started to become upset over something that really didn't matter, it seemed to me the Lord was saying: "Calm down and cheer up! Don't be so intense. Lighten up. Enjoy life!" Then I would think, "Oh, that's right. I'm supposed to enjoy life. I have joy in my salvation, and the Prince of Peace, Who has overcome the world, lives inside me!"

Even after walking in these principles for a while, we need an adjustment every so often. I still have to remind myself to lighten up. Or God may say to me, "Now, Joyce, listen to one of your own messages"!

My nature is to be *extremely* intense, and I come from a background of terrible abuse. If I could lighten up, anyone can!

Some people experience anxiety as a result of deep hurts from the past. Becoming free from emotional bondage is not always easy. But if you will let Him, the Holy Spirit will lead you step-by-step on a path that will take you into freedom!

I found a Scripture which says a woman should enjoy her husband. (See 1 Peter 3:2 AMP.) For years I couldn't enjoy my husband because I was too intense about trying to change him — and my children and myself and everything else in my life.

I had a nice family, but I didn't enjoy them. I was so busy trying to change everyone in it, I never let any of them enjoy life.

I had a nice home, but I didn't enjoy it. I kept it spotlessly clean with everything in its place. But I was so intense about it I didn't enjoy it, and I didn't let anyone else enjoy it either.

My children had some nice toys, but they were never able to enjoy them because I didn't want the toys "strewn out all over the place." I never wanted to get the toys out and play with my children — or let them play with the toys either. I didn't know what fun was. In fact, because of the way I was raised I didn't think anyone was *supposed* to have fun. All I knew was work.

I would tell my kids, "Get out of here and go play." Then when they went someplace to play, I went along behind them saying, "Pick up this mess! Get this room cleaned up right now! All you ever do around here is make more work for me!"

Yet I wondered why I wasn't happy. I couldn't understand why I was plagued by "evil forebodings." That went on until the Lord brought healing and deliverance into my life.

THE PURPOSE BEHIND ANXIETY

...a gentle and peaceful spirit...[is not anxious or wrought up, but] is very precious in the sight of God.

1 PETER 3:4

According to Peter, the kind of spirit God likes is a peaceful spirit that is not anxious or wrought up. To be *wrought up* is to be tense, tied in a knot, upset and disturbed. To be *anxious* is to be worried, disquieted, or distracted.

Why does the devil try to make us tense, get us tied up in knots, upset, disturbed, worried, disquieted, and distracted? He wants to keep us from focusing our attention on the good things God has given us. He wants to keep us from enjoying our relationship with the Lord and the abundant life Jesus died to provide for us.

As a result of the abuse I suffered growing up, I never used to enjoy anything about my life. Because of the way I was treated as a child, I never really got to be a kid, so I didn't know how to be childlike. To me everything was burdensome. Because I was so tense, worried, and wrought up, I blew everything way out of proportion. I made a big deal out of everything. I had to learn to relax, lighten up, and let things go. I had to learn that even if everything did not always work out exactly as I wanted it to, it would not be the end of the world.

Rejoice in *Today*

This is the day which the Lord hath made; we will rejoice and be glad in it.

Psalm 118:24 KJV

Anxiety also means to take thought or being "...apprehensive, or worried about what may happen; concern about a possible future event."[2] The Lord once told me, "Anxiety is caused by trying to mentally and emotionally get into things that are not here yet or things that have already been" — mentally leaving where you are and getting into an area of the past or the future.

Since the Lord gave me that definition I have been trying to learn to lighten up and enjoy life. That doesn't mean I go around acting like an airhead. The Bible says that we believers are to be sober-minded, vigilant, and cautious, on our guard against our enemy, the devil, who is out to devour us. (1 Peter 5:8.)

Many serious things are going on in this world, and we need to be aware of them and prepared for them. But at the same time we need to learn to relax and take things as they come without getting all nervous and upset about them.

We need to learn how to enjoy the good life God has provided for us through the death and resurrection of His Son Jesus Christ. (See John 10:10.) In spite of all the troubling things going on around us in the world, our daily confession should be, "This is the day the Lord has made; I will rejoice and be glad in it."

Something we Christians need to do more of is laugh. We tend to be so heavy about everything — our sin, expecting perfection from ourselves, our growth in God, our prayer life, the gifts of the Spirit, and memorizing Bible verses. We carry around such heavy burdens.

If we would just laugh a little more — *be of good cheer,* "cheer up" — we would find that a little bit of laughter makes that load much lighter. In the world we live in there isn't a great deal to laugh about so we will need to do it on purpose. It is easy to find plenty to worry about. To be happy, we need to work on it a little. We need to laugh and have a good time.

One night my husband and I were in bed and started tickling each other. We were laughing and carrying on like two maniacs, giggling, laughing, tickling. My only problem is that every time I wrestle with Dave, he wins. I've tried ganging up on him with all our kids so that they will hold him down while I tickle him — just having a good time.

Some people are too starchy and religious to tickle anybody. They would rather lie in bed and say, "Hallelujah!"

Some wives whose husbands aren't saved lie there praying in their husband's ear. Instead, they ought to roll over and tickle him. It's OK to lighten up!

DON'T FRET — REJOICE!

Rejoice in the Lord always [delight, gladden yourselves in Him]; again I say, Rejoice!....

Do not fret or have any anxiety about anything, but in every circumstance and in everything, by prayer and petition (definite requests), with thanksgiving, continue to make your wants known to God.

And God's peace [shall be yours, that tranquil state of a soul assured of its salvation through Christ, and so fearing nothing from God and being content with its earthly lot of whatever sort that is, that peace] which transcends all understanding shall garrison and mount guard over your hearts and minds in Christ Jesus.

PHILIPPIANS 4:4,6,7

Twice in this passage the apostle Paul tells us to rejoice. He urges us not to fret or have any anxiety about anything but to pray and give thanks to God *in* everything — not *after* everything is over.

If we wait until everything is perfect before rejoicing and giving thanks, we won't have much fun. Learning to enjoy life even in the midst of trying circumstances is one way we develop spiritual maturity.

In 2 Corinthians 3:18 Paul writes:

And all of us, as with unveiled face, [because we] continued to behold [in the Word of God] as in a mirror the glory of the Lord, are constantly being transfigured into His very own image in ever increasing splendor and *from one degree of glory to another....*

That means there are many stages we must go through in the course of our spiritual growth. We need to learn how to enjoy the glory we are experiencing at each level of our development. It is true we are not yet where we need to be, but, thank God, we are not where we used to be. We are somewhere in the middle, but we are making progress toward our goal — and we ought to be enjoying each stage.

Often young parents delay enjoying their child until he has reached a certain stage of growth. When he is an infant they say, "I'll be glad when he gets out of diapers or quits cutting teeth or learns to walk." Then they say, "I'll be glad when he's in kindergarten." Then it becomes, "I'll be glad when he starts school." Later they say, "I'll be glad when he graduates." On and on it goes until the child is grown and gone, and the parents have never really enjoyed any stage of his life. They were always waiting to be glad *when.*

We postpone being glad until everything is perfect — which we all know is never going to happen in this life. We need to learn to rejoice and be glad in the Lord this day and every day along the way toward our goal.

When I first started out in my ministry and was holding meetings with only about fifty people in attendance, I was constantly saying, "I'll be so glad when I have hundreds in my meetings." But I learned that none of that kind of thing brings happiness or joy because we always want more. I also discovered that every phase of development comes with its own set of problems.

Eventually I found the doorway to happiness. It is expressed in the words of the song to the Lord, "He has made me glad; He has made me glad; I will rejoice for He has made me glad."

The way I was during those days, I should have sung it, "If He does what I want Him to do, He has made me glad; if He doesn't, He has made me sad." Finally the Lord gave me a breakthrough by teaching me that the fullness of joy is found in His *presence* — not in His *presents!* (Psalm 16:11.)

True joy comes from seeking God's face.

People who think they will be glad when God does some particular thing for them usually can't be glad until He does something else for them. They can spend their whole life waiting for some other time to be glad.

One day as I was on my way to a meeting I was singing that song: "You have made me glad, You have made me glad; I will rejoice for You have made me glad." Suddenly the Lord spoke to me and said, "For the first time in your life you're singing it right."

I had sung that song many times, but never from my heart. Once the Lord gave me a breakthrough in that area, I could sing it the way it was meant to be sung — as a hymn of praise and thanksgiving to God for what He has *already done* and not for what He is going to do *when.*

To live in the fullness of the joy of the Lord we must find something to be glad about besides our current circumstances. The world is full of people and situations that are never going to please us. Even those people and things that do please us are only going to do so for a short time. Sooner or later people — even Christians — will fail us, and circumstances will go against us. That's why we must learn to derive our happiness and joy not from the outside but from the Lord inside us. We must learn not to fret or have any anxiety about anything but in everything to give thanks and praise to God. Then the peace that passes all understanding will be ours.

We will always have opportunities to be anxious, worried, and fretful. The devil will see to that because he knows that anxiety in a man's heart weighs it down. When the devil tries to bring anxiety into our heart, we must give that anxiety to the Lord in prayer with thanksgiving, making our requests known to Him. Then the peace that passes all understanding will keep our hearts and minds in Christ Jesus.

I used to worry about my son, fourteen at the time, whom my husband Dave and I had to leave at home while we traveled in our ministry. Several times a day while we were away, the devil would try to make me worry about what was happening to Danny in our absence. Each time Satan would try to lay that burden on me, I would stop and pray: "Father, I thank You that You're taking care of Danny. Thank You, Lord, that You have a good plan for his life and that You are watching over him and working out everything for the best for him. Thank You that he is covered by the blood of Your Son Jesus."

I absolutely refused to allow Satan to weigh me down with worry and anxiety. Instead, I turned to the Lord in prayer, rejoicing in the midst of my trying circumstances. The Lord answered my prayers and gave me the peace and joy He has promised to all those who refuse to give in to worry and fear, but turn to Him in simple faith and trust.

CATEGORIES OF ANXIETY

Many evils confront the [consistently] righteous, but the Lord delivers him out of them all.

PSALM 34:19

Although there are many evils that confront the righteous, there are three main categories of anxiety. Let's look at each of them and see how we are to handle them so they do not drag us down into depression and despair.

1. THE PAST AND THE FUTURE

Keep your foot [give your mind to what you are doing]....

ECCLESIASTES 5:1

My personal definition of *anxiety* is mentally leaving where you are and getting into an area of the past or the future.

One of the things we need to understand is that God wants us to learn to be "now people." That's what the Lord was referring to in the Bible when He said, "Today is the day of salvation" (2 Corinthians 6:2), "Today if you will hear My voice," (Hebrews 3:7,15), "Today if you will believe, you will enter into My rest." (Hebrews 4:7-9.)

Too often we spend our time in the past or the future. We need to learn to live now — mentally as well as physically and spiritually.

One time while I was brushing my teeth, I suddenly realized I was hurrying and rushing with my stomach all tied up in knots. Although I was physically doing one thing, mentally I was onto the next thing I had planned to do as soon as I finished. I was trying to hurry and finish one thing in order to get to the next.

When I was a young housewife I used to get in a nervous fit every day trying to get my husband up and off to work and our young children up and off to school. I would be in such a mental and emotional stew because of all the things I wanted to get done that day I wouldn't be able to concentrate on anything for very long.

In the middle of doing one thing, I would realize I hadn't done something else. I would stop that task and go start another one. I would continue this pattern with one task after another.

Obviously, by the end of the day I would be in a worse mess mentally, emotionally, and physically than when I started out that morning. Everything would be half done, and I would be totally frustrated, stressed out, worn to a frazzle, and anxious about the same thing happening the next day — all because I had neglected to give myself to one thing at a time.

Do you know why we find it so hard to give ourselves to one thing at a time? Because we are more occupied with the past or the future than we are with the present.

In Ecclesiastes 5:1 the Bible tells us to give our mind to what we are doing, to "keep our foot" — our footing. In other words, we are to keep a balance in life. If we don't do that, nothing will ever make any real sense. We must learn to focus on what we are doing. If we don't, we will end up in anxiety and worry because we will be always mentally dealing with yesterday or tomorrow when we should be living today.

There is an anointing on today. In John 8:58 Jesus referred to Himself as "I AM." If you and I, as His disciples, try to live in the past or the future, we are going to find life hard for us because Jesus is always in the present. That's what He meant when He told us in Matthew 6:34: ...*do not worry or be anxious about tomorrow, for tomorrow will have worries and anxieties of its own. Sufficient for each day is its own trouble.*

Jesus has plainly told us we don't need to worry about anything. All we need to do is seek the Kingdom of God, and He will add to us whatever we need, whether it is food or clothing or shelter or spiritual growth. (vv. 25-33.)

We don't need to be concerned about tomorrow, because tomorrow will have problems of its own. We need to concentrate our full attention on today and stop being so intense and wrought up. Calm down and lighten up! Laugh more and worry less. Stop ruining today worrying about yesterday or tomorrow — neither of which we can do anything about. We need to stop wasting our precious "now," because it will never come again.

How many years of my life did I waste, tormenting myself with needless worry and anxiety, trying to handle things that were not mine to handle? I was always a responsible person, but in addition to the *responsibility* for my life I took on the *care* of it. According to the Bible we are to handle our responsibility, but we are to cast our care upon the Lord because He cares for us. (1 Peter 5:7.)

God cares for you. He cares about everything that concerns you. He cares about your life. Don't waste it waiting until everything is perfect before you start enjoying it. Don't waste your precious "now" worrying about yesterday or tomorrow.

The next time you are tempted to get anxious or upset about something — especially something in the past or the future — think about what you are doing and turn your mind to what is going on today. Learn from the past and prepare for the future, but *live in the present.*

2. Confrontations and Conversations

Now when they take you [to court] and put you under arrest, do not be anxious beforehand about what you are to say nor [even] meditate about it; but say whatever is given you in that hour and at the moment, for it is not you who will be speaking, but the Holy Spirit.

MARK 13:11

In this passage Jesus was warning His disciples that when they went out into the world to preach the Gospel to every creature, as He was commanding them to do, they would run into opposition. He was preparing them to face tribulation and persecution. He was telling them that they would be brought before governors and kings for His sake as a testimony to them. (v. 9.)

Jesus finished His remarks by instructing His disciples not to worry about what to say or even try to figure out or meditate upon it, because when they opened their mouths to speak, it would not be them speaking but the Holy Spirit within them.

I spent many years of my life mentally rehearsing what I was going to say to people. I imagined what they would say to me, then I tried to figure out what I was going to say back to them. In my head I would even practice those imaginary conversations over and over.

You may do the same kind of thing, for example, before you go in to ask your boss for a raise or some time off for a special need. If you are filled with anxiety, it may be a sign you think the outcome of that conversation depends upon you and your ability rather than upon the Holy Spirit and His ability.

As in all aspects of life, there is a balance that needs to be maintained. If we are sure we are operating in the Word of God and in obedience to His will, then we do not need to be nervous, worried, or anxious about what we are going to say to others. Of course, we need to be prepared, but if we excessively rehearse the conversation over and over, it is an indication we are not trusting in the anointing of God but in ourselves. In that case, we will not do as well as if we were depending completely on God!

We need to ask the Lord to give us favor with all those to whom we speak. Then we can be confident that whatever the results of our conversation or confrontation, it is the will of God, and it will work out for the best for all concerned. (Romans 8:28.)

3. Duties and Obligations of the Day

Now while they were on their way, it occurred that Jesus entered a certain village, and a woman named Martha received and welcomed Him into her house.

And she had a sister named Mary, who seated herself at the Lord's feet and was listening to His teaching.

But Martha [overly occupied and too busy] was distracted with much serving; and she came up to Him and said, Lord, is it nothing to You that my sister has left me to serve alone? Tell her then to help me [to lend a hand and do her part along with me]!

But the Lord replied to her by saying, Martha, Martha, you are anxious and troubled about many things;

There is need of only one or but a few things. Mary has chosen the good portion [that which is to her advantage], which shall not be taken away from her.

LUKE 10:38-42

In this passage we see one sister, Martha, upset and distracted because she is overly occupied and too busy, while the other sister, Mary, is happily seated at the feet of Jesus enjoying His presence and fellowship.

I can just imagine Martha in this scene. I am sure that as soon as she heard Jesus was coming to her house, she started running around cleaning and polishing and cooking, trying to get everything ready for His visit. The reason I find it so easy to picture Martha in this situation is because I used to be just like her.

One time the Lord said to me, "Joyce, you can't enjoy life because you're too complicated." He was referring to a simple barbecue I was turning into a major production.

My husband and I had invited some friends over on Sunday afternoon, telling them we would throw some hot dogs on the grill, open up some potato chips and a can of pork and beans, make some iced tea, and sit around on the patio visiting or playing games.

Of course, once I got to making preparations for the occasion, everything quickly got out of hand. The hot dogs turned into steaks, the potato chips became potato salad, the barbecue grill had to be cleaned, the lawn had to be mowed, and the whole house had to be spotlessly prepared for guests. Besides all that work, the six people we had originally invited had to be increased to fourteen because I was afraid of offending anyone who might feel left out.

So all of a sudden a simple barbecue with friends turned into a nightmare. All because I had the "Martha syndrome." I had "Martha" written all over me. That's what the Lord meant when He told me I couldn't enjoy life because I was too complicated.

I needed to learn to be more like Mary and less like Martha. Instead of worrying and fretting, I needed to learn to simplify my plans, lighten up, and enjoy life!

3

⌐◦◦⌐

THE ARM OF THE FLESH

Thus says the Lord: Cursed [with great evil] is the
strong man who trusts in and relies on frail man,
making weak [human] flesh his arm, and whose
mind and heart turn aside from the Lord.

JEREMIAH 17:5

The Bible speaks of two vastly different arms: the arm of the flesh and the arm of the Lord. One of these is "our deal," the other is "God's deal"; that is, one is based on human ideas and effort, the other is based on God's plan and power. One is of the flesh, the other is of the Spirit.

In John 3:6, Jesus told Nicodemus, *What is born of [from] the flesh is flesh [of the physical is physical]; and what is born of the Spirit is spirit.* What is begun in the flesh must be maintained in the flesh, but what is begun in the Spirit is maintained by the Spirit. When we try to operate in the arm of the flesh we end up frustrated, but when we operate in the arm of the Lord we end up victorious.

It is hard work to carry out the plans and schemes we ourselves have devised. But when God starts something, He carries it through to completion without any struggle on our part.

Many times when we face struggles, we assume the devil is causing us problems, so we try to rebuke him! Sometimes it is the devil trying to stop God's plan for our lives. But often the problem is not the devil but ourselves. We are trying to accomplish our will and plan, not the will and plan of God.

No amount of rebuking the devil will do any good when we are operating in the arm of the flesh rather than the arm of the Lord. If the work was begun by the Lord, He will finish it.

OPPORTUNITY BRINGS ADVERSITY

For a wide door of opportunity for effectual [service] has opened to me [there, a great and promising one], and [there are] many adversaries.

1 CORINTHIANS 16:9

It is true that whenever we do anything for God, the adversary will oppose us. But we must remember that greater is He Who is in us than he who is in the world. (1 John 4:4.) According to the Word of God, if we are operating in obedience to His will and plan, although the enemy may come at us one way, he will have to flee from us seven ways. (Deuteronomy 28:7.)

We should not have to spend our lives struggling against the devil. Sometimes we spend more time talking about Satan than we do talking about God.

In His earthly ministry, Jesus did not spend a great deal of time fighting against local demons. When Jesus appeared on the scene, they either fled in terror or were driven out by Him with a word. When we minister in His name, we have the same power and authority He had. Instead of wearing ourselves out trying to fight spiritual enemies, we should learn to stand strong in the authority given us by Jesus.

The best way to overcome the devil and his demons is simply to stay in God's will and plan by operating in the arm of the Lord and not the arm of the flesh. James 4:7 KJV says: *Submit yourselves therefore to God. Resist the devil, and he will flee from you.*

Many people try to resist the devil without submitting themselves to God! We should submit our will to God's will.

Without recognizing it, we sometimes have a problem with lusting after something *we* think should be in the plan for us. This is not sexual desire — I am talking about a desire for what we think we must have in order to be happy. It is possible to lust after something that is good, even something God Himself wants us to have. In my own case, there was a time when I lusted after my ministry.

As soon as we start wanting anything so much we try to take matters into our own hands to get it, we are asking for trouble. It takes a mature individual to be patient and wait on the Lord to work out things according to His perfect will and timing. Immature people rush ahead of God and end up frustrated. They don't realize that nothing is going to work out right unless it comes from God and is carried out in the Spirit in accordance with His divine plan and purpose.

Many people are frustrated and unhappy simply because they are trying to operate in the arm of the flesh rather than in the arm of the Lord. I spent many, many years in that state because I was trying to do things my own way and in my own power. I was out ahead of God, giving birth to Ishmaels instead of Isaacs.

ISHMAEL OR ISAAC?

Now Sarai, Abram's wife, had borne him no children. She had an Egyptian maid whose name was Hagar.

31

> And Sarai said to Abram, See here, the Lord has restrained me
> from bearing children. I am asking you to have intercourse
> with my maid; it may be that I can obtain children by her.
> And Abram listened to and heeded what Sarai said.
>
> GENESIS 16:1,2

In Genesis 15:1-5, the Lord came to Abraham ("Abram" at
that time) and promised him that He would bless him and give
him an heir from his own body so that his descendants would
be as numerous as the stars in the heavens.

Just one chapter later, in Genesis 16:1,2, Sarah ("Sarai" at
that time) came up with a plan to produce an heir for Abraham
by having him take her handmaid Hagar as his "secondary
wife." (v. 3.)

In Chapter 17, the Lord appeared to Abraham and again
promised to bless him and make him the father of many
nations. (vv. 1-6.) He then went on to bless Sarah and
promised to give Abraham a son by her in their old age. (vv. 15-
19.) It was through this promised son, Isaac, and not through
the natural son, Ishmael, that God's covenant of blessings was
to be fulfilled.

Isaac was God's idea and plan; Ishmael was Sarah's idea
and plan. One was the child of promise, the child of the Spirit;
the other was the child of human effort, the child of the flesh.

Abraham had to wait twenty years for the fulfillment of
God's promise to him that he would have the son through
whom the Lord would fulfill His covenant promises. When
Isaac was finally born, Ishmael caused problems in the household, so Abraham had to send Ishmael and his mother Hagar
away. (Genesis 21:1-14.)

Many times the reason we are having problems is because
we have produced Ishmaels rather than Isaacs. We are reaping

the consequences of trying to carry out our own ideas and plans rather than waiting for God to bring forth His ideas and plans. When things don't turn out the way we expect, we get angry at God because He is not making everything work out as we want it to.

But the problem is not God's doing; it is ours. What we fail to remember is that what is born of the Spirit is spirit, and what is born of the flesh is flesh.

The Spirit Versus the Flesh

It is the Spirit Who gives life [He is the Life-giver]; the flesh conveys no benefit whatever [there is no profit in it]....

John 6:63

Jesus has told us it is the Spirit Who is important, not the flesh, because the Spirit gives life while the flesh profits nothing. The apostle Paul went even further when he said, *For I know that nothing good dwells within me, that is, in my flesh...* (Romans 7:18).

If you and I are to fulfill God's will and plan for us in this life, the flesh — the selfish, rebellious sin nature within us — has to die.

Often we are not aware of what is on the inside of us because we are so caught up in the outer life. It is from within us that the energy of the soul comes forth to cause us all kinds of problems on the outside.

Paul testified to having this same problem when he went on to write in that same verse, *...I can will what is right, but I cannot perform it. [I have the intention and urge to do what is right, but no power to carry it out.]* In that passage, he described

33

how miserable he was because he failed to practice the good deeds he desired to do, but succeeded in doing the evil deeds he did not want to do. In his misery and frustration, he ended up crying out, *O unhappy and pitiable and wretched man that I am! Who will release and deliver me from [the shackles of] this body of death?* (v. 24).

I know that feeling. I used to work hard all day trying to do right and then go to bed at night frustrated and depressed because I had failed again. I would cry out to the Lord, "Father, I just don't understand. I tried hard all day, Lord. I did my very best — and it was all in vain."

My problem was that I was operating in the arm of the flesh, and the flesh was profiting me nothing.

I lived that way for years and years. I would get up in the morning all ready to "plan my work and work my plan." I was determined to make my ministry grow. I wanted so much for doors of opportunity to open for me, just as they had for Paul. But I was convinced that, like Paul, I was being confronted with "adversaries." I rebuked them until my "rebuker" was worn out. I cast them out until there could not have been a demon left in my entire town. Still the doors were not opening.

I fasted and prayed, alone and with others. I commanded crowds to come to my meetings from the north, south, east, and west. But nothing worked. I was still holding meetings of fifty people in basements or banquet halls where we had to clean fried crab legs and chicken bones off the tables and floor before we could begin our services. Sometimes there would be no heat or the air conditioning would not work properly. It seemed no matter how hard I tried to make things work, everything that could go wrong would go wrong.

All of that was a testing ground, one which we all must go through. Do you know what the purpose of the testing ground is? To teach us to deny the flesh and depend on the Spirit in order to build character in us as we go through the hard times and refuse to give up.

If we are committed to doing what God has told us to do, we will succeed despite our adversaries and their devices. Our problem is that instead of getting God's plan and being obedient to Him as He works it out, we try to make up our own plan and get Him to bless it. If He doesn't do that, we get angry at Him; we get confused and often very negative in our emotions and conversations.

There is no telling how many frustrated, depressed people there are in our world who have basically given up on God because He didn't make *their* plan work. I used to be one of them.

One time a friend of mine and I cooked up an idea to increase my ministry. We decided to write every pastor in St. Louis, where my ministry was located, informing them I was called of God and had a strong teaching gift. We were going to suggest to the pastors they have me come to their churches to minister. Fortunately the Lord stayed our hand, and for that I am so grateful. Just imagine how I would feel now if we had carried through with our plan instead of waiting for the Lord to work out His plan.

What my friend and I were planning was a work of the flesh. As is often the case, we were trying to kick doors open and make our own way. Instead, we needed to wait on the Lord, believe and trust in Him, and enjoy where we were and what we were doing until He opened the doors for us.

As Christians, we all have a work to do. Our work is to believe, not to cook up all kinds of plans and schemes to try to make things happen. All of that kind of conniving and manipulating comes from the flesh and profits nothing. If

God is not in our work, it will be frustrating and depressing. We must learn to discern between what God is truly leading us to do and what we are "trying" to do.

For years I had a work — or so I thought. It was changing my husband Dave. I tried everything in my power to manipulate, coerce, pressure, and force him to do what I thought he needed to do — which was basically to give up sports and pay more attention to me and the things I was interested in.

I was convinced Dave had a problem. It never occurred to me I might have a problem. That was out of the question. It was not even in my thinking.

One day as I was praying I said, "Oh, Lord, You have *got* to change Dave!"

Suddenly the voice of the Lord came to me, saying, "Excuse Me, Joyce, but Dave is not the one with the problem."

"Well, then, Lord," I asked, "who is?" since there were only the two of us, Dave and me. I thought, *Surely it can't be me!* My foolish pride had me judging Dave while I was blinded to my own faults.

Proverbs 21:2 says, *Every way of a man is right in his own eyes, but the Lord weighs and tries the hearts.* That is true for all of us. We all think we are right. It was a great revelation to me to discover I was wrong sometimes.

I was trying so hard to change Dave, change my children, change myself, change everything in our lives. I was trying to prosper, get healed, make my ministry grow, and on and on. I was wearing myself out trying to change everything and everybody, and feeling miserable about it. I was constantly praying, trying to get God to bless my plans and efforts and make them successful. What I was doing was what the Galatians were doing in Paul's day: I was trying to live by the flesh, by works, rather than by the Spirit.

THE TWO COVENANTS

For it is written that Abraham had two sons, one by the bondmaid and one by the free woman.

But whereas the child of the slave woman was born according to the flesh and had an ordinary birth, the son of the free woman was born in fulfillment of the promise.

Now all this is an allegory; these [two women] represent two covenants. One covenant originated from Mount Sinai [where the Law was given] and bears [children destined] for slavery; this is Hagar.

Now Hagar is (stands for) Mount Sinai in Arabia and she corresponds to and belongs in the same category with the present Jerusalem, for she is in bondage together with her children.

But the Jerusalem above (the Messianic kingdom of Christ) is free, and she is our mother.

GALATIANS 4:22-26

The Bible speaks of two covenants. We know them as the old covenant and the new covenant, but they can be called the covenant of works and the covenant of grace.

The first covenant is based on man's doing everything on his own, struggling, striving, and laboring to be acceptable to God. That kind of covenant steals joy and peace. That was the kind of covenant the Galatians were trying to return to, and Paul had to write to them to remind them of the futility of trying to live by their works rather than by the grace of God. (Galatians 3:1-7.)

The second covenant, the covenant of grace, is based not on what man can do, but on what Christ has already done. Under this covenant, we are justified not by our works or our righteousness, but by our faith and confidence in Christ. That takes the pressure off of us to perform. We can give up our outward efforts and allow God to work through us by the power of His Holy Spirit within us.

One covenant brings bondage; the other covenant brings liberty. Under one we give birth to things of the flesh, because what is born of the flesh is flesh. Under the other we allow God to give birth to things of the Spirit, because what is born of the Spirit is spirit.

Under the first covenant, we believe we have to do it all; under the second covenant all we have to do is believe, and as part of our believing lifestyle, act on what God tells us to do.

As we saw in the introduction, Romans 15:13 tells us those who believe are full of hope, joy, and peace. The problem is that today, as in Paul's day, so many people in the Church are not believing. They are trying to live by their works rather than by God's grace. Therefore, they have no hope, peace, or joy.

As we saw, the Word of God has promised us if we will operate in simple, childlike faith, we will be bubbling over with joy. We will also see much more positive results in our lives.

REJOICE!

For it is written in the Scriptures, Rejoice, O barren woman, who has not given birth to children; break forth into a joyful shout, you who are not feeling birth pangs, for the desolate woman has many more children than she who has a husband.

GALATIANS 4:27

After Paul describes the difference between the two covenants represented by the two women, Hagar and Sarah, he goes on to say to the barren woman, "Rejoice!"

For years I read this verse and wondered what Paul was talking about. It was only later I discovered that Galatians 4:27 was a cross reference to Isaiah 54:1, which says basically the same thing: Those who do not labor to bring forth their own results but who depend entirely upon the grace of God will enjoy more results than those who wear themselves out trying to produce by their own efforts.

The Church is not seeing the results we want today because God's people are trying to do with the arm of flesh what can only be done by the arm of the Lord.

Instead of trusting in the arm of flesh, we believers are supposed to be trusting in the arm of the Lord. Like the barren woman in these Scriptures, instead of grieving we are supposed to be rejoicing.

Why would a barren woman rejoice? Because the writers of these Scriptures are talking about spiritual, not natural, children. The barren woman is barren of her own works. She has given up trying to give birth the natural way. Instead, she has learned to put her faith and trust in God to give birth spiritually. She has ceased from her labor and has entered the rest of God.

As we read in Hebrews 4:10, those who have entered the rest of God have given up all their own labor and striving — the weariness and pain of trying to give birth to things in a natural way — and simply are resting, waiting upon the Lord to do for them what they cannot do for themselves. As a consequence, they end up having more children — enjoying more and better results — than those who try to produce by their own works.

THE FRUSTRATION OF WORKS

[You should] be exceedingly glad on this account, though now for a little while you may be distressed by trials and suffer temptations,

So that [the genuineness] of your faith may be tested, [your faith] which is infinitely more precious than the perishable gold which is tested and purified by fire. [This proving of your faith is intended] to redound to [your] praise and glory and honor when Jesus Christ (the Messiah, the Anointed One) is revealed.

Without having seen Him, you love Him; though you do not [even] now see Him, you believe in Him and exult and thrill with inexpressible and glorious (triumphant, heavenly) joy.

1 PETER 1:6-8

I don't believe we lack joy because we have problems. The Bible says that we can have inexpressible, glorious, triumphant, heavenly joy right in the very midst of our trials and temptations.

If we are not experiencing that kind of "joy unspeakable" (as the *King James Version* calls it), we need to ask why not. In my own life, I did not begin to experience a sense of joy despite my outward circumstances until I discovered and learned the real meaning of the second covenant.

The blessings of that covenant were available to me, just as they are to all believers. But something can be available to us yet never be of any benefit to us because we never avail ourselves of it. As long as we live in ignorance or neglect of the blessings that are ours under the covenant of grace, we will live in the frustration of works.

In fact, that is what the Lord told me: "Frustration equals works of the flesh." In other words, we only benefit from the blessings of the covenant of grace by living under grace. As long as we live under works, we will be frustrated and depressed because we are trying to do God's job.

God has given us His Holy Spirit to be our Helper in life. (John 16:7.) But stubborn, independent people don't want any help. They want to do everything for themselves. If they do ask for help of any kind, it is only because they have exhausted every avenue of self-help and have come to the inevitable conclusion that they just cannot do it alone.

I used to be that way. I would worry and fret and work myself to a frazzle over simple things like trying to open a jar of mayonnaise before I would finally have to give up and ask Dave to come to the kitchen and open the jar for me. What made me act that way? Pure stubbornness — and pride. I wanted to prove that I didn't need anybody's help, that I could do everything for myself. But I couldn't, and that frustrated me.

The way we receive help — and thus avoid the frustration of works — is by simply asking for it. But only the humble among us will do that, because asking for help is an acknowledgment that we are not able to do everything for ourselves.

PRIDE VERSUS HUMILITY

...Clothe (apron) yourselves, all of you, with humility [as the garb of a servant, so that its covering cannot possibly be stripped from you, with freedom from pride and arrogance] toward one another. For God sets Himself against the proud (the insolent, the overbearing, the disdainful, the presumptuous, the boastful) — [and He opposes, frustrates, and defeats them], but gives grace (favor, blessing) to the humble.

41

Therefore humble yourselves [demote, lower yourselves in your own estimation] under the mighty hand of God, that in due time He may exalt you,

Casting the whole of your care [all your anxieties, all your worries, all your concerns, once and for all] on Him, for He cares for you affectionately and cares about you watchfully.

1 PETER 5:5-7

We can see from this passage how important humility is to God. If we are full of pride and doing things our own way without listening to Him, we will end up in situations that will result in anxiety and stress.

God's reasons for asking us to do things in the way He asks are not to take anything away from us. He is trying to set us up for a blessing. Or He may be trying to protect us from something we don't know about. We must always be on our guard against pride because it will keep us from experiencing peace and joy in this life.

One time after one of our meetings in which I taught on this subject, a lady came to me and said, "I'm looking for one of your cassette albums, but I don't see it on the tape table."

"Which one is it?" I asked.

"The one about exchanging pride for humility," she answered.

"We don't usually carry it with us," I told her, "because there is not much demand for it. Those who are humble don't need it, and those who need it are too proud to pick it up."

That would be amusing if it weren't so true.

James tells us God gives us more and more grace — power of the Holy Spirit — to overcome all of our evil tendencies. In the same verse he goes on to say exactly what Peter said in his first letter to the believers: ...*God sets Himself against the proud and haughty, but gives grace [continually] to the lowly (those who are humble enough to receive it)* (James 4:6).

James then urges us, just as Peter did, *Humble yourselves [feeling very insignificant] in the presence of the Lord, and He will exalt you [He will lift you up and make your lives significant]* (v. 10).

We receive the grace of God by humbling ourselves before Him, casting all our cares upon Him, and trusting Him to take care of them as He has promised in His Word.

Proud people won't do that, because they think they can handle everything for themselves. Only the humble will do that, because they know they can't handle everything — only God can.

The Lord Builds the House

Except the Lord builds the house, they labor in vain who build it; except the Lord keeps the city, the watchman wakes but in vain.

It is vain for you to rise up early, to take rest late, to eat the bread of [anxious] toil — for He gives [blessings] to His beloved in sleep.

PSALM 127:1,2

What should we let God build in our lives? The first thing we need to let Him build is *us*.

In Matthew 16:18 Jesus said that He would build His Church. In 1 Corinthians 3:9 Paul tells us that we are that Church: ...*you are God's garden and vineyard and field under cultivation, [you are] God's building.*

We are the building, and Jesus is the Chief Cornerstone. (Ephesians 2:20.) We are being built up, one brick at a time, day by day, from glory to glory.

But *how* do we get built? The answer is found in Paul's letter to the Galatians who needed to be reminded of the difference between works and faith.

BEGUN BY FAITH, FINISHED BY FAITH

Are you so foolish and so senseless and so silly? Having begun [your new life spiritually] with the [Holy] Spirit, are you now reaching perfection [by dependence] on the flesh?

Have you suffered so many things and experienced so much all for nothing (to no purpose) — if it really is to no purpose and in vain?

Then does He Who supplies you with His marvelous [Holy] Spirit and works powerfully and miraculously among you do so on [the grounds of your doing] what the Law demands, or because of your believing in and adhering to and trusting in and relying on the message that you heard?

GALATIANS 3:3-5

We need to ask ourselves what Paul was asking the "foolish," "senseless," and "silly" Galatians: Having begun our new lives in Christ by dependence on the Spirit, are we now trying to live them in the flesh?

Just as we were saved by grace (God's unmerited favor) through faith, and not by works of the flesh (Ephesians 2:8,9), so we need to learn to live by grace (God's unmerited favor) through faith, and not by works of the flesh.

When we were saved, we were in no condition to help ourselves. What kind of condition are we in now that we have been saved by grace through faith in the finished work of Jesus Christ? We are still in no condition to help ourselves! Why then do we keep trying to make things happen that are never going to happen?

The only way we are ever going to be ...*built [into] a spiritual house, for a holy (dedicated, consecrated) priesthood, to offer up [those] spiritual sacrifices [that are] acceptable and pleasing to God through Jesus Christ* (1 Peter 2:5) is by submitting ourselves to God and letting Him do the work in us that needs to be done.

The flesh profits us nothing. Only the Spirit can cause us to grow up into the perfection of Christ.

ARE YOU INTERESTED IN BEING PERFECTED?

His intention was the perfecting and the full equipping of the saints (His consecrated people), [that they should do] the work of ministering toward building up Christ's body (the church),

[That it might develop] until we all attain oneness in the faith and in the comprehension of the [full and accurate] knowledge of the Son of God, that [we might arrive] at really mature manhood (the completeness of personality which is nothing less than the standard height of Christ's own perfection), the measure of the stature of the fullness of the Christ and the completeness found in Him.

EPHESIANS 4:12,13

Are you interested in being perfected? I am. I want to grow up in the Lord. I want to mature and be Christlike in my attitude and behavior. Like Paul, I want to know Jesus and the power of His resurrection. (Philippians 3:10.) I want to measure up to His stature and operate in the fruit of His Spirit. (Galatians 5:22,23.)

But I cannot do all that on my own. I cannot change myself from what I am to what I want to be. All I can do is be *willing* to be changed and humbly submit myself to the Lord, allowing Him to build me into the person He wants me to be. And the only way that can be done is through faith.

What Is Faith?

For we have heard of your faith in Christ Jesus [the leaning of your entire human personality on Him in absolute trust and confidence in His power, wisdom, and goodness] and of the love which you [have and show] for all the saints (God's consecrated ones).

COLOSSIANS 1:4

According to this verse, faith is the leaning of the entire human personality on God in absolute trust and confidence in His power, wisdom, and goodness.

That means we need to lean all of ourselves on God, believing only He has the ability to do for us what needs to be done in us. Our only job is to abide in Him, to lean on Him totally and completely, to put our trust and confidence in Him.

When the Holy Spirit convicts us of our sins, what do we do? The first thing we do is confess those sins. We get into agreement with God about them. The second thing we do is acknowledge our inability to do anything about our sins. The more we try to change ourselves, the worse we get.

So what are we to do in order to do the work of God? The answer is found in John 6:28, 29 in which the disciples came to Jesus and asked this same question:

> They then said, What are we to do, that we may [habitually] be working the works of God? [What are we to do to carry out what God requires?]

> Jesus replied, This is the work (service) that God asks of you: that you believe in the One Whom He has sent [that you cleave to, trust, rely on, and have faith in His Messenger].

Our Work Is To Believe

The work that God requires of us is to *believe,* and believing requires that we cleave to, trust in, rely on, and have faith in Him and His Son Jesus Christ. If we truly have faith in God, if we truly lean our entire personality on Him in absolute trust and confidence in His power, wisdom, and goodness, we will not be anxious or worried. We will quit trying to build ourselves and will allow Him to build us and equip us.

The Master Builder

> For [of course] every house is built and furnished by someone, but the Builder of all things and the Furnisher [of the entire equipment of all things] is God.

HEBREWS 3:4

God is the Master Builder. Jesus is the Chief Cornerstone. God is the One Who has to build us and equip us for the work of the Lord Jesus Christ.

In Philippians 1:6 the apostle Paul writes to assure us: ...*He Who began a good work in you will continue until the day of Jesus Christ [right up to the time of His return], developing [that good work] and perfecting and bringing it to full completion in you.* What he was saying to us is simply this: "It was God Who started this work in you, and it is God Who will finish it!"

That means we should leave God alone to do His work. We need to stay out of His business and mind our own. There are certain things only God can do. We are to do our part and let Him do His. We are to handle our responsibility but cast our care on Him.

We are to confess our sins and failures to the Lord, confident that He will forgive us of those sins and failures and cleanse us from all unrighteousness, as He has promised in His Word. (1 John 1:9.) We are to trust to Him the job of perfecting us for the work He has for us to do in this life. That takes the pressure off of us, which relieves us of the worry and anxiety we feel so often as we try to perfect ourselves.

LET GO AND LET GOD

Abstain from evil [shrink from it and keep aloof from it] in whatever form or whatever kind it may be.

And may the God of peace Himself sanctify you through and through [separate you from profane things, make you pure and wholly consecrated to God]; and may your spirit and soul and body be preserved sound and complete [and found] blameless at the coming of our Lord Jesus Christ (the Messiah).

Faithful is He Who is calling you [to Himself] and utterly trustworthy, and He will also do it [fulfill His call by hallowing and keeping you].

1 THESSALONIANS 5:22-24

Here are God's instructions to us for finding peace and joy: Stay away from wrong behavior and allow the Lord of peace Himself to sanctify us, preserve us, complete us, hallow us, and keep us.

These verses are our call from God to a certain kind of holy living. They are also our assurance that it is not we who bring about this holy life, but God Himself, Who can be trusted utterly to do the work in us and for us.

What then is our part? What is the work that we are to do? What does God require of us? Our part is to *believe.* Our work is to trust the Lord. His requirement is that we let go and let God.

LET GOD BUILD

And now [brethren], I commit you to God [I deposit you in His charge, entrusting you to His protection and care]. And I commend you to the Word of His grace [to the commands and counsels and promises of His unmerited favor]. It is able to build you up and to give you [your rightful] inheritance among all God's set-apart ones (those consecrated, purified, and transformed of soul).

ACTS 20:32

God, the Master Builder, has promised to build us if we will allow Him to do so. What areas in our lives do we need to allow Him to build?

The first area, which we have already discussed, is ourselves. The second area, which is really a part of the first, is our ministry. The third and final area is our reputation.

GOD AND OUR REPUTATION

Now am I trying to win the favor of men, or of God? Do I seek to please men? If I were still seeking popularity with men, I should not be a bond servant of Christ (the Messiah).

GALATIANS 1:10

The apostle Paul said that in his ministry he had to choose between pleasing men and pleasing God. That is a choice each of us must make.

In Philippians 2:7 KJV, we read that Jesus made Himself of no reputation. Our Lord did not set out to make a name for Himself, and neither should we.

The Lord once commanded me, "Tell My people to stop trying to build their own reputation, and let Me do it for them." If it is our goal to build a name for ourselves, it will cause us to live in fear of man rather than in fear of God. We will try to win favor with people rather than with the Lord.

For years I tried to build my own reputation among believers by trying to win the favor of men. I manipulated and connived and played all the fleshly games to get in with the right group of church people. Through bitter experience, I learned that if we are to be truly free in the Lord we must do as Paul has told us in Galatians 5:1: *In [this] freedom Christ has made us free [and completely liberated us]; stand fast then, and do not be hampered and held ensnared and submit again to a yoke of slavery [which you have once put off].*

There is nothing the devil uses more to keep people out of the will of God than the threat of rejection. In my own case, when I made a full commitment to follow the will of God for my life, many of my former friends abandoned me and some even turned against me. Like Paul, I soon learned I had to choose between pleasing people and pleasing God. If I had chosen to be popular with people I would not be standing in the place of ministry I occupy today.

The followers of Jesus have faced this same choice since the very beginning. In John 12:42, 43 we read:

> And yet [in spite of all this] many even of the leading men (the authorities and the nobles) believed and trusted in Him. But because of the Pharisees they did not confess it, for fear that [if they should acknowledge Him] they would be expelled from the synagogue;

> For they loved the approval and the praise and the glory that come from men [instead of and] more than the glory that comes from God. [They valued their credit with men more than their credit with God.]

Today you and I are faced with a decision. Are we going to go on trying to build ourselves, our ministries, and our reputations, or are we willing to give up all our own human efforts and simply trust God? Are we ready to stop operating in the arm of the flesh and start operating in the arm of the Lord?

4

The Arm of the Lord

*...to whom has the arm (the power) of the Lord
been shown (unveiled and revealed)?*

John 12:38

The arm of the Lord is in direct contrast to the arm of the flesh which we discussed previously. While the arm of the flesh is based on the covenant of works, the arm of the Lord is based on the covenant of grace. The first depends upon law, the second depends upon faith.

Under the first covenant we wear ourselves out trying to make things happen on our own. Under the second covenant we enter into the rest of God and depend upon Him to do for us what we cannot do for ourselves. To fulfill the first covenant we must be full of fleshly zeal. To fulfill the second covenant we must be full of God.

In Romans 12:1 we are told to present our bodies as a living sacrifice, holy and well pleasing to God, which is our reasonable service and spiritual worship. The Lord revealed to me that in order to be filled with His Spirit and be pleasing to Him, we must be 1) willing, 2) yielded, and 3) empty. We must be willing for God to use us as He sees fit. We must be willing to follow His plans rather than our own. We must be empty of ourselves.

To be pleasing to God, we must give up all our human efforts to build ourselves, our ministries, and our careers and allow the Lord to build them for us according to His will and plan for us. We must learn to be satisfied where we are and with what we are doing. We must quit worrying and fretting and simply allow the Lord to do the work in us and through us that He knows needs to be done.

To be pleasing to God, we must quit looking to the arm of the flesh and start looking to the arm of the Lord.

But God... Was With Him

And the patriarchs [Jacob's sons], boiling with envy and hatred and anger, sold Joseph into slavery in Egypt; *but God* was with him.

ACTS 7:9

As a young man, Joseph had a dream in which he saw himself being honored by all the members of his family. The mistake he made was telling that dream, because it was one of the things that made his brothers so hateful, envious, and angry that they tried to get rid of him by selling him into slavery.

Joseph was a little overly exuberant. That's why God had to spend several years doing a work in him before He could use him to fulfill His plan to bless him and his family and many, many others.

Often we are like young Joseph. We make the same mistake he did. When God reveals to us His dream and vision for our life, we share it with others who are not as thrilled about it as we are and who may even cause us problems, just as Joseph's brothers did for him. As a result of the rashness of Joseph and his brothers, Joseph ended up alone in a prison cell in Egypt far from home and family with no one to turn to but the Lord.

If you and I are going to enjoy the fullness of God in our lives, we must go through periods in which we have to stand alone. Sometimes that is good for us because we get too caught up with people. Sometimes we must be left with nobody so we will learn to depend solely upon the Lord. Like Joseph, with all the people and things we were leaning on stripped away, we will be forced to place our entire faith and trust in God. The Lord wants us to be rooted and grounded in Him, able to stand alone, with Him upholding us.

When God called me out of my job in St. Louis and into full-time ministry, I had to go through some hard, lonely times. I found myself out on the road in a traveling ministry pursuing a dream and a vision which I had not yet really proven was from God. Those were rough years. I went through such hard, lonely times I cried out to God, begging Him to give me groups of people to support me in what I was trying to do for Him.

In my loneliness I would pray, "Lord, I've got to have someone to talk to. I have nobody."

"You've got Me," He would say. "Talk to Me."

"But, Lord," I would cry, "I don't know how to do this. I need to be around people I can ask about it."

But the Lord didn't want me talking to anybody else about what He had told me to do. He wanted me to seek His direction and guidance, not the opinions and advice of other people. As in the case of Joseph, God wanted me to depend upon the arm of the Lord and not the arm of the flesh. It is not wrong to ever seek advice from others, but in my case I was so insecure and fearful of rejection, I would have followed the advice people gave me instead of seeking God's direction.

God does not want us to be a clone of somebody else. He wants us to be unique and creative. He is looking for something new and fresh in us. He wants us to operate by His Spirit.

One of the things God taught me during that hard, lonely period of my life was the difference between many types of birds and eagles. Most birds fly in flocks, but eagles fly alone. Each of us must decide whether we want to fly along as one of the many birds in a flock or be an eagle. If we want to be an eagle, we must learn to fly alone.

There were many times when Joseph had to fly alone. He had to face hard, lonely times in his life, especially during the period he spent in prison in a foreign country. Yet despite all the adversity that came against him, notice what the Scriptures say about his situation: Joseph was sold into slavery by his own brothers, *but God* was with Him. That phrase "but God" occurs several times in this story, as we will see.

IN HIS BUSINESS GOD DELIVERS

And [God] delivered him [Joseph] from all his distressing afflictions and won him goodwill and favor and wisdom and understanding in the sight of Pharaoh, king of Egypt, who made him governor over Egypt and all his house.

ACTS 7:10

God built Joseph's reputation and career. He put him in the right place at the right time. He gave him favor with the right people and promoted him when the time was right, just as He will do for us: *For not from the east nor from the west nor from the south come promotion and lifting up* (Psalm 75:6).

You and I do not have to depend upon the arm of the flesh in our efforts to overcome adversity and opposition and earn favor and win promotion. When God is ready to move in our lives, He will *give* us favor and promotion — and no devil or person on earth will be able to prevent it from happening: ...*If God is for us, who [can be] against us? [Who can be our foe, if God is on our side?]* (Romans 8:31).

It doesn't matter what people think of us. Our weaknesses and inabilities don't make any difference to God. His criteria for using people is not their talents, gifts, and abilities. He is looking for people who are willing, yielded, and empty. Let God build you, your ministry, and your reputation and career. When the time is right, He will deliver you just as He delivered Joseph. Then you will see the fulfillment of your dream, just as Joseph did.

BUT GOD...MEANT IT FOR GOOD

Then his brothers went and fell down before him, saying, See, we are your servants (your slaves)!

And Joseph said to them, Fear not; for am I in the place of God? [Vengeance is His, not mine.]

As for you, you thought evil against me, *but God* meant it for good, to bring about that many people should be kept alive, as they are this day.

GENESIS 50:18-20

Whatever may have happened to us in the past, it does not have to dictate our future. Regardless of what people may have tried to do to us, God can take it and turn it for good: *We are assured and know that [God being a partner in their labor] all things work together and are [fitting into a plan] for good to and for those who love God and are called according to [His] design and purpose* (Romans 8:28).

Joseph's brothers meant evil to him, *but God* meant good to him. They devised a plan to destroy him by selling him into slavery in Egypt. But in the end Joseph became second in command to Pharaoh and was the instrument used by God to save his own family and many thousands of others. That is a good example of the arm of the Lord triumphing over the arm of the flesh.

Sometimes we forget how big our God is. Through everything that happened to him, Joseph kept his eyes on God. He didn't sit around and gripe and complain and hold a "pity party." Despite what others — even his own brothers — did to him, he didn't allow himself to be filled with bitterness, resentment, and unforgiveness. He knew it didn't matter who was against him, because God was for him and would eventually work out everything for the best for all concerned.

Joseph knew that whatever happened, God was on his side. He let God build his life, his reputation, and his career. That is what you and I need to do. We need to put no confidence in the arm of the flesh, but rather trust ourselves entirely to the arm of the Lord.

DON'T TRUST THE FLESH

A voice says, Cry [prophesy]! And I said, What shall I cry? [The voice answered, Proclaim:] All flesh is as frail as grass, and all that makes it attractive [its kindness, its goodwill, its mercy from God, its glory and comeliness, however good] is transitory, like the flower of the field.

The grass withers, the flower fades, when the breath of the Lord blows upon it; surely [all] the people are like grass.

The grass withers, the flower fades, but the word of our God will stand forever.

Isaiah 40:6-8

When I first began to follow God's call into the ministry, there were many people who told me I couldn't do it, for a variety of reasons. The main two were that 1) I was a woman and 2) I didn't have the personality to be a minister of the Gospel. *But God* wanted to use me, a woman, and He changed my personality.

Those people were wrong about my not being able to function as a minister because I was a woman, but they were right about my not having the kind of personality needed to minister. I was not a very nice person. I was harsh and hard, crude and rude, loud and overbearing, rebellious and stubborn. *But God* went to work on me and began to change me. He will do the same for you, if you will keep your eyes on Him and not on yourself.

No Confidence in the Flesh

For we [Christians]...worship God in spirit and by the Spirit of God and exult and glory and pride ourselves in Jesus Christ, and put no confidence or dependence [on what we are] in the flesh and on outward privileges and physical advantages and external appearances.

Philippians 3:3

You and I are going to lean either on the arm of the flesh or on the arm of the Lord. Either we will spend our lives trying to take care of ourselves or we will let go and let God take care of us as we put our faith and trust in Him.

Through Isaiah the prophet, the Lord has told us not to trust in the flesh, because all flesh is as frail as grass. Like the flowers of the field, it is here today and gone tomorrow.

We can put no confidence at all in the flesh. Apart from the Lord, we can do nothing. We must humble ourselves under His mighty hand and wait upon Him to exalt us in His good time.

ACKNOWLEDGE GOD

In all your ways know, recognize, and acknowledge Him, and
He will direct and make straight and plain your paths.

PROVERBS 3:6

Do you know what it means to acknowledge the Lord in all our ways? It means to submit all our plans to Him to work them out according to His will and desire for us. And what He wants is for us to come to know Him in the power of His resurrection and to behold Him in all His beauty and glory. (Philippians 3:10.)

We need to seek after one thing, and one thing only, and that is to dwell in His presence, because only there can we experience the fullness of joy. (Psalm 27:4; 16:11.) It is a sign of maturity to seek God for Who He is, not only for what He can do for us.

If my husband returned from a long trip away from home, I would meet him at the airport thrilled to see *him*. Because I care about him, he delights in giving me things to show me his love. However, if I met him at the airport excited, not over his being home, but over finding out what *gift* he had brought me, he might be hurt and offended.

I have found that when I seek God's face (His Presence) to get to know our wonderful, loving heavenly Father better, His hand is always open to me.

As His children, God is waiting for us to grow up in all things unto the stature of His Son Jesus Christ. (Ephesians 4:13.) Babies cry every time they don't get what they want, but not adults.

The Bible teaches that a child should be brought up in the nurture and admonition of the Lord, promising if he is trained in the way he should go, he will not depart from it. (Ephesians 6:4 KJV; Proverbs 22:6 KJV.) God is training us up, His children, in the way we should go — not the way we *want* to go, but the way we *should* go.

THE LORD KNOWS THE BEST PLAN!

Come now, you who say, Today or tomorrow we will go into such and such a city and spend a year there and carry on our business and make money.

Yet you do not know [the least thing] about what may happen tomorrow. What is the nature of your life? You are [really] but a wisp of vapor (a puff of smoke, a mist) that is visible for a little while and then disappears [into thin air].

You ought instead to say, If the Lord is willing, we shall live and we shall do this or that [thing].

JAMES 4:13-15

It took me a long time to learn to want what God wants more than what I want. Now I want God's will more than my

61

own will. I know if I want something and God says no, it may hurt my feelings and be hard for me to accept, but it will be better for me in the long run.

One time I was sitting in my golf cart with my husband Dave making plans for our next vacation. We were having such a good time where we were, I was already planning our return to that same spot the next year. Suddenly the Lord spoke to me the words of James 4:13-15. I didn't even know they were in the Bible until I searched them out for myself.

The Lord was not telling me I shouldn't plan for the future. He was telling me not to get ahead of myself or to think too highly of myself and my schemes. He was letting me know that all my bright ideas are not worth two cents; it is His will and purpose that really matter. That was what I should have been seeking, not my own wants and desires. I had to learn the flesh profits nothing. Frequently, we make our own plans and expect God to bless them. I was showing Him disrespect by not acknowledging Him in my plans.

My problem was I had a haughty spirit. In Proverbs 16:18 we are warned: *Pride goes before destruction, and a haughty spirit before a fall.* The key to the abundant, joyful, peaceful life Jesus died to give us is humility. We need to learn to humble ourselves under the mighty hand of God so that He may exalt us in due time. One way we humble ourselves is by waiting on the Lord, refusing to move in the energy of the flesh. We need to learn to live one day at a time, being content where we are and with what we have until the Lord leads us to something better.

It is not wrong to plan a vacation, but it honors God when we acknowledge Him. When we honor Him, He honors us — and frequently gives us our heart's desire!

The real issue here is attitude. If my attitude had been right, I would have begun with lifting my heart up to the Lord and saying something such as, "Lord, if it is all right with You, I would really like to come back here next year. We are starting to make plans, but if You don't approve, we will be happy for You to interrupt our plans anytime You want to. We want Your will!"

EMPTY OUT AND BE FILLED

Now the wife of a son of the prophets cried to Elisha, Your servant my husband is dead, and you know that your servant feared the Lord. But the creditor has come to take my two sons to be his slaves.

Elisha said to her, What shall I do for you? Tell me, what have you [of sale value] in the house? She said, Your handmaid has nothing in the house except a jar of oil.

Then he said, Go around and borrow vessels from all your neighbors, empty vessels — and not a few.

And when you come in, shut the door upon you and your sons. Then pour out [the oil you have] into all those vessels, setting aside each one when it is full.

So she went from him and shut the door upon herself and her sons, who brought to her the vessels as she poured the oil.

When the vessels were all full, she said to her son, Bring me another vessel. And he said to her, There is not a one left. Then the oil stopped multiplying.

Then she came and told the man of God. He said, Go, sell the oil and pay your debt, and you and your sons live on the rest.

2 KINGS 4:1-7

The key to value and worth is knowing who we are in Jesus. When we know that, there is nothing for us to do but stand in awe of the Lord and give Him thanks and praise for what He has done for us in Christ. Like this poor widow, the first step to fullness is to recognize we are empty.

All of us are empty vessels. None of us has anything in us of any value except the power of God that is resident there to flow out of us. What do we have to offer to God? Nothing. God is not needy. He doesn't need you or me. He can do His own work without us. We are not indispensable.

I don't say that to tear us down or make us feel bad about ourselves. I say it to make a point. If we don't get rid of our highmindedness and haughtiness, the Lord will not be able to use us as He desires.

We do have value, but only the value the Lord assigns to us because of the blood of His Son Jesus Christ. We have nothing in and of ourselves. In Christ, we are and have everything. But in our flesh, there is nothing of any value or worth. What is born of the flesh is flesh, and it profits us nothing.

When I first started ministering, I wanted to help people. The Lord spoke to me then and said: "When you are empty of yourself so that all you have left within you is the ability to depend on the Holy Spirit, when you have learned that everything you are and have comes from Him, then I'll send you around to your neighbors to fill their empty vessels with the life I have poured into your empty vessel."

Arriving at the place of being empty of ourselves is not an easy task and is rarely ever a quick one. A deep work must be done in each of us before we can say with the apostle Paul:

I have been crucified with Christ [in Him I have shared His crucifixion]; it is no longer I who live, but Christ (the

Messiah) lives in me; and the life I now live in the body I live by faith in (by adherence to and reliance on and complete trust in) the Son of God, Who loved me and gave Himself up for me.

GALATIANS 2:20

I spent many years wondering if I would ever reach a place of manifesting humility instead of pride — of being dependent on God instead of independent, of trusting in His arm instead of in my own. If you feel the same way, let me encourage you that as long as you don't give up, you are making progress.

It may seem as though reaching the place you desire is taking forever, but ...*He who began a good work in you will continue until the day of Jesus Christ [right up to the time of His return], developing [that good work] and perfecting and bringing it to full completion in you* (Philippians 1:6).

If we press on and are sincere about spiritual maturity, we will all eventually be like the woman in 2 Kings 4:1-7 — empty of ourselves and ready to be used by God to fill other empty people.

It is only after we have realized it is not us; it is all the Lord, that we can even begin to serve Him as we should. Someone has said, "It remains to be seen what God can do through a man or woman who will give Him all the glory."

We must come to realize the battles we face in this life are not ours, but God's. If we stop trying to win them by relying on the arm of the flesh, we will find the arm of the Lord moving on our behalf and doing for us what we could never do on our own.

To know and experience what God can do, we must first realize and acknowledge what we cannot do. We must get our eyes off of ourselves and our limited ability, and totally onto Him and His infinite power.

THREE IMPORTANT PRINCIPLES

After this, the Moabites, the Ammonites, and with them the Meunites came against Jehoshaphat to battle....

And Judah gathered together to ask help from the Lord; even out of all the cities of Judah they came to seek the Lord [yearning for Him with all their desire].

And Jehoshaphat stood in the assembly of Judah and Jerusalem in the house of the Lord before the new court

And said, O Lord, God of our fathers, are You not God in heaven? And do You not rule over all the kingdoms of the nations? In Your hand are power and might, so that none is able to withstand You....

And now behold, the men of Ammon, Moab, and Mount Seir, whom You would not let Israel invade when they came from the land of Egypt, and whom they turned from and did not destroy —

Behold, they reward us by coming to drive us out of Your possession which You have given us to inherit.

O our God, will You not exercise judgment upon them? For we have no might to stand against this great company that is coming against us. We do not know what to do, but our eyes are upon You.

2 CHRONICLES 20:1,4-6,10-12

In verse 12 of this passage we see three important statements that apply to us today as much as they did to the people of Judah who faced overpowering enemies: 1) "We have no might to stand against this great company that is coming against us," 2) "We do not know what to do," 3) "But our eyes are on You."

When we reach the place of being able to make these three statements to the Lord in total honesty and complete dependence upon Him, He will be free to move on our behalf, as He did for the people in this story.

Sometimes we wonder why it seems God is not moving in our lives. The answer may be that we are still too full of ourselves. The reason God may not be taking control of our situation is that we won't let go of it. That is part of what the Bible means when it says the battle is not ours, but God's.

THE BATTLE IS NOT YOURS, BUT GOD'S...

And all Judah stood before the Lord, with their children and their wives.

Then the Spirit of the Lord came upon Jahaziel...a Levite of the sons of Asaph, in the midst of the assembly.

He said, Hearken, all Judah, you inhabitants of Jerusalem, and you King Jehoshaphat. The Lord says this to you: Be not afraid or dismayed at this great multitude; for the battle is not yours, *but God's*.

Tomorrow go down to them. Behold, they will come up by the Ascent of Ziz, and you will find them at the end of the ravine before the Wilderness of Jeruel.

You shall not need to fight in this battle; take your positions, stand still, and see the deliverance of the Lord [Who is] with you, O Judah and Jerusalem. Fear not nor be dismayed. Tomorrow go out against them, for the Lord is with you.

And Jehoshaphat bowed his head with his face to the ground, and all Judah and the inhabitants of Jerusalem fell down before the Lord, worshiping Him.

2 CHRONICLES 20:13-18

Before we begin to shout what we read in verse 15, "O God, the battle is not mine, but Yours," we must do what we are told in verse 12: 1) acknowledge we have no power to save ourselves, 2) admit we do not know what to do about our situation, and 3) turn our eyes upon the Lord, placing our faith and trust in Him to deliver us.

Once we stop looking to the arm of the flesh for our solution, God will begin to give us His instructions for what to do. Often it will be what He told the people in this passage: "Be still."

In Psalm 46:10 KJV the Lord says to us, *Be still, and know that I am God: I will be exalted among the heathen, I will be exalted in the earth.* In Isaiah 40:31 we are told that *...those who wait for the Lord [who expect, look for, and hope in Him] shall change and renew their strength and power; they shall lift their wings and mount up [close to God] as eagles [mount up to the sun]; they shall run and not be weary, they shall walk and not faint or become tired.*

It will not be the end of the world if we do absolutely nothing for a month or two except fall to our knees and say, "Lord, I am waiting on You. I worship You and wait for You to move against my enemies and bring forth my deliverance."

When the Israelites were journeying from Egypt, the land of bondage, to Canaan, the land of promise, the cloud of the Lord went before them, leading the way. Each time the Ark of the Covenant was lifted up and carried out before them, Moses would cry out to God, *...Rise up, Lord; let Your enemies be* *scattered; and let those who hate You flee before You* (Numbers 10:35). I love that verse. I believe it should be our war cry: "Let God arise and His enemies be scattered!"

We need to remember that when the Lord rises up, every knee shall bow and every tongue shall confess that Jesus Christ is Lord, to the glory of God the Father. (Philippians 2:10,11.)

Many in the Body of Christ have lost sight of the greatness of God. We tend to think of Him and His abilities from our limited human perspective. We serve a great and mighty God. Every enemy will crumble before Him. It is so important that we keep our eyes on Him and not on ourselves.

In verse 16 of this passage God began to give directions to His people through His prophet. He told them to take up their positions, stand still, and see the deliverance of the Lord. They were not to be afraid or dismayed, for God was with them.

Hearing that news, King Jehoshaphat and all the people bowed their faces to the ground and worshipped the Lord. Faced with their enemies, that was the position of God's people in this situation — and it should be our position today.

We need to spend more time in worship and praise and less time in planning, scheming, and trying to tell God what He needs to do. We need to remember that God resists the proud, but gives grace to the humble.

God Helps the Helpless

...Clothe (apron) yourselves, all of you, with humility [as the garb of a servant, so that its covering cannot possibly be stripped from you, with freedom from pride and arrogance] toward one another. For God sets Himself against the proud (the insolent, the overbearing, the disdainful, the presumptuous, the boastful) — [and He opposes, frustrates, and defeats them], but gives grace (favor, blessing) to the humble.

1 PETER 5:5

God wants us to learn we cannot succeed by trusting in ourselves and our own human knowledge, wisdom, strength, and ability, but in Him.

The world says, "God helps those who help themselves." That statement is totally unscriptural. In some matters we do help ourselves: God won't send an angel to clean our cars and houses for instance. We need to be in charge of that. We also need to go out and look for a job to earn our own living. God gives us wisdom and strength, but we need to use our own arm of the flesh in these matters.

The Bible tells us God helps those who *cannot* help themselves in the sense that we are to depend not upon our own efforts, plans, and schemes to get us through this life and solve all our own problems, but on Him.

Saying that God helps those who help themselves is not only unscriptural, but misleading. This statement tends to make people feel as though they need to do all they possibly can for themselves before ever asking God to help. No wonder it is a "worldly statement" frequently accepted as Scripture.

Satan, the god of this world's system (see 2 Corinthians 4:4) would like nothing better than for us to believe that lie and spend our lives in frustration trying to take care of ourselves rather than leaning on God.

God does not help those who help themselves; He helps those who know they cannot help themselves, those who, like King Jehoshaphat and the people of Judah, realize they are totally dependent upon Him for their deliverance.

THE EVERLASTING ARMS

The eternal God is your refuge and dwelling place, and underneath are the everlasting arms; He drove the enemy before you and thrust them out, saying, Destroy!

DEUTERONOMY 33:27

We often sing that old hymn, "Leaning on the Everlasting Arms." As we sing it, we should feel the everlasting arms of the Lord coming down and lifting us up. We should experience the manifest presence of God with us as we make the conscious decision to no longer lean on the arm of the flesh, but on the arm of the Lord.

WITH US IS THE LORD OUR GOD

Be strong and courageous. Be not afraid or dismayed before the king of Assyria and all the horde that is with him, for there is Another with us greater than [all those] with him.

With him is an arm of flesh, but with us is the Lord our God to help us and to fight our battles....

2 CHRONICLES 32:7,8

When the Assyrians came in great strength to invade Judah and lay siege to Jerusalem, King Hezekiah encouraged the people with these words: "Be strong and full of courage. Don't be fearful or discouraged because of our enemy, the king of Assyria, and the huge army with him. The One Who is with us is greater than all of them put together. The king of Assyria will fail, and we will be victorious, because he is depending on the arm of the flesh, but we are trusting in the arm of the Lord."

That is the attitude you and I need to have in the face of our seemingly overwhelming problems. Rather than looking at our past failures, our present fallacies, or our future fears, we should be looking to the Lord and trusting in His wisdom, strength, and power. We should be reminding ourselves that no matter how many problems may be facing us, the One Who is with us is greater than all those who oppose us. With them is the arm of the flesh, but with us is the arm of the Lord.

In Jeremiah 17:5-8 we read that those who put their trust in the arm of the flesh are cursed with great evil. They are like a plant in the desert that is dry and destitute. They will not see any good come. But those who put their trust in the arm of the Lord are blessed. They are like a tree planted by a river. They do not cease to produce fruit even in the midst of a drought. No matter what comes, they will flourish and ...*shall not be anxious and full of care...* (v. 8).

We are not to lean on the arm of flesh, but on the arm of the Lord. That means we are not to lean on ourselves or on other people, but on God. People will disappoint us, and we will end up devastated, but God will never fail us or forsake us. Like Jesus, we need to love people, but not trust ourselves to them.

LOVE MAN, TRUST GOD

But when He was in Jerusalem during the Passover Feast, many believed in His name [identified themselves with His party] after seeing His signs (wonders, miracles) which He was doing.

But Jesus [for His part] did not trust Himself to them, because He knew all [men];

And He did not need anyone to bear witness concerning man [needed no evidence from anyone about men], for He Himself knew what was in human nature. [He could read men's hearts.]

JOHN 2:23-25

Jesus loved people, especially His disciples. He had great fellowship with them. He traveled with them, ate with them, and taught them. But He did not put His trust in them, because He knew what was in human nature.

That does not mean He had no trust in His relationship with them; He just didn't open Himself up to them and give Himself to them in the same way He trusted God and opened Himself up to His heavenly Father.

That is the way we should be. We should love people, but trust God.

Many times we become devastated because we form relationships with people we should not be involved with. We become too familiar with them, start depending upon then idolizing them, and looking to them when we should be looking to God.

I love my husband. He and I have a wonderful relationship together. I don't think I could find a better man to be married to than Dave Meyer. He is good to me. He respects me. He treats me the way a husband should treat his wife. But, being human, he still sometimes says and does things that hurt me, just as I sometimes say and do things that hurt him.

Why does that happen even in the best of human relationships? It happens because we are not perfect. Only God can be counted on never to fail us, disappoint us, hurt us, or do us wrong. As much as we may love, honor, cherish, and respect others — especially our spouse or our family members

— we must not place our trust in the weak arm of the flesh, but only in the strong arm of the Lord.

When we expect things from people they are not able to give us, we always end up disappointed and hurt.

5

THE WARFARE OF REST

*For we who have believed (adhered to and trusted
in and relied on God) do enter that rest....*

HEBREWS 4:3

The importance of entering into God's rest through believing and trusting in Him is very important, as previously mentioned. There is a warfare of rest. We can defeat what the devil is trying to do in our life simply by refusing to become upset. In this chapter we will examine how to enter and stay in that place of rest.

The world we live in today fits the description in 2 Timothy 3:1 below. As you read the following Scriptures, keep in mind that believers operate from a different world than that of unbelievers — we are in this world, but not of it.

But understand this, that in the last days will come (set in) perilous times of great stress and trouble [hard to deal with and hard to bear].

We are in hard times: *hard to deal with and hard to bear.* Verses 2 - 5 continue describing what we recognize as the times we are living in today and one action we are to take.

For people will be lovers of self and [utterly] self-centered, lovers of money and aroused by an inordinate [greedy] desire for wealth, proud and arrogant and contemptuous boasters. They will be abusive (blasphemous, scoffing), disobedient to parents, ungrateful, unholy and profane.

[They will be] without natural [human] affection (callous and inhuman), relentless (admitting of no truce or appeasement); [they will be] slanderers (false accusers, troublemakers), intemperate and loose in morals and conduct, uncontrolled and fierce, haters of good.

[They will be] treacherous [betrayers], rash, [and] inflated with self-conceit. [They will be] lovers of sensual pleasures and vain amusements more than and rather than lovers of God.

For [although] they hold a form of piety (true religion), they deny and reject and are strangers to the power of it [their conduct belies the genuineness of their profession]. Avoid [all] such people [turn away from them].

We are living in the times these Scriptures describe.

In verse 11 after Paul describes the persecutions and sufferings he endured, he then states, *out of them all the Lord delivered me*. He continues:

Indeed all who delight in piety and are determined to live a devoted and godly life in Christ Jesus will meet with persecution [will be made to suffer because of their religious stand].

But wicked men and imposters will go on from bad to worse, deceiving and leading astray others and being deceived and led astray themselves.

But as for you, continue to hold to the things that you have learned and of which you are convinced, knowing from whom you learned [them].

2 TIMOTHY 3:12-14

In chapter 4 Paul starts to explain what our response to living in this kind of atmosphere and situation should be. He says:

> Herald and preach the Word! Keep your sense of urgency [stand by, be at hand and ready], whether the opportunity seems to be favorable or unfavorable. [Whether it is convenient or inconvenient, whether it is welcome or unwelcome, you as preacher of the Word are to show people in what way their lives are wrong.] And convince them, rebuking and correcting, warning and urging and encouraging them, being unflagging and inexhaustible in patience and teaching.
>
> For the time is coming when [people] will not tolerate (endure) sound and wholesome instruction, but, having ears itching [for something pleasing and gratifying], they will gather to themselves one teacher after another to a considerable number, chosen to satisfy their own liking and to foster the errors they hold,
>
> And will turn aside from hearing the truth and wander off into myths and man-made fictions.
>
> 2 TIMOTHY 4:2-4

There are people with "itching ears" in the church today. If they hear teaching that doesn't suit them, they won't listen to it. Instead of stopping to check with their heart to see if it is right, they find someone who teaches what they want to hear and go there.

Sometimes people in counseling have "itching ears." They want someone to counsel them who will tell them what they want to hear. If the person counseling them tells them the truth, they don't go back. It is very dangerous to not listen to truth — to teaching and counsel based on God's Word!

Paul admonishes us to keep our sense of urgency in preaching the Word, *rebuking and correcting, warning and urging and encouraging* people, to convince them where their lives are wrong, so that they won't move further away from the truth.

In verse 5, Paul tells us what our response is to be to all the trouble in the world, all the trouble in our lives, the people that are hard to deal with or hard to bear:

> As for you, be calm and cool and steady, accept and suffer unflinchingly every hardship, do the work of an evangelist, fully perform all the duties of your ministry.

This is a glorious Scripture! *As for you, be calm and cool and steady.*

Our response to trouble is to be, "I am to be calm, cool and collected"!

When trouble starts in someone's life, the first thing they usually do is run around wildly, saying, "What can I do, what can I do, what can I do?" They react immediately in the flesh instead of seeking the Lord for direction.

I call this "a wild spirit"! They start doing all sorts of different things, reacting emotionally rather than remaining calm, cool, and steady and acting in accordance to the leading of the Holy Spirit. They start rebuking devils. Then they say, "I know what I'll do — I'll fast for two weeks. I'll get ten people from church over here, and we'll pray and pull these strongholds down."

Sometimes God does have us do such things, but we need to make sure we are acting in obedience to the leading of the Lord and not just reacting out of emotion. We must remember that works not energized by God are "dead works" and do not produce any good result.

THE WARFARE OF REST

Therefore put on God's complete armor, that you may be able to resist and stand your ground on the evil day [of danger], and, having done all [the crisis demands], to stand [firmly in your place].

EPHESIANS 6:13

We are to take a stand, after having done all in our power that God has led us to do. When faced with challenges, there are things we are to do.

But we must realize what we do to overcome one crisis may not be what we are to do to handle the next crisis that arises. The reason it may not work the second time is that the solution to the problem is not in the procedure, it is in the power — which God gives us to accomplish what *He* directs us to do.

God uses different methods for different people and in different situations. One time Jesus healed a blind man by spitting on the man's eyes and then laying hands on Him, twice. (Mark 8:22-25.) Another time He healed a man blind from birth by spitting on the ground and making mud which He rubbed on the man's eyes and sent him to wash in the Pool of Siloam. (John 9:1-7.) On another occasion He healed a blind man by simply speaking a word. (Mark 10:46-52.)

It was not any of the methods Jesus used that opened the blind eyes of these men so they could see. The thing that brought their healing was the power of God flowing through Jesus. The different methods were simply the different means used by Jesus to release the faith within each person to whom He ministered.

The key to unleashing the power of God is faith.

No Faith, No Rest

For indeed we have had the glad tidings [Gospel of God] proclaimed to us just as truly as they [the Israelites of old did when the good news of deliverance from bondage came to them]; but the message they heard did not benefit them, because it was not mixed with faith (with the leaning of the entire personality on God in absolute trust and confidence in His power, wisdom, and goodness) by those who heard it....

For we who have believed (adhered to and trusted in and relied on God) do enter that rest, in accordance with His declaration that those [who did not believe] should not enter when He said, As I swore in My wrath, They shall not enter My rest; and this He said although [His] works had been completed and prepared [and waiting for all who would believe] from the foundation of the world.

HEBREWS 4:2,3

In order to release our faith and activate the power of God on our behalf, sometimes we must fast and pray. At other times we must speak forth the Word of God over ourselves or our situation. Sometimes we must rebuke the devil and command him to depart in the name of Jesus. But whatever the Lord may lead us to do, it will do us no good if we do not remain in the rest of God, because if we are not abiding in His rest, we are not operating in true faith.

Hebrews 11:6 tells us that without faith it is impossible to please God. None of the methods we use mean anything if they are not mixed with faith.

According to Hebrews 4:2, 3, rest is a place. I believe it is the secret place spoken of in Psalm 91:1. That secret place is the presence of the Lord. When we are in that secret place, we don't have to worry or fret or have any anxiety. We don't have to try to figure out everything. Our flesh may be screaming at us to do something, but we can remain calm, cool, and steady. We don't have to get wild. We can relax and be secure knowing that in the presence of the Lord there is joy, peace, and rest.

PRACTICING THE PRESENCE OF GOD

Moses said to the Lord, See, You say to me, Bring up this people, but You have not let me know whom You will send with me. Yet You said, I know you by name and you have also found favor in My sight.

Now therefore, I pray You, if I have found favor in Your sight, show me now Your way, that I may know You [progressively become more deeply and intimately acquainted with You, perceiving and recognizing and understanding more strongly and clearly] and that I may find favor in Your sight. And [Lord, do] consider that this nation is Your people.

And the Lord said, My Presence shall go with you, and I will give you rest.

EXODUS 33:12-14

When Moses complained to God that He had not let him know whom He was going to send with him on his mission, he asked Him to show him His way so he could get to know Him better. The Lord then assured Moses His presence would be with him and give him rest. This was considered by God to be a great privilege. To Him, it was all that Moses needed.

What was true for Moses is true for us. As much as we would like to know God's plans and ways for us, all we really need to know is that His presence will be with us wherever He sends us and in whatever He gives us to do.

Moses had a big job on his hands, so naturally he was concerned about it, just as we are concerned about what God has called us to do in our lives. But all Moses needed was the knowledge and assurance God would go with him and help him. That is all we need to know too.

With all the challenges in our ministry as we try to bring hope and healing to others, sometimes we are tempted to get upset and bothered. But the Lord has taught us to remain calm, cool, and steady. He has shown us we must be adaptable and keep our eyes on Him, not on our plans. If things don't work out the way we want them to, we have to stay relaxed and trust Him to show us what to do.

When something goes wrong with our plan, often we are tempted to say, "Well, that does it! Now my plan is ruined!" If it was God Who ruined our plan, we had the wrong plan to begin with. If it was the devil who ruined our plan, the Lord will give us another plan, one that will be ten times better than the one that failed.

Too often when things don't work out just as we want them to, we start rebuking the devil. Yes, we do have authority over the devil. But what good does it do us to rebuke Satan and get wild and emotionally distraught? Psalm 91:1 tells us that he who dwells in the secret place of the Lord will remain stable and fixed under the shadow of the Almighty, Whose power no foe can withstand.

Too often in the midst of our troubles we talk to the wrong person. Instead of getting all upset and rebuking the devil every time something goes wrong, we need to learn to turn to the Lord and say, "Father, You are my Refuge and my Fortress, my God; on You I lean and rely, and in You I confidently trust."

THE PROMISES DEPEND ON THE PRESENCE

For [then] He will deliver you from the snare of the fowler and from the deadly pestilence.

[Then] He will cover you with His pinions, and under His wings shall you trust and find refuge; His truth and His faithfulness are a shield and a buckler.

You shall not be afraid of the terror of the night, nor of the arrow (the evil plots and slanders of the wicked) that flies by day,

Nor of the pestilence that stalks in darkness, nor of the destruction and sudden death that surprise and lay waste at noonday....

For He will give His angels [especial] charge over you to accompany and defend and preserve you in all your ways [of obedience and service].

PSALM 91:3-6,11

Verses 1 and 2 of Psalm 91 speak of the person who dwells in the secret place of the Most High, who claims the Lord as his Refuge and Fortress, and who leans, relies, and confidently trusts in Him.

The rest of the psalm (verses 3 though 16) then goes on to list all the promises of God's provision and protection. I have listed only a few of them here. We will look at the rest of these blessings more carefully in Chapter 5 of this book.

In *The Amplified Bible* there is a footnote at the bottom of the page on which Psalm 91 appears, which reads: "The rich promises of this whole chapter are dependent upon one's meeting exactly the conditions of these first two verses (see

Exodus 15:26)." What are the conditions of these first two verses? Basically, they are that we stay in rest.

You and I need to be delivered from the "wild spirit" that so often motivates us to lose our self-control so that we say and do things that cause pain and problems for us as well as for others. We need to remember that the promises of the Lord depend upon the presence of the Lord, which is always accompanied by the peace of the Lord.

PRACTICING THE PEACE OF THE LORD

Peace I leave with you; My [own] peace I now give and bequeath to you. Not as the world gives do I give to you. Do not let your hearts be troubled, neither let them be afraid. [Stop allowing yourselves to be agitated and disturbed; and do not permit yourselves to be fearful and intimidated and cowardly and unsettled.]

JOHN 14:27

Just before He was to go to the cross, Jesus told His disciples He was leaving them a gift — His peace. After His resurrection, He appeared to them again, and the first thing He said to them was, ...*Peace to you!* (John 20:19). To prove to them Who He was, He showed them His hands and His side, and then said to them once more, ...*Peace to you!*...(v. 21). Eight days later, He again appeared to them, and again His first words to them were, ...*Peace to you!* (v. 26).

Obviously Jesus intends for His followers to live in peace despite what may be going on around them at the time. What He was saying to His disciples — and to us — is simply, "Stop allowing yourselves to be anxious, worried, and upset."

In Psalm 42:5, the psalmist asks, *Why are you cast down, O my inner self? And why should you moan over me and be disquieted within me? Hope in God and wait expectantly for Him, for I shall yet praise Him, my Help and my God.* In verse 11 of that psalm he says basically the same thing: *Why are you cast down, O my inner self? And why should you moan over me and be disquieted within me? Hope in God and wait expectantly for Him, for I shall yet praise Him, Who is the help of my countenance, and my God.*

When we begin to become cast down and disquieted within, we need to hope in God and wait expectantly for Him, Who is our Help and our God.

When we begin to lose our *peace,* we need to remember our *place.*

OUR PLACE

But God — so rich is He in His mercy! Because of and in order to satisfy the great and wonderful and intense love with which He loved us,

Even when we were dead (slain) by [our own] shortcomings and trespasses, He made us alive together in fellowship and in union with Christ; [He gave us the very life of Christ Himself, the same new life with which He quickened Him, for] it is by grace (His favor and mercy which you did not deserve) that you are saved (delivered from judgment and made partakers of Christ's salvation).

And He raised us up together with Him and made us sit down together [giving us joint seating with Him] in the heavenly sphere [by virtue of our being] in Christ Jesus (the Messiah, the Anointed One).

EPHESIANS 2:4-6

Where is our place? In Christ Who, according to Ephesians 1:20, is seated at the right hand of God the Father in heavenly places. The fact that Jesus is seated is a key issue. If you and I are in Him, and He is seated, then we should be seated also.

In many biblical references to Jesus following His ascension, Jesus is depicted as being seated. (Ephesians 1:20; 2:6; Colossians 3:1; Hebrews 1:3,13; 8:1; 10:12; 12:2; 1 Peter 3:22; Revelation 4:2.)

Let's look at a couple of these instances because they reveal to us Jesus' place, which determines our place since we are in Him.

JESUS' PLACE

He [Jesus] is the sole expression of the glory of God [the Light-being, the out-raying or radiance of the divine], and He is the perfect imprint and very image of [God's] nature, upholding and maintaining and guiding and propelling the universe by His mighty word of power. When He had by offering Himself accomplished our cleansing of sins and riddance of guilt, He sat down at the right hand of the divine Majesty on high....

Besides, to which of the angels has He [God] ever said, Sit at My right hand [associated with Me in My royal dignity] till I make your enemies a stool for your feet?

HEBREWS 1:3,13

Here we see not only the *nature* of Jesus as the Word of God, and the *role* of Jesus as the Upholder, Sustainer, and Redeemer of the universe, we also see the *place* of Jesus — at the right hand of God on high.

Although it was never hard for me to believe Jesus was seated at the right hand of the Father in heaven, it was a revelation to me to learn it was God Who made the devil into a footstool. I had always thought it was my job to put Satan in his place.

Satan's Place

Then the devil who had led them astray [deceiving and seducing them] was hurled into the fiery lake of burning brimstone, where the beast and false prophet were; and they will be tormented day and night forever and ever (through the ages of the ages).

Revelation 20:10

I realize by speaking forth the Word of God in faith we can vocalize authority over the devil. Jesus has given us authority over Satan, and sometimes we need to give expression to that authority. There are times when we need to "put the devil in his place" by saying, "No, I'm not going to listen to you because you are a liar!" But at the same time, we need to recognize we are not the ones who exercise *ultimate* power and authority over the enemy.

It helped me to understand that when Jesus ascended into heaven, He was greeted there by His Father Who said to Him, "Welcome, My Son. Well done. Your work is finished. Sit here at the right hand of My throne until I make Your enemies a footstool for Your feet."

Who are the feet of Christ? We are. We are the Body of Christ, which includes His feet. That means although Jesus has given us power and authority over the devil and his demons on this earth, in the end it is God Himself Who is ultimately going to take away from Satan every bit of his power and send him to his final place of eternal punishment.

SEATED WITH CHRIST

Whereas this One [Christ], after He had offered a single sacrifice for our sins [that shall avail] for all time, sat down at the right hand of God,

Then to wait until His enemies should be made a stool beneath His feet.

HEBREWS 10:12,13

Why is it so important that Christ is seated in heavenly places and that we are seated there with Him waiting for His enemies to be placed under His feet by the Father?

This issue does not relate to us as strongly as it did to the ancient Jews. Under the old covenant, the Jewish high priest had to go into the earthly Holy of Holies once a year to make atonement for his own sins and for the sins of the people, which he did by sprinkling the blood of animals on the altar.

Within the earthly Holy of Holies there were no chairs because under the covenant of works the people were not allowed to sit down and rest. The Sabbath rest would not be instituted until after Jesus had gone into the true Holy of Holies and sprinkled His own blood on the heavenly altar: *For Christ (the Messiah) has not entered into a sanctuary made with [human] hands, only a copy and pattern and type of the true one, but [He has entered] into heaven itself, now to appear in the [very] presence of God on our behalf* (Hebrews 9:24).

All the time the Jewish high priest was in the earthly Holy of Holies, he had to be ministering to the Lord. God had commanded that bells be attached to the skirts of his robe: *...and its sound shall be heard when he goes [alone] into the Holy of Holies before the Lord and when he comes out, lest he die there* (Exodus 28:35).

Under the old covenant, the covenant of works, the high priest had to keep moving while in the Holy of Holies; he was not allowed to sit down and rest. But once Jesus had finished the work of salvation through His shed blood, when He entered into heaven His Father did not say to Him, "Stand up, Son, and keep moving." Instead, He said to Him, "Well done. Your work is finished. Sit here at My right hand until I make Your enemies Your footstool."

That is the same message God is giving you and me today. He wants us to know we are seated at His right hand with His Son Jesus Christ. That is a part of our inheritance as the saints of the Lord. Now instead of running around trying to please God and win His favor through works of the flesh, we can enter into His throne room and find rest for our souls.

Rest for Our Souls

Come to Me, all you who labor and are heavy-laden and overburdened, and I will cause you to rest. [I will ease and relieve and refresh your souls.]

Take My yoke upon you and learn of Me, for I am gentle (meek) and humble (lowly) in heart, and you will find rest (relief and ease and refreshment and recreation and blessed quiet) for your souls.

Matthew 11:28,29

Just as we can be involved in outward activity, we can be involved in inward activity. God wants us not only to enter into His rest in our body, He also wants us to enter into His rest in our soul.

To me, finding rest, relief, ease, refreshment, recreation, and blessed quiet for my soul means finding freedom from mental activity. It means not having to constantly try to figure out what I should do about everything in my life. It means not having to live in the torment of reasoning, always trying to come up with an answer I don't have. I don't have to worry; instead, I can remain in a place of quiet peace and rest.

When something goes wrong, instead of getting all upset and just rebuking the devil, I can speak to my raging soul and tortured mind just as Jesus spoke to the wind and waves by simply saying: "Peace, be still." (Mark 4:39 KJV.) The Lord has taught me in trying times I can "possess my soul." In doing this we are walking in authority over Satan.

POSSESS YOUR SOUL

By your steadfastness and patient endurance you shall win the true life of your souls.

LUKE 21:19

The *King James Version* of this verse reads, *In your patience possess ye your souls.* That is something we all need to learn to do.

I am the kind of person who likes to be in control. I don't like it when things get out of hand and start going the way I don't want them to go. One of my daughters is the same way. She and I have the same kind of personality. We like to plan our work and work our plan. When things start happening that are out of our control, we start getting upset and sometimes even fearful.

All of us need to learn not to let our mind and emotions get the best of us, especially when it involves things we have no control over. For example, suppose we are on our way to an important interview and we get caught in a traffic jam. How do we react? Is it worth getting all upset and unleashing a wild spirit? Wouldn't it be much better for us and everyone else if we just remained calm, cool, and steady, even if we were late for that interview? If we have done our best, God will do the rest.

One time a lady came to one of our meetings in Louisiana. She told us she had just learned her husband had been injured in an accident and was at that very moment undergoing surgery in a hospital in Arkansas. Yet there she was in the back of the church filled with the peace of the Lord. But why not? It would not have done her any good at all to be worrying and fretting and weeping and wailing, "Oh, why did this happen? Here I am trying to be a good Christian, and while I'm in church a tree falls on my husband and causes a disaster in our lives. I just don't understand why such things happen to us believers."

One day a lady was sitting in a boat reading and quoting Psalm 91:11 which promises that the angels of the Lord will take charge over us and defend us and protect us in all our ways. Just then something happened to the chair she was sitting on, and she fell over and cracked her head on the side of the boat. It hurt so bad her soul leaped up, and she started complaining to God, "I don't understand how this could have happened. Here I was reading and quoting Psalm 91:11 about how You send Your angels to watch over me and protect me, and look what happened! Where were You, Lord?"

Immediately God spoke to her and said, "Well, you're not dead, are you?" We often become so upset over what happened, we fail to realize what God protected us from.

We love to confess the Word of God by saying, "My steps are ordered of the Lord" (Psalm 37:23 KJV) — until He takes us someplace we don't want to go. Then all of a sudden it's, "I rebuke you, Satan!" What we don't realize is, God may be taking us right into the middle of a traffic jam to keep us from having a terrible wreck farther down the road.

We need to refuse to get wild. We need to refuse to allow our mind, will, and emotions to rule our spirit. In our patience we need to learn to possess our souls and not give the devil a foothold in our lives.

Don't Give the Devil a Foothold

When angry, do not sin; do not ever let your wrath (your exasperation, your fury or indignation) last until the sun goes down.

Leave no [such] room or foothold for the devil [give no opportunity to him].

EPHESIANS 4:26,27

Sometimes when my husband wants me to do something I don't want to do, my soul rises up and causes strife.

Dave and I have a long-standing difference of opinion about getting to the airport. He likes to get there at least an hour ahead of departure time and quietly wait. Since I hate to wait, I would rather get there twenty minutes before the plane takes off — and maybe end up chasing it down the runway yelling, "Hold that plane!" But that is just one aspect of our totally different personality types.

I am a high-energy, hang-from-the-chandelier type who is always in high gear. Dave, on the other hand, is Mr. Cast Your

Care. He is always peaceful, quiet, and collected. Nothing is a problem to him; he can adapt to any situation or circumstance.

(Is it any wonder he has always been in the best of health while I always used to be going to the doctor for backaches, neck aches, headaches, stomachaches, and colon problems?)

Every time Dave and I would plan a trip by air, which for us was usually three or four times a month, he would make me arrive at the airport so early it would upset me. Although I might not show it on the outside, on the inside I was wild.

"This is so stupid," I would say to myself. "Here I am sitting and waiting an hour and sometimes an hour and a half for an airplane to take off. I spend half my life waiting in airports. I have better things to do than this!"

I used to try to talk to Dave, to reason with him. I begged him. I got mad at him. I argued with him. But no matter what I said or did, he was unmoved.

"We are getting to the airport an hour early," he would say. "We are not going to miss our flight. We are not going to go through life running after airplanes or getting to our destination late. It's just not wise."

It would have been much easier if I had just said, "Okay. I'll take a good book and read while we wait or carry a pillow with me and take a nap." But instead, I fussed and fumed and made myself sick — all because I had not learned to rule my soul rather than letting it rule me.

Dave and I used to disagree about the silliest things. We would come home at night and fight about what to watch on television. When an old movie came on we liked, we would get into an argument about who the actors were.

Dave used to have this funny idea that everybody in the movies was Henry Fonda. Even if it was John Wayne, Dave would say it was Henry Fonda. I couldn't stand it. It would make me so mad I would say, "Dave, you're wrong, that is not Henry Fonda."

"Oh, yes, it is," he would answer.

"No, it's not!"

"Yes, it is."

"NO, IT ISN'T!"

We would stay up to midnight waiting for the credits to roll so I could *prove* to him I was right.

One day the voice of the Lord came to me and said, "Joyce, it won't make any difference to anybody's eternal salvation if Dave lives his whole life and comes home to Me thinking every actor he sees is Henry Fonda." So I had to learn to bite my tongue and let Dave think he was right even when I really believed he wasn't.

Another argument we used to have was about the location of a certain hardware store. There were actually two stores named Central Hardware in our town. To get to one of them, we had to turn right on our way out of our subdivision, and to get to the other we had to turn left. I thought one of the stores was closer to our house, and Dave thought the other was closer. When we would start out to go buy some hardware, I would tell him to turn one way, and he would invariably turn the other way.

"You're going the wrong way," I would say.

"No, I'm not."

"Yes, you are!"

"No, I'm not."

"YES, YOU ARE!"

A wild spirit would get the best of me every time. My soul would rise up within me and cause a conflict. I needed to tell it, "Soul, sit down, and get back into your place." Instead, I would start a fight.

Finally, one day Dave and I were driving out of our subdivision headed for the hardware store when the Holy Spirit spoke to me and said, "Joyce, just let the man go the way he wants to go." It was one of the hardest things I ever did to keep my mouth shut and let him go where I thought was the "wrong way."

Another time while we were ministering in Louisiana, some people sent Dave and me to a restaurant we didn't particularly care for because it served Cajun food, which we were not used to eating. I had found another restaurant I thought would be better for us, but it was some distance away, and Dave didn't want to drive that far. So he suggested a third restaurant. I was convinced I would not like it at all, but since it was obvious that was where Dave wanted to go, I gave in. All the way to the restaurant, I had to talk to my soul and ask the Lord to help me keep it under control because I was not at all enthusiastic about where we were going. As it turned out, we had one of the best meals we had eaten in a long time.

That's the way the Christian life is. Many times the thing we think we don't want is the best thing for us. That's why we need to learn to "go with the flow" and not cause so many problems over things that don't really matter. After all, what difference does it really make where we eat?

So often we make mountains out of molehills. We blow things up all out of proportion. We make major issues out of minor situations that are of no real importance whatsoever. We need to learn to adapt, to let things go, to quit allowing our souls to rule our lives. We need to learn to walk by the Spirit and not by the flesh.

When we get all upset about unimportant things, we throw open the door for the devil. We give him an opportunity to come in and wreak havoc. Often it is really not the devil's fault, it is ours.

It is amazing what the Lord would deliver us from, sovereignly and supernaturally, if we would choose to honor Him by staying in peace. We must learn to control our emotions and not let them control us. That doesn't mean we are to have no feelings. It just means we need to manage our feelings and not let them manage us. In the midst of our anger and upset, we are to possess our souls. We are to keep them in their place and give no room to the devil. In trying times we are to be constant and fearless.

CONSTANT AND FEARLESS

And do not [for a moment] be frightened or intimidated in anything by your opponents and adversaries, for such [constancy and fearlessness] will be a clear sign (proof and seal) to them of [their impending] destruction, but [a sure token and evidence] of your deliverance and salvation, and that from God.

PHILIPPIANS 1:28

According to this verse, the clear sign, proof, seal, token, and evidence to our enemies of their defeat and destruction and of our deliverance and salvation is our constancy and fearlessness.

What is the sign to the devil he cannot control us? It is not our great confession of our power and authority over him. It is our constancy and fearlessness in the face of his onset.

Why then does our deliverance sometimes seem to take so long? Often it is because God is waiting to see if we really trust Him or not. If we do, we will remain seated, *fully satisfied and assured that God* [is] *able and mighty to keep His Word and to do what He* [has] *promised* (Romans 4:21). We will say to Him, "If there is something You want me to do, Father, tell me and I'll do it. The battle is Yours, Lord, not mine. My eyes are on You. On You do I wait, and in You do I trust."

The devil does not want us to think we can relax, rest, and enjoy life while we are having problems. He wants us to think we have to be up and running around doing something, like the Old Testament priests in the Holy of Holies. He will whisper in our ear, "This is a terrible situation; what are you going to do?" He will send our closest friends and most trusted family members to say, "I heard about your problem; what are you going to do?" In times of adversity, it may seem that everybody we meet wants to know what we are going to do.

Our answer should be, "I'm going to stay seated in Christ and enjoy the rest of the Lord while He handles this situation and uses it to bless me."

CALM IN THE DAY OF ADVERSITY

Blessed (happy, fortunate, to be envied) is the man whom You discipline and instruct, O Lord, and teach out of Your law,

That You may give him power to keep himself calm in the days of adversity, until the [inevitable] pit of corruption is dug for the wicked.

PSALM 94:12,13

God uses the events and people of our lives to build our spiritual character as well as our spiritual power.

We think God just wants to empower us to overcome every problem of life by rebuking the devil. But the Lord has a much greater goal and purpose in mind than that. He is working to get us to the point where, no matter what is going on around us, we remain the same, rooted and grounded in Christ and His love, standing firm on the Rock of our salvation.

God is working in our lives to discipline, instruct, and teach us so He can give us power to keep ourselves calm in the days of adversity.

With that power, we are able to wait patiently and confidently for our promised deliverance and salvation, and for the impending destruction of all our enemies.

Seated with Christ at the right hand of God in heavenly places, trusting not in the arm of the flesh but in the arm of the Lord, we can truly be anxious for nothing.

Part 2

Cast All Your Care

Introduction

The Bible says we can cast all our care on God because He cares for us. (1 Peter 5:7.) That means God wants to take care of us, but in order for Him to do that, there is something we must do: We must stop taking the care upon ourselves and start casting it upon Him.

In His Word the Lord promises us if we will give Him our care, He will give us something in return.

Blessings for Messes

The Spirit of the Lord God is upon me, because the Lord has anointed and qualified me to preach the Gospel of good tidings to the meek, the poor, and afflicted; He has sent me to bind up and heal the brokenhearted, to proclaim liberty to the [physical and spiritual] captives and the opening of the prison and of the eyes to those who are bound,

To proclaim the acceptable year of the Lord [the year of His favor] and the day of vengeance of our God, to comfort all who mourn,

To grant [consolation and joy] to those who mourn in Zion — to give them an ornament (a garland or diadem) of beauty instead of ashes, the oil of joy instead of mourning, the garment [expressive] of praise instead of a heavy, burdened, and failing spirit — that they may be called oaks of righteousness [lofty, strong, and magnificent, distinguished for uprightness, justice, and right standing with God], the planting of the Lord, that He may be glorified.

ISAIAH 61:1-3

In this passage God promises to give us several positive things in exchange for the negative things in our lives. One of the positive exchanges He promises to make is to give us beauty for ashes. But God cannot give us His beauty if we do not give Him our ashes.

One time the Lord spoke to me and said, "A lot of people want to wallow around in the ashes of their past failures and disappointments, yet they expect Me to give them beauty."

If we are to receive the blessings God wants to bestow upon us, we must be willing to give Him the messes in our lives.

Blessings for messes — that's quite an exchange!

What a great trade. We give God all our worry, concern, anxiety, and care, and in return He gives us the peace and joy that come from knowing He is taking care of all those things for us.

THE FOUR ISSUES OF CARE

The thief comes only in order to steal and kill and destroy. I came that they may have and enjoy life, and have it in abundance (to the full, till it overflows).

JOHN 10:10

In Part 1 of this book we learned we are not to be anxious about anything but to turn from the arm of the flesh and depend upon the arm of the Lord as we remain calm — quietly, and confidently seated with Christ in heavenly places.

In Part 2 we are going to deal with several issues relating to our care. In Chapter 6 we will learn to cast all of our care on the Lord, because He cares for us. In Chapter 7 we will learn to cast our care, but not our responsibility. In Chapter 8 we will learn no matter how bad our situation or circumstance may be, we are to say of it, "This too shall pass." And in Chapter 9 we will examine the great advantage that comes from retiring from care.

It is my prayer that through these pages you will gain the insight you need to live to the full the joyful, abundant, overflowing life God wills for us and has provided for us through His Son, our Lord Jesus Christ.

6

⌾◦◦

HE CARETH FOR YOU

He who dwells in the secret place of the Most
High shall remain stable and fixed under the
shadow of the Almighty [Whose power
no foe can withstand].

I will say of the Lord, He is my Refuge and
my Fortress, my God; on Him I lean and rely,
and in Him I [confidently] trust!

PSALM 91:1,2

I n our study of casting our care upon the Lord because He cares for us, we will be looking again at Psalm 91, this time in more detail.

As we have seen, verses 3 through 16 of this psalm contain many of the blessings offered us by the Lord in exchange for our "messes." But, as we noted in Chapter 5, in order to receive those blessings, we must do something. We must meet the conditions of the first two verses quoted here, which is that we dwell in the secret place of the Most High, remaining stable and fixed under the shadow of the Almighty.

Specifically, there are three aspects of Psalm 91:1, 2 that determine our ability to receive God's richest blessings. First, we must *dwell*, which means "to remain...to settle...continue...sit (-down)."[1] This same word is used in John 15:4 in which Jesus told His disciples, *Dwell in Me, and I will dwell in you. [Live in Me, and I will live in you.] Just as no branch can bear fruit of itself without abiding in (being vitally united to) the vine, neither can you bear fruit unless you abide in Me.*

Second, we must dwell in the *secret place* of the Most High, meaning a hiding place, a place of protection, a place with a covering over it so we will be kept safe from all our enemies.

Third, we must remain under the *shadow* of the Almighty, meaning we must make the Lord our Refuge and our Fortress, leaning and relying on Him and confidently trusting in Him.

FOR THEN...

For [*then*] He will deliver you from the snare of the fowler and from the deadly pestilence.

[*Then*] He will cover you with His pinions, and under His wings shall you trust and find refuge; His truth and His faithfulness are a shield and a buckler.

You shall not be afraid of the terror of the night, nor of the arrow (the evil plots and slanders of the wicked) that flies by day,

Nor of the pestilence that stalks in darkness, nor of the destruction and sudden death that surprise and lay waste at noonday.

A thousand may fall at your side, and ten thousand at your right hand, but it shall not come near you.

Only a spectator shall you be [yourself inaccessible in the secret place of the Most High] as you witness the reward of the wicked.

PSALM 91:3-8

When we do the things required of us in verses 1 and 2, *then* the Lord will fulfill His wonderful promises to us set forth in the rest of the psalm. He will deliver us, cover us, keep us from fear and terror, and protect us against evil plots and slander so that we have no fear of pestilence, destruction, or sudden death, even though others may be falling from these things all around us.

Angelic Protection and Deliverance

Because you have made the Lord your refuge, and the Most High your dwelling place,

There shall no evil befall you, nor any plague or calamity come near your tent.

For He will give His angels [especial] charge over you to accompany and defend and preserve you in all your ways [of obedience and service].

They shall bear you up on their hands, lest you dash your foot against a stone.

You shall tread upon the lion and adder; the young lion and the serpent shall you trample underfoot.

Because he has set his love upon Me, therefore will I deliver him; I will set him on high, because he knows and understands My name [has a personal knowledge of My mercy, love, and kindness — trusts and relies on Me, knowing I will never forsake him, no, never].

He shall call upon Me, and I will answer him; I will be with him in trouble, I will deliver him and honor him.

With long life will I satisfy him and show him My salvation.

Psalm 91:9-16

The Amplified Bible version of this passage makes it very clear God promises angelic protection and deliverance to those who are serving Him and walking in obedience to Him.

A cross-reference to verse 13 is Luke 10:19 in which Jesus tells His disciples, *Behold! I have given you authority and power to trample upon serpents and scorpions, and [physical and mental strength and ability] over all the power that the enemy [possesses]; and nothing shall in any way harm you.* That describes our place in God. We believers are in a position of power and authority over Satan and his demons and devices.

We are also in a position of favor and influence with God. Because of our personal knowledge of Him and His mercy, love, and kindness, because we trust and rely on Him, knowing He will never leave us or forsake us, we have been given His precious promise to be with us, answer us, deliver us, and honor us with long and abundant life. What else could we ask for?

Saying we have angelic protection does not mean we will never have any trials or afflictions. It means we are protected from what Satan ultimately has planned for us as long as we keep our trust in God and say the right things of Him.

But there is one important thing we must learn about this angelic protection and deliverance. It is a *process.* In verses 15 and 16, the Lord promises us when we call upon Him, He will answer us and be with us *in* our troubles and will strengthen us and accompany us through them to victory, deliverance, and honor.

It took me many years to see the pattern: God was with me in my trials and troubles, then He began to deliver me out of them, and afterwards He honored me. That is a process, a progression, and we must be aware of it if we are to find peace and joy in the Lord.

One Thing

One thing have I asked of the Lord, that will I seek, inquire for, and [insistently] require: that I may dwell in the house of the Lord [in His presence] all the days of my life, to behold and gaze upon the beauty [the sweet attractiveness and the delightful loveliness] of the Lord and to meditate, consider, and inquire in His temple.

For in the day of trouble He will hide me in His shelter; in the secret place of His tent will He hide me; He will set me high upon a rock.

And now shall my head be lifted up above my enemies round about me; in His tent I will offer sacrifices and shouting of joy; I will sing, yes, I will sing praises to the Lord.

PSALM 27:4-6

At one time in my life I was asking the Lord for much more than just one thing. Then, later on, the Lord started transforming my life. When He did, this was the passage of Scripture He used to start the process.

Now when things start to go wrong in my life, instead of getting all anxious and upset and weeping and wailing, I go into the secret place of the Lord and lift up shouts of joy while the devil is trying to destroy me. I find refuge and remain stable and fixed under the shadow of the Almighty. If I worship and seek God, He fights my battles.

Under the Shadow

O God, You are my God, earnestly will I seek You; my inner self thirsts for You, my flesh longs and is faint for You, in a dry and weary land where no water is.

So I have looked upon You in the sanctuary to see Your power and Your glory.

Because Your loving-kindness is better than life, my lips shall praise You.

So will I bless You while I live; I will lift up my hands in Your name.

My whole being shall be satisfied as with marrow and fatness; and my mouth shall praise You with joyful lips

When I remember You upon my bed and meditate on You in the night watches.

For You have been my help, and in the shadow of Your wings will I rejoice.

PSALM 63:1-7

My husband Dave received a revelation from God on what it means to dwell under the shadow of His wings. A shadow is a shade, a protection from the heat or the sun. It is also a border between light and dark. We are either in the shadow of something or we are not.

In the same way there are definite borders or limits within which we must stay if we are to remain under the shadow of God's wings — that is, under His protection against the world or the devil.

When we are outside in the summertime, we can choose to stand in the shade or the shadow of a tree, or we can choose to walk back out into the full, direct sunlight. One place will usually be a lot cooler than the other and will offer much more protection against the damaging rays of the sun than the other.

That is the way it is with the Lord. As long as we choose to remain under the shadow of His wings, we will be much more comfortable and much better protected against danger than when we choose to walk out from under those wings.

A border is an intermediate area or boundary between two qualities or conditions. We can choose to live under one set of conditions or under a different set of conditions. The wise thing is not only to choose to stay under the shadow of the Almighty, but to take up permanent residence there.

When we drive down the highway, as long as we stay within the dividing lines between lanes and obey the signposts along the road, we are in much less danger of being involved in an accident than if we ignore those boundaries and instructions. Those lines and signs are put there for our benefit and protection.

In the spiritual realm, the "lines and signs" that keep us on the way of the Lord and out of danger are trust and confidence. As long as we place our trust and confidence in the Lord, He will keep us under the shadow of His wings and protect us from all danger and harm.

PRAYER PRODUCES PEACE

Do not fret or have any anxiety about anything, but in every circumstance and in everything, by prayer and petition (definite requests), with thanksgiving, continue to make your wants known to God.

And God's peace [shall be yours, that tranquil state of a soul assured of its salvation through Christ, and so fearing nothing from God and being content with its earthly lot of whatever sort that is, that peace] which transcends all understanding shall garrison and mount guard over your hearts and minds in Christ Jesus.

PHILIPPIANS 4:6,7

In this passage the apostle Paul does not say, "Pray and worry." Instead, he says, "Pray and don't worry." Why are we to pray and not worry? Because prayer is supposed to be the way we *cast our care* upon the Lord.

When the devil tries to give us care, we are supposed to turn and give that care to God. That's what prayer is, our acknowledgment to the Lord that we cannot carry our burden of care, so we lay it all on Him. If we pray about something and then keep on worrying about it, we are mixing a positive and a negative. The two cancel each other out so that we end up right back where we started — at zero.

Prayer is a positive force, worry is a negative force. The Lord has told me the reason many people operate at zero power level spiritually is that they cancel out their positive prayer power by giving in to the negative power of worry.

Too often we pray and give a positive confession for a while, and then worry and give a negative confession for a while. We go back and forth between the two extremes. That is like driving down the highway going from one side of the road to the other. If we keep doing that, sooner or later we are going to end up in trouble.

As long as we are worrying, we are not trusting God. It is only by trusting, by having faith and confidence in the Lord, that we are able to enter into His rest and enjoy the peace that transcends all understanding.

PRAYER PRODUCES REST

For we who have believed (adhered to and trusted in and relied on God) do enter that rest....

HEBREWS 4:3

If we are not at rest, we are not believing, because the fruit of believing is rest.

For many years of my life I would claim, "Oh, I'm believing God; I'm trusting the Lord." But I was not doing either of those things. I didn't know the first thing about believing God or trusting the Lord. All I did was worry and fret, talk negative and try to figure out everything on my own. I was anxious and panicky, irritable and on edge all the time. And yet I called myself believing and trusting.

If we are truly believing God and trusting the Lord, we have entered into His rest. We have prayed and cast our care upon Him and are now abiding in the perfect peace of His holy presence.

Prayer Produces Patience and Hope

Through Him also we have [our] access (entrance, introduction) by faith into this grace (state of God's favor) in which we [firmly and safely] stand. And let us rejoice and exult in our hope of experiencing and enjoying the glory of God.

Moreover [let us also be full of joy now!] let us exult and triumph in our troubles and rejoice in our sufferings, knowing that pressure and affliction and hardship produce patient and unswerving endurance.

And endurance (fortitude) develops maturity of character (approved faith and tried integrity). And character [of this sort] produces [the habit of] joyful and confident hope....

ROMANS 5:2-4

It is easy to say, "Don't worry." But to actually do that requires experience with God. I don't think there is any way a person can fully overcome the habit of worry, anxiety, and fear and develop the habit of peace, rest, and hope without years of experience.

That's why it is so important to continue to have faith and trust in God in the very midst of trials and tribulations. It is so important to resist the temptation to give up and quit when the going gets rough — and keeps on getting rougher over a long period of time. It is in those hard, trying times that the Lord is building in us the patience, endurance, and character that will eventually produce the habit of joyful and confident hope.

When you and I are in the midst of battle against our spiritual enemy, every round we go through produces valuable experience and strength. Each time we endure an attack, we become stronger. If we hang in there and refuse to give up, sooner or later we will be more than the devil can handle. When that happens, we will have reached spiritual maturity.

For years the devil controlled and manipulated me. He doesn't do that anymore. It is because I have had years of experience. I have learned to stop running to people and start turning to God. I have learned to pray to Him and cast my care upon Him — in secret. The Lord has revealed to me that we need to learn to endure our personal suffering privately.

There is a time to share what we are going through, and there is a time to keep things between us and God. Often we talk so much about "what we are going through" that the intended work never gets accomplished. God works out things for our good that Satan intends for our harm. The thing may be bad, but we serve a God Who is so good He can take a bad thing and actually work good in us from it.

Suffering in Silence

He was oppressed, [yet when] He was afflicted, He was submissive and opened not His mouth; like a lamb that is led
to the slaughter, and as a sheep before her shearers is dumb,
so He opened not His mouth.

Isaiah 53:7

In the Old Testament, the prophet Isaiah foretold what
would happen when the Messiah was led away to be sacrificed
for the sins of the world. He prophesied that He would be
silent and submissive, a sign of His inner strength and stability.

In my early Christian life and ministry I wanted to get to
the point where I was strong and stable like Jesus. I wanted to
reach the point where I was not fretful or worried or filled with
reasoning or anxiety.

My husband was the type person who found it easy to cast
his care upon the Lord and leave it with Him, believing He
would provide for all our needs. I wasn't that way. In the midst
of all our financial problems, I would be in the kitchen poring
over our unpaid bills and working myself into a frantic mess,
while Dave would be in the living room watching television
and playing with the kids. I was trying so hard to believe, to
trust, to have confidence in the Lord, but I just didn't have the
experience to *know* He would work out everything in His own
way and in His own time.

It is in just such trying times we get to know the Lord and,
like the apostle Paul, learn to be quiet and confident in whatever circumstances we may find ourselves.

CONTENT IN WHATEVER STATE

...I have learned how to be content (satisfied to the point where I am not disturbed or disquieted) in whatever state I am.

PHILIPPIANS 4:11

Paul had the ability to be content in whatever state he found himself. He knew how to cast his cares upon the Lord and remain in the secret place under the shadow of His wings. In spite of all the challenges he faced and all the hardships he had to go through, Paul knew how to live day by day without being disturbed or disquieted.

If that is not true of you, don't become discouraged, because Paul said it was something he had *learned* to do — and that takes time and experience. You may not have that ability yet, but if you keep following the Lord, being faithful and obedient to Him regardless of what may happen to you, sooner or later you will begin to develop the ability to be content in whatever state you may find yourself.

TRUST THE LORD — TOTALLY

Lean on, trust in, and be confident in the Lord with all your heart and mind and do not rely on your own insight or understanding.

In all your ways know, recognize, and acknowledge Him, and He will direct and make straight and plain your paths.

PROVERBS 3:5,6

As you and I travel down the road of life, we will have many opportunities to veer off the road to one side or the other. Because the devil knows we are making progress toward our goal, he will try to distract us. He will continually tempt us to "take the road of worry" so he can lead us off into destruction.

But if we keep within the lines and obey the signs along the way, we can remain within the boundaries of God's guidance and protection. Instead of trying to figure out everything for ourselves, we need to trust the Lord to lead us in the way we should go and get us safely to our final destination.

It is not difficult to tell when we have begun to cross over the boundary; it is when we begin to lose our peace. A loss of peace is a sure sign we have moved out from under the protection of the shadow of the Almighty. Usually it is an indication we have started worrying or have sinned and been unrepentant or have mistreated others without acknowledging our wrong and making an effort to set things right between us. Whatever the problem may be, we need to be sensitive to our lack of peace and find the reason for it so we can correct the problem and move back into the way of the Lord.

In this passage from Proverbs we are told to trust in the Lord not just with our heart, but with our heart *and* our mind. As we have seen, faith is the leaning of the *entire* human personality on God in absolute trust and confidence in His power, wisdom, and goodness. When God says to lean on Him, He means totally, completely. He means we are to trust Him mentally and emotionally as well as spiritually.

I used to think I was believing God and trusting the Lord. Spiritually, I may have been doing that. But mentally, I was still planning and scheming, trying to figure out how to handle everything on my own. Emotionally, I was still worrying and fretting, trying to find peace of mind and heart by keeping everything under my control.

Despite my claim to be believing God and trusting the Lord, I was in constant turmoil and confusion — which is always a sign we are getting over the line and headed for trouble.

SEEK GOD, NOT SECURITY

Therefore I tell you, stop being perpetually uneasy (anxious and worried) about your life, what you shall eat or what you shall drink; or about your body, what you shall put on. Is not life greater [in quality] than food, and the body [far above and more excellent] than clothing?

Look at the birds of the air; they neither sow nor reap nor gather into barns, and yet your heavenly Father keeps feeding them. Are you not worth much more than they?

And who of you by worrying and being anxious can add one unit of measure (cubit) to his stature or to the span of his life?

And why should you be anxious about clothes? Consider the lilies of the field and learn thoroughly how they grow; they neither toil nor spin.

Yet I tell you, even Solomon in all his magnificence (excellence, dignity, and grace) was not arrayed like one of these.

But if God so clothes the grass of the field, which today is alive and green and tomorrow is tossed into the furnace, will He not much more surely clothe you, O you of little faith?

Therefore do not worry and be anxious, saying, What are we going to have to eat? or, What are we going to have to drink? or, What are we going to have to wear?

For the Gentiles (heathen) wish for and crave and diligently seek all these things, and your heavenly Father knows well that you need them all.

> But seek (aim at and strive after) first of all His kingdom and His righteousness (His way of doing and being right), and then all these things taken together will be given you besides.

Matthew 6:25-33

This is a wonderful passage of Scripture in which Jesus Himself talks to us directly about the futility of worry and anxiety. Every time we are tempted to worry or be anxious about anything in life, we should read these verses out loud.

In verse 25 our Lord commands us specifically to stop being perpetually uneasy, worried, and anxious. That is reason enough in itself for us to quit torturing ourselves with negative thoughts and feelings, because when we do that we are not only harming ourselves, we are also being disobedient to God.

In verse 26 Jesus commands us to look at the birds of the air. Have you ever seen a bird in a tree having a nervous breakdown? Just as God feeds the birds and animals and even clothes the grass and flowers of the field, so He will feed and clothe those of us who put our faith and trust in Him.

In verse 32, Jesus assures us our heavenly Father knows all the things we have need of and that He has promised to provide them for us. So why should we worry?

Finally, in verse 33 Jesus gives us the key to living in the peace of the Lord. We are to seek first God's Kingdom and His righteousness, and then all these other things will be given to us as well. In other words, the reason we worry and fret and live in anxiety and fear is simply because we have the wrong priorities. We are seeking security in the things of this world rather than in the Creator of this world.

As the Body of Christ, *we are supposed to seek God, not the answer to our problems.* If we will seek Him and His righteousness, He has promised to provide all the answers we need.

We spend too much time seeking things and not enough time seeking God. Nowhere in the Word of God are we told to spend all our time seeking the perfect mate or a happy home or a successful career or ministry, though God wants us to have all these good things. Instead, we are told to seek God and His righteousness, trusting Him to provide all these other things He knows we need in accordance with His divine plan and timing.

CAST YOUR CARE

Humble yourselves therefore under the mighty hand of God, that he may exalt you in due time:

Casting all your care upon him; for he careth for you.

1 PETER 5:6,7 KJV

In Psalm 27 we saw the psalmist had the right idea when he wrote the one thing he asked of the Lord was that he might dwell in the presence of the Lord and behold His beauty all the days of his life.

In Psalm 91 we saw if we seek to dwell in the secret place of the Most High, leaning and relying on Him in confidence and trust, He will add to us all the blessings He has promised in the rest of that psalm.

In Matthew 6:25-33 we saw we are not to seek after the things of this life, but to seek first God's Kingdom and His righteousness. In verse 34 of that passage we saw we are not to be worried or anxious about tomorrow, because tomorrow will have worries and anxieties of its own; it is enough for us to deal with each day's cares as they arise.

Now in this passage we are told *how* we are to deal with each day's cares — by casting them all on the Lord Who cares for us affectionately and cares about us watchfully.

Several times in Psalm 37 we are told to fret not ourselves and to avoid anxious thoughts, which can quickly become irritating. Instead, we are to place our faith and confidence in the Lord, Who is our Refuge and our Fortress. (Psalm 91:2.)

God As Our Refuge and Fortress

I love You fervently and devotedly, O Lord, my Strength.

The Lord is my Rock, my Fortress, and my Deliverer; my God, my keen and firm Strength in Whom I will trust and take refuge, my Shield, and the Horn of my salvation, my High Tower.

I will call upon the Lord, Who is to be praised; so shall I be saved from my enemies.

PSALM 18:1-3

The psalmist says God is everything he needs: his Lord, his keen and firm Strength, his Rock, his Fortress, his Deliverer, his Shield, the Horn of his salvation, and his High Tower. In Psalm 61:2 he calls God ...*the rock that is higher than I....* In Psalm 62:2 he says of the Lord, *He only is my Rock and my Salvation, my Defense and my Fortress, I shall not be greatly moved.*

David said God *only* was his Rock and Fortress. That should be our testimony also. Our Rock of security should not be God plus something else, but God only.

A rock is a type of a sure foundation. When the waters of trial threaten to rise up and overwhelm us, we need to do as David did and climb up on the rock that is higher than we are.

David also called the Lord his Fortress. A fortress is a castle, a fort, a defense, a place into which we go when we are being hunted or attacked. It is not a hiding place, as we have discussed before, in which our enemy cannot find us. It is a place of protection in which we can see and be seen but cannot be reached because we are safe in God's protection.

David also called the Lord his High Tower — another lofty and inaccessible place — and his Shield and Buckler — which are part of the protective armor that surrounds the believer. (Ephesians 6:10-17.)

In Psalm 125:1, 2 we read: *Those who trust in, lean on, and confidently hope in the Lord are like Mount Zion, which cannot be moved but abides and stands fast forever. As the mountains are round about Jerusalem, so the Lord is round about His people from this time forth and forever.* God is not just above us and around us, He is even underneath us, because the psalmist tells us *...the Lord upholds the [consistently] righteous* (Psalm 37:17). God is holding us up by His powerful right hand and is surrounding us as the mountains surround the holy city of Jerusalem.

The devil is against us, but God is for us, and over us, and with us, and in us. Because He cares for us, He watches over us and keeps us so we can find rest and peace under the shadow of His wings as we cast all our care upon Him.

7

CAST YOUR CARE,
NOT YOUR RESPONSIBILITY

Therefore humble yourselves [demote, lower
yourselves in your own estimation]
under the mighty hand of God,
that in due time He may exalt you,

Casting the whole of your care [all your anxieties,
all your worries, all your concerns, once and for
all] on Him, for He cares for you affectionately
and cares about you watchfully.

1 PETER 5:6,7

It is important that we learn to cast our care, but not our responsibility. So often we do just the opposite; we cast our responsibility, but keep our care.

There is a difference between casting our care and being passive. We need to understand that difference. As we saw in John 6:28,29, Jesus has told us that as believers our first responsibility is to believe. That should not be a struggle, because if God has told us something, we should have no problem believing it and doing what He says for us to do. And one thing He has told us to do is to cast our care upon Him, which itself can be something of a violent matter.

THE KINGDOM SUFFERS VIOLENCE

And from the days of John the Baptist until the present time, the kingdom of heaven has endured violent assault, and violent men seize it by force [as a precious prize — a share in the heavenly kingdom is sought with most ardent zeal and intense exertion].

MATTHEW 11:12

Casting is a violent word. It refers to throwing, hurling, arising, sending, striking, thrusting, driving out, or expelling — all rather forceful terms.[1] In Matthew 11:12 Jesus said that since the days of John the Baptist, the Kingdom of God has endured violent assault, and violent men have seized it by force.

In a way, then, we are going to have to get violent — spiritually violent — about casting our care upon the Lord and abiding in the secret place of the Most High, under the shadow of the Almighty. Part of that violence is expressed in our absolute refusal to live any longer under guilt and condemnation, which can actually be worry about past mistakes.

Because I was abused for so long in my childhood, I developed a shame-based nature. I felt bad about myself all the time. I carried a load of guilt with me all my life.

When I began to get into the Word of God and discover Jesus had set me free from that burden of guilt and condemnation, it took me years to feel I was totally free of it. Although I knew mentally and spiritually I had been made the righteousness of God in Him because of what He had done for me on Calvary, I still had a hard time accepting it and living in it emotionally. The devil kept attacking my feelings, making me *feel* guilty and condemned. I worried about my past — how could I ever overcome it? I fought against those feelings for years until finally I got fed up. I told the devil, *"No! I am not going to live under guilt and condemnation! Jesus has made me the righteousness of God, and I have made up my mind I am going to have what He died to give me!"*

The apostle Paul said he pressed on to take hold of those things for which Christ Jesus had laid hold on him. (Philippians 3:12.) That was what I was doing. I knew from the Bible I had been made right with God through the shed blood of His Son Jesus Christ. I had the Scriptures in my heart and was confessing them with my mouth, but the enemy was still attacking me in my feelings — until there arose up in me a holy anger that finally set me free.

Sometimes we have to get angry enough to rise up against the principalities, powers, and wickedness in high places that try to keep us from enjoying all the blessings bought for us by Jesus Christ. Often we get mad at other people when we should be mad at the devil and his demons.

Just as anger at Satan can be a form of righteous violence, so can casting our care on the Lord. We can resist and resist Satan and the guilt, condemnation, worry, and anxiety he tries to place on us, until we get so fed up we react with a holy anger. When he tries to force us to carry a burden of care, we can stop and violently take back what Satan is trying to take from us by saying, *"No! I will not carry that care. I am casting it upon the Lord!"*

Everyone has their own set of problems, but has become very good at hiding them. Many people struggle with worry or guilt, anxious to the point of tears at times, on their way to church. When they get out of the car in the parking lot, they put on their "church face" and go into the building praising the Lord. They leave the same way — until they are alone again. Then they go right back to their misery and shame.

To be free of that kind of charade, we need to engage in some holy violence. When we feel the devil starting to lay any kind of guilt, condemnation, and care upon us, we need to take it and cast it upon the Lord.

In each one of us there are certain spiritual issues that need to be settled once and for all. Whatever the issues may be that are keeping us from walking in the fullness of joy, peace, and rest the Lord intends for us, we need to cast them upon Him.

The Bible says we are to cast *all* our care upon God. What is a care? The Greek word translated *care* in 1 Peter 5:7 means "'to draw in different directions, distract' hence signifies 'that which causes this, a care, especially an anxious care.'"[2]

Why does the devil try to give us care? To distract us from our fellowship with God. That is his whole purpose. That's why we need to learn to cast our care, but not our responsibility. In order to do that, we need to know what our responsibility is and what it is not.

THE PROBLEM OF INDEPENDENCE

Having cast all your anxiety on Him, because He careth for you.

1 PETER 5:7 WORRELL

In a footnote to this verse the *Worrell New Testament* says: "*Having cast all your anxiety upon Him:* the Greek tense here indicates a momentary and complete casting of one's anxiety, once for all, upon God. This, in a sense, is done when one makes a complete surrender of himself and his all to God for Him to manage at His will. When one puts the whole management of his life in God's hands, he may reach the place where all anxiety leaves him, regardless of the outward testings that may fall to his lot."[3]

Too often we are guilty of the sin of independence, which causes many problems.

A desire for independence is a sign of an immature Christian. A small child thinks he can do anything. Instead of asking for help, he wants to do everything for himself. He tries to put on his own shoes, tie his own laces, and dress himself. Often he gets the shoes on the wrong feet, ties the laces together so he trips, and gets his clothes on backward or inside out.

That's the way we are sometimes in our Christian life. Our heavenly Father tries to help us, but we don't want His help; we want to do everything for ourselves — and we end up making a terrible mess of things.

God wants to manage our life. He wants to handle our affairs for us as a blessing to us. But many times we reject His help and try to do things on our own. Often the result is disastrous. If we want to experience the peace of the Lord, we must learn to cast all our care upon Him permanently, as we see in Worrell's study notes:

"Instead of casting one's burden on the Lord, and letting it remain with Him, many Christians go to the Lord in prayer, and get some temporary relief; and then go away, and soon find themselves under the same old burden. Christians of this type have never experienced the crucifixion fully; but after this crucifixion has been well passed through, one may live without any anxious care; nothing disturbing the deep peace of the soul. But no one can reach this blissful state of mind and heart, until he first surrenders his whole being to God, receives the Holy Spirit to dwell within him, and Christ becomes real to his heart, as Ruler of that realm."[4]

The way we overcome a spirit of independence is by placing ourselves totally into God's hands and allowing Him to be the Manager of our life.

Here is a good prayer for that submission: "Lord, in this situation in which I find myself, if there is anything You want me to do, show it to me and help me do it. I am waiting on You, leaning on You. I will pray and praise, but I will not get into works of the flesh, trying to make something happen. If there is nothing I can do to solve this situation, give me the grace to leave it alone for You to work out in accordance with Your divine will and in Your perfect timing."

So our first responsibility is to trust God. The second is not to try to take His place.

DON'T TRY TO PLAY GOD

However, I am telling you nothing but the truth when I say it is profitable (good, expedient, advantageous) for you that I go away. Because if I do not go away, the Comforter (Counselor, Helper, Advocate, Intercessor, Strengthener, Standby) will not come to you [into close fellowship with you]; but if I go away, I will send Him to you [to be in close fellowship with you].

And when He comes, He will convict and convince the world and bring demonstration to it about sin and about righteousness (uprightness of heart and right standing with God) and about judgment.

JOHN 16:7,8

We must learn to distinguish between our part and God's part — and then leave His part to Him, refusing to "play God."

For example, we cannot change other people. I know, because for years I tried to change my husband. The more I tried to change him, the worse the tension between us became.

128

Finally, I received the revelation that *people cannot change people.* Only God can change people.

For years I had been trying to do something I did not have the power to do. What I needed to do was simply submit my husband to the Lord, believing He would do for him what was best in His own way and time.

It is the Holy Spirit's job to bring conviction to sinners. It is not our job to drop little hints to make them feel guilty — like leaving the Bible open at just the right place or putting a verse of Scripture up on the bathroom mirror so they will see it.

The Bible says it is the Holy Spirit Who convicts and convinces of sin and of righteousness. Yet for years I tried to convict my husband and my children of what I thought were their sins. I also tried to convince them of my righteousness. No wonder I was always in such a struggle! I was trying to do the work of the Holy Spirit.

So in addition to submitting ourselves entirely to the Lord, trusting Him to work out things for us as He knows best, we must stop trying to play God in our own life and in the lives of other people. We must let God be God.

LET GOD BE GOD

For who has known or understood the mind (the counsels and purposes) of the Lord so as to guide and instruct Him and give Him knowledge?....

1 CORINTHIANS 2:16

It is not our job to give God guidance, counsel, or direction. In His Word He makes it clear He doesn't need us to inform Him of what is going on or tell Him what He needs to do about it: *For My thoughts are not your thoughts, neither are your ways My ways, says the Lord. For as the heavens are higher than the earth, so are My ways higher than your ways and My thoughts than your thoughts* (Isaiah 55:8,9).

It is our job to listen to God and let Him tell us what is going on and what we are to do about it — leaving the rest to Him to work out according to His knowledge and will, not ours.

Sometimes we forget that fact, so the Lord has to say to us, "Who do you think you are? Get back in your place of submission and quit trying to be My boss."

I remember one time when I was trying so hard to figure out something while God was trying to free me from the burden of reasoning. Finally, He said to me, "Joyce, don't you realize if you ever figured Me out, I would no longer be God?"

God is God — and we aren't. We need to recognize that truth and simply trust ourselves to Him, because He is greater than we are in every aspect and area. We are created in His image, but He is still above us and beyond us. His thoughts and ways are higher than ours. If we will listen to Him and be obedient to Him, He will teach us His ways. But we are never going to figure Him out. We shouldn't even try.

DON'T QUESTION OR CRITICIZE GOD

But who are you, a mere man, to criticize and contradict and answer back to God? Will what is formed say to him that formed it, Why have you made me thus?

Has the potter no right over the clay, to make out of the same mass (lump) one vessel for beauty and distinction and honorable use, and another for menial or ignoble and dishonorable use?

ROMANS 9:20,21

It is not our place to cross-examine God. He is not on trial.

"Lord," we say, "I don't understand why You don't answer my prayers." Yet it never occurs to us that maybe we are praying out of the will of God. It has been noted that the biggest problem for most Christians is their inability to distinguish between God's will and personal ambition.

"Oh, but I know what I'm asking is God's will."

What makes us think that? Usually it's because what we are asking is what we want, so we assume it must be what God wants too.

There are many things in this life that are not clearly laid out in Scripture, so we must have some discernment from the Lord about whether they are His will for us. Even if they are His will for us, we must also consider His timing, and often that takes patience and trust on our part.

For years I struggled with these matters, usually because I already had my mind made up about the way things were supposed to be, even before I went to God in prayer about them. Too often my prayers were really just PR sessions in which I tried to manipulate God to get what I wanted from Him.

If I didn't get what I asked for in prayer, I would assume it was because the devil was trying to keep it from me. So I would spend hours rebuking Satan and ordering him to get his hands off my answer and let it manifest. When that didn't work, I would call in a bunch of my friends to agree with me in prayer. Together we would pray and confess and rebuke and agree, but usually none of it did any good at all. I couldn't understand why it didn't work when I was so sure I knew the will of God in that area.

I would go to the Lord and say, "Father, what's wrong? Why aren't You answering my prayers as You promised?"

In essence, I was questioning and criticizing God. I was saying, "Lord, I'm doing my part, so why aren't You doing Yours? What's going on here?"

Finally, the Lord showed me in His Word what the problem was. Although I was asking, I was doing so with the wrong purpose and motives.

WRONG PURPOSE AND MOTIVES

What leads to strife (discord and feuds) and how do conflicts (quarrels and fightings) originate among you? Do they not arise from your sensual desires that are ever warring in your bodily members?

You are jealous and covet [what others have] and your desires go unfulfilled; [so] you become murderers. [To hate is to murder as far as your hearts are concerned.] You burn with envy and anger and are not able to obtain [the gratification, the contentment, and the happiness that you seek], so you fight and war. You do not have, because you do not ask.

[Or] you do ask [God for them] and yet fail to receive, because you ask with wrong purpose and evil, selfish motives....

JAMES 4:1-3

The first thing the Lord showed me in this passage is that we often get into struggles and strife because we try to make things happen on our own instead of simply asking that His will be done.

Then He showed me the second part of this passage which says even when we do ask, the reason we don't get our prayers answered is that we ask with the wrong purpose or with the wrong motives.

The Lord said to me, "Joyce, anytime You ask Me for something and you don't get it, it's not because I don't want to bless you or because I'm holding out on you. It's because I have something better in mind for you, but you are not yet spiritually mature enough to know how to ask Me for it."

LET GOD MAKE THE DECISIONS

Trust (lean on, rely on, and be confident) in the Lord and do good; so shall you dwell in the land and feed surely on His faithfulness, and truly you shall be fed.

Delight yourself also in the Lord, and He will give you the desires and secret petitions of your heart.

Commit your way to the Lord [roll and repose each care of your load on Him]; trust (lean on, rely on, and be confident) also in Him and He will bring it to pass.

PSALM 37:3-5

Since the Lord spoke to me about what was wrong with the way I was praying, I have learned not to ask Him for anything out of His will. If I am not sure what His will is in a situation, I always pray for what I want to have or would like to see happen, but I follow my request with this statement: "Lord, if what I am asking for is not Your will, please don't give it to me. I want Your will more than I want my own."

I have learned to seek first His will and His righteousness, trusting Him to add to me all the things He knows I really need, the things that will bless me and not be a burden to me or draw me away from Him.

For years I prayed for and sought a big ministry. But God knew that was not what I needed at the time. I wasn't ready for it — I wasn't mature enough to handle everything that goes with success. By continuing to pray for and seek something that wasn't right for me, all I was doing was retarding my growth. Once I started seeking God rather than a big ministry, my ministry started to grow.

For years I sought God for prosperity. I had other needs that were greater. I needed to walk in love and display the fruit of the Spirit. I needed to be freed from selfishness, stubbornness, independence, and many other things. God wanted me to give and believe that His laws of prosperity worked, but He did not want me to spend my time seeking things.

If we seek God for money or things without seeking Him, even if He gives them to us, having them will only cause us to sin. I always say our branches cannot be any wider than our roots are deep. Trees are like that — however far the branches extend, which is the part we see, below the surface of the ground where we can't see, the roots extend as deep as the branches are wide. Otherwise the tree would topple over in a storm.

If our spiritual life does not go as deep as our outward blessings, we only get in trouble. Our spiritual maturity must match our prosperity and success. God must become and always remain first in our lives for anything else to work properly.

In Deuteronomy 8 we see God give the Israelites a warning. He told them He was going to bless them and then said this: *And if you forget the Lord your God and walk after other gods and serve them and worship them, I testify against you this day that you shall surely perish* (v. 19).

Many things can become gods to us. A job a person believed God to help them get can become a god to them. A ministry, a home, a spouse, children — literally any blessing of the Lord can get us in trouble if we don't keep our lives in balance and turn the blessing into a god. We must regularly examine our priorities and be sure they are in proper order.

It is such a deliverance to turn the management of our life over to God. Does that mean we are to become passive and stop resisting the enemy when he attacks us? No, not at all. It simply means we are to trust in the Lord and put our confidence in Him. We are to wait on Him and listen to Him. He will show us when we need to rise up against the evil spirits that come to deceive us and destroy us. If we listen to Him, we will not be so quick to start rebuking every situation that arises or every circumstance in which we find ourselves.

It is God's will to bless us, but not necessarily on our terms. Sometimes what we think would be a wonderful blessing would not bless us at all.

In all our seeking, struggling, and striving — even in prayer — we must be careful not to give birth to Ishmaels. If we do, we will have to spend the rest of our days taking care of them. Instead, we need to learn to wait for God to bring forth the Isaacs in our life. They will be a blessing to us for as long as we live.

DO NOT STRIVE WITH YOUR MAKER

Woe to him who strives with his Maker! — a worthless piece of broken pottery among other pieces equally worthless [and yet presuming to strive with his Maker]! Shall the clay say to him who fashions it, What do you think you are making? or, Your work has no handles?

Woe to him [who complains against his parents that they have begotten him] who says to a father, What are you begetting? or to a woman, With what are you in travail?

> Thus says the Lord, the Holy One of Israel, and its Maker:
> Would you question Me about things to come concerning
> My children, and concerning the work of My hands [would
> you] command Me?

ISAIAH 45:9-11

In Romans 9:20, 21 we saw we are not to criticize, contradict, or answer back to God. We are not to ask God, "Why did You make me this way?"

For years I did not like the way I was, the way God had put me together. I didn't like my strong, aggressive, bold personality. I wanted to be sweet, meek, and quiet — because sweet, meek, and quiet people don't get into as much trouble as people like me.

To tell the truth, I didn't like anything about myself. So I would pray and ask God, "Why have You made me this way? It's so easy for Dave to cast his care, and I just seem to worry about everything. Why God, why? Why did You give me this deep voice? Why couldn't I have had a nice, sweet little voice like most other ladies do?"

The fact is, my voice has turned out to be a blessing because it commands attention. I can't remember how many people have told me, "I was turning the radio dial when suddenly I heard this voice..." In fact, it is so commanding that Carman, the popular Christian singer, refers to me as "the Voice."

But at the time I was praying to God and striving with my Maker about how He had made me, I didn't understand. All I wanted to know was why I couldn't be "normal," why I couldn't be content to stay home and keep house, grow tomatoes, and wash and iron and sew.

I really didn't want to do those ordinary things, I wanted to have a great ministry. But it seemed I just didn't have what it takes to do that. So I cried out to God, asking Him why He made me the way He did instead of the way I wanted to be.

Who can say why God puts us together the way He does? But He is the Potter, and we are the clay. It is none of our business why He forms and fashions us as He does.

Not only do we question God about why He made us the way He did, we also question Him about why He made others as they are.

In the beginning of our marriage, my husband Dave prayed and asked God, "Lord, why did You give Joyce the gift of preaching instead of me?" Neither of us could understand why God seemingly reversed the order in our case. He gave me the gift of preaching and teaching, and He gave Dave the gift of administration and support. That didn't seem "normal" to us. It was not the way other husband-wife ministry teams that we knew worked. But as long as Dave and I questioned the Lord about it, we were miserable.

As long as you and I argue with God and strive with our Maker, we are going to be unhappy. Once we accept God's will, as Dave and I finally did, then we can be used and blessed by Him as He sees fit.

In Romans 9:21, Paul asks, "Doesn't the potter have the right to take a lump of clay and make one vessel for beauty and distinction and honorable use, and another for menial or ignoble or dishonorable use?" That does not mean dishonorable in God's eyes. It means dishonorable in the eyes of those who do not understand God's purpose, those who think some people are more honorable and some work more important than others.

Some may look at me and think my job is more important than Dave's simply because I am in front of the microphone and the camera, and he is behind them. But we are where we are because God Himself has placed us there. I did not ask for this position of prominence any more than Dave asked for his work behind the scenes in the ministry of helps. But we must each accept the role God has assigned us and submit ourselves to Him to mold and make us after His will and plan, and not ours.

We have to remember that as long as we function in the position God has created us for, His grace is with us. But the moment we get out of our God-ordained role, we are operating outside of His anointing.

We must never forget that ...*we are God's [own] handiwork (His workmanship), recreated in Christ Jesus, [born anew] that we may do those good works which God predestined (planned beforehand) for us [taking paths which He prepared ahead of time], that we should walk in them [living the good life which He prearranged and made ready for us to live]* (Ephesians 2:10). We must not question Him, criticize Him, contradict Him, answer back to Him, or strive with Him.

In 1 Corinthians 13:12 we are told that now we know only in part. That is the best answer we can find to the question of why God does anything the way He does. It is not our job to question God, or even try to explain Him. It is our job to trust and obey Him and to cast our care upon Him.

THE FIRST THREE RESPONSIBILITIES

As for you,...fully perform all the duties of your ministry.

2 TIMOTHY 4:5

As ministers of the Gospel of Jesus Christ, which is what we are all called to be, we have certain basic duties or responsibilities.

We have already discussed our first responsibility, which is to trust God. Our second responsibility is to pray without worry. Our third responsibility is to avoid works of the flesh.

When there is something that greatly concerns us, like the salvation of our spouse or children, we can be so intense we become obsessive about it, even in our prayer life. Excessive prayer, especially in the area of spiritual warfare, can become just another work of the flesh.

In my life there have been certain relatives I have prayed for over a period of months or years. But I did not pray for each one of them by name day in and day out. I might pray for one of them on a particular day and then go for a full year without praying specifically for that person again. Then all of a sudden I might be moved to weep and travail for that individual even though I might not have seen him or her for months. I didn't do that every day, only when I felt led to do so by the Holy Spirit.

In our prayers, as in every other aspect of our Christian life, we need not be afraid of being led by the Spirit. Sometimes if we don't sense that the Spirit of God is leading us to do something, we lead ourselves to do it. After all, we reason, we ought to be doing something. We seem to have the mistaken idea if we are not actively doing something, God can't work. We forget we are to cast on Him our care, not our responsibility.

It is our responsibility to trust, to pray without worry, and to avoid works of the flesh. When we go beyond that responsibility and start to pray *and* worry, we cancel out our prayers. They become nothing more than a work of the flesh, an attempt to change things by our own energy and effort.

FRUSTRATION EQUALS WORKS OF THE FLESH

I do not frustrate the grace of God....

GALATIANS 2:21 KJV

God is not against *work*, He is against *works*. There is a difference.

Work is doing by the grace of God what He has called us to do. It is the expending of our energy and effort to see the will of God come to pass in our life. But *works* is doing by our own strength and ability what we want done. It is the expending of our energy and effort to try to make happen what only God can make happen.

When we do the work God has called us to do, He gives us superhuman energy.

In our meetings sometimes we work until very late in the evening ministering to people. The next day we may be up at six, getting everything ready to move on to our next destination. Physically we may be tired, but spiritually we are renewed and refreshed by the Spirit of the Lord. That is a good example of the difference between works of the flesh and the work of the Spirit. We work hard but seek to avoid works of the flesh.

Works of the flesh include worry, reasoning, and trying to figure out what to do to make things happen according to our will and timing. They are one of the biggest problems among God's people today.

As we have seen, the opposite of works is grace. As long as we are trying to live the Christian life by works of the flesh, we are never going to be really, truly happy.

The devil uses works of the flesh to rob us of our joy. Satan doesn't want us to be filled with contentment, peace, and rest.

He wants us to be worried, confused, and upset. Instead of trusting in the Lord and waiting for Him to move in His own way and timing, the devil wants us to take things into our own hands, as Abraham and Sarah did in the Old Testament.

SHIFTING RESPONSIBILITY

Then Sarai said to Abram, May [the responsibility for] my wrong and deprivation of rights be upon you! I gave my maid into your bosom, and when she saw that she was with child, I was contemptible and despised in her eyes. May the Lord be the judge between you and me.

But Abram said to Sarai, See here, your maid is in your hands and power; do as you please with her....

GENESIS 16:5,6

In Part 1, we read how Sarah, despairing of ever having a child of her own in her old age, suggested to Abraham that he take her Egyptian maid Hagar as his "secondary wife" and have a child by her. Abraham agreed and did as Sarah suggested.

In Genesis 16:5, 6 we see the immediate consequences of that action. As soon as Hagar saw she was pregnant with Abraham's child, she despised Sarah and began to treat her with contempt. Sarah complained to Abraham saying, "May the responsibility for this terrible situation be upon you!"

At first, that accusation may seem to be totally unfair and unjustified. After all, it was not Abraham's idea that he have a child by Hagar, it was Sarah's idea. But in a way, Sarah was right; Abraham was to blame. Why? Because by agreeing with Sarah's suggestion, he failed to fulfill his God-given responsibility. Instead of waiting for the Lord to supernaturally produce the promised heir, Abraham joined his wife in a foolish attempt to produce an heir on their own through totally human effort. The result was trouble and unhappiness for all concerned: Sarah, Abraham, Hagar, Ishmael, and Isaac.

The reason Abraham failed to fulfill his responsibility was that he was passive. Instead of truly casting his care upon the Lord and trusting Him to work out His divine plan, Abraham went along with his wife's misguided scheme.

Often that is our problem. Instead of casting our care on the Lord, we cast our responsibility. We become passive, often due to laziness. It just seems to be too much trouble to take a stand on the Word of God and wait for Him to act on our behalf as we confidently trust in Him.

When Sarah came up with the idea of trying to produce a child through Abraham and Hagar, Abraham passively went along with it. Later, when Hagar became pregnant and treated Sarah cruelly, Abraham again shifted his responsibility by telling Sarah, "Well, she's your maid, do whatever you want to with her."

Just as he failed to correct Sarah when she made a foolish suggestion, Abraham also refused to get involved when her suggestion produced problems in the household. In both cases, he avoided his God-given responsibility by trying to shift it to his wife. The same kind of thing happened with Adam in the Garden of Eden.

When God questioned Adam about eating from the forbidden tree of the knowledge of good and evil, Adam's excuse was, ...*The woman whom You gave to be with me — she gave me [fruit] from the tree, and I ate* (Genesis 3:12). Like Abraham, Adam tried to shift his responsibility from himself to his wife. He even went so far as to imply it was God's fault for giving Eve to him in the first place.

Too often today men try to avoid accepting their personal responsibility by shifting it onto someone else — usually their wives, or even God. I believe the devil has done a marvelous job of getting men to be spiritually passive and leave the responsibility for spiritual matters to the women in their lives. Thank God, we are seeing a change as more and more men begin to seek God and become the spiritual leaders in their marriages and families.

THE LAST THREE RESPONSIBILITIES

...See to it that you complete the work you have received in the Lord.

COLOSSIANS 4:17 NIV

So our first three duties or responsibilities are to trust God, to pray without worry, and to avoid works of the flesh.

Our final three duties or responsibilities are to continue in obedience during the time of waiting, to continue to bear good fruit, and to offer God a sacrifice of praise. Let's look at each of these three separately.

CONTINUE IN OBEDIENCE

...Whatever He says to you, do it.

JOHN 2:5

Jesus' first recorded miracle took place while He was attending a wedding celebration. When the marriage couple ran out of wine to serve their guests, Mary asked her Son to do something about the situation, telling the servants, "Whatever He tells you to do, do it." Jesus ordered them to fill up several huge water pots. When they had done so, He directed them to draw out of the vessels the water which by then had been miraculously changed into wine. (vv. 1-11.) Because of their obedience to Him, the physical needs of many were met that day.

The first rule of miracles is obedience.

If you are looking for a miracle in your life, make sure you are sowing seeds of obedience, because the Lord has promised us that if we do so in patient confidence and trust in Him, we will eventually reap: *And let us not lose heart and grow weary and faint in acting nobly and doing right, for in due time and at the appointed season we shall reap, if we do not loosen and relax our courage and faint* (Galatians 6:9).

Sometimes when things are not working out the way we think they should, or we are not receiving the answers to our prayers as quickly as we would like, we get the idea, "Well, since God's not doing anything, why should I? Why should I be obedient if it isn't producing results?" In such times we must realize that God is always working. We just may not be able to see it, because He usually works in secret.

God's Secret Work

My frame was not hidden from You when I was being formed *in secret* [and] intricately and curiously wrought [as if embroidered with various colors] in the depths of the earth [a region of darkness and mystery].

Your eyes saw my unformed substance, and in Your book all the days [of my life] were written before ever they took shape, when as yet there was none of them.

Psalm 139:15,16

The psalmist wrote that long before his actual appearance in this world, he was being formed in secret by the Lord.

God put together a perfect work in the form of King David of Israel, just as He is putting together a perfect work in our lives. David did not make his appearance in this world until the Lord determined the time was right. In the same way, God will bring forth His perfect work in us when He knows everything is right for us.

Even though it may seem God is doing nothing, He is secretly working behind the scenes. We may not be able to hear it or see it, but we can accept it by faith.

If you would like something to cheer you up in the midst of all your trials and troubles, get a good Bible concordance and look up every reference to the words *work(s)*, *worketh*, *working*, etc. You will see right away that ours is a working God, as Jesus told us in John 5:17: ...*My Father has worked [even] until now, [He has never ceased working; He is still working] and I, too, must be at [divine] work.*

At this very moment while you are reading this book, God is at work in your life and in your present situation, if you believe He is: ...*According to your faith be it unto you* (Matthew 9:29 KJV).

If you have cast your care upon the Lord and left it with Him to handle, He is working on your behalf right now. He wants you to untie His hands. You do that by refusing to worry and by dwelling in the secret place of the Most High, hidden away safe and secure under the shadow of His wings.

While you are abiding in the Lord and resting in His peace, waiting for Him to do His part, your part is to continue to bear good fruit for His Kingdom.

CONTINUE TO BEAR GOOD FRUIT

[Most] blessed is the man who believes in, trusts in, and relies on the Lord, and whose hope and confidence the Lord is.

For he shall be like a tree planted by the waters that spreads out its roots by the river; and it shall not see and fear when heat comes; but its leaf shall be green. It shall not be anxious and full of care in the year of drought, nor shall it cease yielding fruit.

JEREMIAH 17:7,8

While you and I are waiting on the Lord, we need to be bearing good fruit. We should be like a tree planted by the water, drawing strength and life from its source because its roots go down deep into the ground. Even in times of drought, such a tree will continue to bear good fruit.

If you and I are firmly planted in Jesus Christ and deeply rooted in His love (Ephesians 3:17), even though we may have all kinds of problems in our lives, we will still bear the fruit of the Spirit described in Galatians 5:22, 23: ...*love, joy (gladness), peace, patience (an even temper, forbearance), kindness, goodness (benevolence), faithfulness, gentleness (meekness, humility), self-control (self-restraint, continence). Against such things there is no law [that can bring a charge].*

Sometimes we seem to think because we are going through hard times we have a license to be miserable and ugly. That kind of attitude and behavior will not bring our answer. The Bible teaches we are not to give in to such "evil tendencies" (James 4:6), but rather to continue to bear fruit, giving thanks and praise to God even in the midst of negative circumstances.

Offer the Sacrifice of Praise

Through Him, therefore, let us constantly and at all times offer up to God a sacrifice of praise, which is the fruit of lips that thankfully acknowledge and confess and glorify His name.

Hebrews 13:15

In Psalm 139:15,16 we saw that David acknowledged God had been working secretly in his life from before his birth. In verses 13 and 14 he praised the Lord for Who He is and for His wonderful works on his behalf: *...You did form my inward parts; You did knit me together in my mother's womb. I will confess and praise You for You are fearful and wonderful and for the awful wonder of my birth! Wonderful are Your works, and that my inner self knows right well.*

That is what we are to do in the midst of our problems. While we are waiting to see the fulfillment of our prayers, we are to be continually offering up to God the fruit of lips that thankfully acknowledge and confess and glorify His name.

It is not our responsibility to worry and fret or try to play God by taking into our own hands things that should be left to Him alone. Instead, it is our responsibility to cast our care upon the Lord, trusting Him, praying without worry, avoiding works of the flesh, continuing in obedience, bearing good fruit, and offering Him the sacrifice of praise.

8

THIS TOO SHALL PASS

...and it shall come to pass....

GENESIS 4:14 KJV

In the beginning chapters of the book of Genesis we see a prophetic word that things will "come to pass." In fulfillment of this word, the expression "it came to pass" is used hundreds of times throughout the *King James Version* of the Bible. For example, in Genesis 39 KJV, which describes some of Joseph's experiences in Egypt where he was sold into slavery and rose to second in command of the entire nation, the phrase "and it came to pass" appears eight times. The last book of the Bible, Revelation, speaks of *...things which must shortly come to pass...* (Revelation 1:1 KJV).

That should tell us in this life whatever exists now, or will exist in the future, is not permanent, but temporary. The good news is, no matter how dismal our current situation or outlook, we are assured by God, "This too shall pass."

Life is a continual process in which everything is constantly changing. If we can grasp that truth, it will help us make it through the difficult times in which we find ourselves. It will also help us not to hold on too tightly to the good times, thinking, "If I ever lose all this, I just can't make it."

God wants us to enjoy all of life — not just its destination, but also the trip itself.

ENJOY THE TRIP!

Behold, what I have seen to be good and fitting is for one to eat and drink, and to find enjoyment in all the labor in which he labors under the sun all the days which God gives him — for this is his [allotted] part.

ECCLESIASTES 5:18

Years ago the church my husband and I belonged to at the time offered a nine-month Bible course called "The Elisha Program." Dave and I enrolled in it because we felt it was God's will that we start our training for ministry. The course met two or three nights a week, which was quite a commitment, especially for Dave because he was working so hard during the day.

That course seemed like a major undertaking until the Lord gave me a vision about having goals and reaching them. In the vision I saw the horizon ahead of me, which in this case represented graduating from the course. As I began moving toward the horizon in the vision, it faded from sight and another would rise up.

The Lord was showing me in our lives we are always going to be moving toward some goal or objective. As soon as we finish one, another will be there. We as believers are always extending our faith for something. Whatever we are believing God for right now may have manifested a year from now, but by that time we will be believing God for something else. The Lord was teaching me that since we are going to spend our entire lives waiting for something, we should learn to enjoy life as it unfolds. If we don't, life will pass us up and we will never enjoy where we are right now.

DON'T DESPISE THE DAY OF SMALL THINGS

Who [with reason] despises the day of small things?....

ZECHARIAH 4:10

I wasted years being miserable where I was, waiting to get to the next horizon before I really started enjoying life.

As I look back on the early days of my ministry, I can remember "the day of small things," which would have been so easy to despise. When I first started out, my meetings would draw just a handful of people, maybe fifty at the most. It is just as hard to preach to fifty as it is to preach to five thousand, so I had to put the same amount of time and effort into my lessons then as I do now.

When my ministry team started traveling, we needed a vehicle to transport us and our equipment from one place to another. The first van we bought cost us twenty-six hundred dollars. It had bald tires and rust spots on it. We would leave St. Louis, Missouri, our hometown, and go to a little place in Illinois called Quincy, where there would be from 70 to 125 people in attendance at our meeting.

Since we didn't have enough money to spend the night in a motel, we would have to drive back home that same evening after the services had closed. We would usually get back about three o'clock in the morning. On the way home we would get so tired we would have to pull off on the side of the road and get ten or fifteen minutes of sleep before driving on.

I hated those days while they were going on, but now I can see their value. They were important because they were times of preparation for the greater days the Lord knew lay ahead. I sincerely believe my ministry would not have grown to the point of reaching so many people as it does today if I had not been faithful enough to press through the hardships of those early times.

It is sad that today many times people give up in the hard times and never get to enjoy the fruit of all their labor.

It is easy to start something, but it is much harder to finish it. In the beginning, we are filled with emotion, and usually have all kinds of enthusiastic support. Everybody cheers us on. But as the days go by and the great and glorious cause becomes a matter of daily, consistent hard work, often we are left with nobody to support us and urge us on but ourselves and God.

That's when we have to decide if we are going to see it through to the finish. That's when we have to realize everything we are going through at the moment will one day pass and we will enjoy the fruit of our labor. In the meantime, we need to enjoy where we are while we are on the way to where we are going.

"THIS IS IT!"

Six days after this, Jesus took with Him Peter and James and John and led them up on a high mountain apart by themselves. And He was transfigured before them and became resplendent with divine brightness.

And His garments became glistening, intensely white, as no fuller (cloth dresser, launderer) on earth could bleach them.

And Elijah appeared [there] to them, accompanied by Moses, and they were holding [a protracted] conversation with Jesus.

And Peter took up the conversation, saying, Master, it is good and suitable and beautiful for us to be here. Let us make three booths (tents) — one for You and one for Moses and one for Elijah.

For he did not [really] know what to say, for they were in a violent fright (aghast with dread).

MARK 9:2-6

I get so encouraged when I read about Peter. Who else would have had the audacity to talk in a situation like that? No one except Peter — and maybe me.

Can you imagine the scene? Jesus is being transfigured before the very eyes of the astonished disciples and is having a personal conversation with Elijah and Moses — and Peter "takes up the conversation." In his babbling, bubbling enthusiasm, he offers to build tents for the three of them. Although he doesn't really know he is saying it, what he means is, "This is it! There's no place to go from here! This is wonderful! Let's just camp here!"

That's exactly what I thought when I received the baptism of the Holy Ghost: "This is it! There's nothing greater than this!" But I soon discovered there were other things God wanted to do in my life.

It is interesting to me that in the Gospels we never find Jesus saying, "This is *it!*" Instead, what we often find Him saying is, "This is *that* which was prophesied and has now come to pass." Then He moves on.

One of our problems is, we get caught up in the "This is it" mentality. We like to think that things, especially pleasant things, are never going to change. When we win a victory, we like to think that is the end of our troubles, and we will never have to fight another battle. But the Lord is trying to tell us that is not so. As soon as we overcome one problem, we will have another one to overcome.

One season always leads to another.

If the situation we are in at the moment is not very pleasant, it will at least prepare us for the next situation, which may be more to our liking. In the same way, a pleasant situation may have to change for a while so we can be prepared for something even better. That has happened to me in my life.

I once had a job in a church in St. Louis which I thought I would never leave. I had been a part of that nice little group of people whom I loved and admired so much for a long time. My name was on my office door and my parking place, plus I had a front row seat in the sanctuary. I felt important! I would have been perfectly content to stay there the rest of my life — but God had other ideas for me.

Then it was hard for me to leave that place and situation I loved so much, but now I am seeing the fulfillment of God's plan in having me give it up to move on with Him.

When the Lord first called me out of that church into independent ministry, at first things did not go well at all. I left a comfortable position in a stable environment to go running around the countryside in a rusty van with four bald tires, no money, no place to sleep at night — and the number of people who came out to hear me was not always that great either.

I remember one place I preached where the total audience was no more than twenty people — and they all looked like they were dead. I felt like I was preaching a funeral. In fact, I have been in funerals that were cheerier than that service.

It was so discouraging to stand up and try to tell that handful of unresponsive people something that was going to make a difference in their lives. Finally, at the end of the service I thought I would walk back to the tape table and cheer myself up by finding out how many tapes we had sold during the meeting.

"Did you sell a lot of tapes?" I asked Dave, who was manning the table.

"No," he answered, "but somebody did return one."

In that dismal service, not only did I feel that I had not reached my sparse audience, but I had not sold a single teaching tape. BUT SOMEBODY DID RETURN ONE!! What an insult. I was so discouraged and embarrassed that I wanted to run and hide. I felt like quitting.

The church had also arranged a dinner for me after the service at a local restaurant. They had invited the church staff and other people they knew, as well as Dave and me. When we got to the restaurant only about forty percent of the people they invited showed up. Even the dinner was a failure. I could not understand at the time why these kinds of things had to happen. Why, God, why?

I later realized that kind of thing had to happen to prepare me for what is taking place now in my ministry. We are now enjoying phenomenal success and explosive growth. Before I could enjoy the fruit of my labor for the Lord, I had to go through some hard things. These trying times help us get more deeply rooted in God. They work humility in us and cause us to be very thankful when the blessings come. I had to grow and develop. Like all of God's children, I had to go through some training, correction, and discipline.

WHOM GOD LOVES, HE DISCIPLINES

You must submit to and endure [correction] for discipline; God is dealing with you as with sons. For what son is there whom his father does not [thus] train and correct and discipline?

Now if you are exempt from correction and left without discipline in which all [of God's children] share, then you are illegitimate offspring and not true sons [at all].

Moreover, we have had earthly fathers who disciplined us and we yielded [to them] and respected [them for training us]. Shall we not much more cheerfully submit to the Father of spirits and so [truly] live?

For [our earthly fathers] disciplined us for only a short period of time and chastised us as seemed proper and good to them; but He disciplines us for our certain good, that we may become sharers in His own holiness.

For the time being no discipline brings joy, but seems grievous and painful; *but afterwards* it yields a peaceful fruit of righteousness to those who have been trained by it [a harvest of fruit which consists in righteousness — in conformity to God's will in purpose, thought, and action, resulting in right living and right standing with God].

HEBREWS 12:7-11

In verse 11 notice the phrase "but afterwards." No training, correction, or discipline seems pleasant at the time it is being administered to us, "but afterwards" we come to appreciate it.

GOD'S PROMISES

Because he has set his love upon Me, therefore will I deliver him; I will set him on high, because he knows and understands My name [has a personal knowledge of My mercy, love, and kindness — trusts and relies on Me, knowing I will never forsake him, no, never].

He shall call upon Me, and I will answer him; I will be with him in trouble, I will deliver him and honor him.

With long life will I satisfy him and show him My salvation.

PSALM 91:14-16

In this passage God promises us three things if we are in trouble: 1) He will be with us, 2) He will deliver us and honor us, and 3) He will grant us long life and will show us His salvation.

I believe the message the Lord is giving us in these verses is simply this: "No matter what you are going through at the moment, sooner or later it will pass. Someday it will all be over and done. In the meantime, cast your care upon Me and trust Me to work out everything for the best."

THIS TOO SHALL PASS

Heaven and earth will perish and pass away, but My words will not perish or pass away.

MARK 13:31

When my three children were small, I thought they would drive me crazy, especially my daughter Laura.

I was Mrs. Neat-n-Clean. To me, there was a place for everything and everything was supposed to be in its place. Laura would have none of that. Her personality was totally different from mine. The moment she came in the house, one of her shoes would fly in one direction, and the other shoe would go in the other direction. From the front door on, she would start strewing her car keys, her purse, her books, her clothes. If I wanted to know where Laura was, all I had to do was follow the trail of her belongings through the house.

But eventually "it came to pass" that Laura grew up, got married, and started a family of her own. When she got her own home, she discovered if she didn't clean up her messes, they would stay right there forever. So "it came to pass" that she started cleaning up after herself.

Now when I go visit her, everything is nice and clean. We have a wonderful relationship together. She is one of my best friends, and we spend a lot of time with one another.

But when she was younger, I thought, "I can't stand this!" How many times did I tell the Lord, "Father, You have got to do something about this daughter of mine. You have got to change her!" I have since learned God doesn't always change those people we want Him to change; instead, He often uses them to change us.

I finally realized that what we believe to be our worst enemy often, in actuality, is our best friend. In my case it was those difficult years, the ones that have now "come to pass." I thought those years would never end, but they did, and they changed me into a better person. God uses things to change us that we think are absolutely too difficult to endure.

One time a woman came to me upset because she was pregnant and already had a house full of kids. Because she was a Christian, she wanted God's will, but she also didn't want to have that baby. She was really distraught.

"This too shall pass," I told her. "Just think, a few months from now you will have a cute little baby, and you'll love it so much everything will be fine."

That seemed to settle the issue for her.

Sometimes we need to look ahead with the eye of faith to the time when the situation will be over.

When God is dealing with you, don't look at the training, correction, and discipline you are going through for the moment. Look at the fruit you are going to bear "afterwards." When you don't see the manifestation of your prayers, realize that God is building faith in you, and "afterwards" that faith will be used to bring you into a greater realm of blessing.

My husband enjoys life so much it used to irritate me. For the first few years of our marriage, he was always happy while I was always mad. When I got mad, I refused to talk. He would say to me, "Joyce, you may as well talk to me, because this time next week you're going to be talking to me anyway."

What he was saying was, "This too shall pass."

As I was preparing this message, Dave said to me, "Joyce, do you know how I was able to get through those early years of our marriage?"

"How?" I asked.

"I just remembered I had asked God for a wife," he answered. "And I had asked Him to give me somebody who needed help!"

The funny thing is, three weeks after we were married, Dave looked at me and asked, "What's wrong with you?"

The truth is, there were a lot of things wrong with me. Because I had been abused as a child, I had all kinds of problems. But I really didn't think there was anything wrong with me. I thought everybody else had a problem, not me. So when Dave did something I didn't like, I would refuse to talk to him. That was my way of trying to control our relationship, which was part of my problem — I thought I always had to be in control of everything in my life.

Later, Dave told me how he got through those trying times with me: he kept telling himself, "In three days' time she won't be this way; four more days and she'll be different; a year from now God will have changed her."

Again, his message to himself was, "This too shall pass."

A Time for Everything

To everything there is a season, and a time for every matter or purpose under heaven.

ECCLESIASTES 3:1

God has shown me the devil offers us *two lies:* the *forever lie* and the *never lie.* He tells us the negative things in our life will be that way forever; then concerning positive things, he wants us to believe that if they ever do change, we couldn't stand it. Both of these lies create fear in our hearts. Both are untrue because sooner or later, everything changes. If we continue to believe God and place our trust in Him, bad things ultimately give way to better things.

When we do have good things going on in our lives, they may not stay exactly the same forever. We might go through another hard time, but eventually through Christ, the difficulty will be changed into even better times than the ones we had previously.

For example: If you've never had a vacation, the devil would like to believe you'll never get to have one. On the other hand, if you are on vacation and enjoying it, the enemy would like you to "dread" ever having to go back to work. He wants you to feel that things will never change, and if you believe his lies, then you won't be ready for the changes that surely will come.

Yes, things are always changing. Sometimes changes are exciting — sometimes they're hard. But Jesus never changes — and as long as we keep our eyes on Him, we will make it through the changes in our life and continue growing from glory to glory.

The psalmist warns us, *...if riches increase, set not your heart on them* (Psalm 62:10). And the writer of Proverbs adds, *For riches are not forever; does a crown endure to all generations?* (Proverbs 27:24). In other words, nothing lasts forever, everything changes, this too shall pass.

When the Bible tells us we are not to set our hearts on the things of this world, it means we are not to get too wrapped up in anything in this life. That includes not only our money — our assets, bank accounts, investments, retirement funds, etc. — it also means our job, our possessions, and even our spouse or family.

As believers, our attachment is to be to the Lord alone and not to anyone or anything else. We are to enjoy what we have while we have it, but we are never to get to the point where we think we could not live without it.

One time the Lord had to deal with me along these lines in regard to my husband. At the time I had become very dependent upon Dave. He has always been so good to me and for me. He has helped me so much in my ministry, as well as in my personal life.

When I began to realize how dependent I was upon him, fear started gripping my heart, as I wondered what I would do if something happened to him. I was so upset I went to the Lord in prayer, asking, "Father, what's going on here? Are You preparing me for the fact that Dave is going to die, or is the devil trying to frighten me with that possibility?"

The more I thought about it, the more disturbed I became. "Oh, my," I thought, "what *would* I do without Dave? I don't think I could make it!"

Finally, the Lord spoke to me and said, "I'll tell you what you would do if Dave died; you would do exactly what you're doing right now, because it's not Dave who is holding you up, it's Me."

God was not trying to drive a wedge between Dave and me, but even in a marriage relationship that will last until death or the sound of the last trumpet, there is a fine line which must not be crossed. To do so is to court disaster. We must remember Who is ultimately holding us up and sustaining us.

I am enjoying my ministry right now. Many good things are happening. We are in a period of growth. It is so gratifying to look back on those times when we were traveling around the countryside in a worn-out van with bald tires and rusty fenders, sleeping on the side of the road, holding meetings for a handful of half-dead people, and going to our tape table to find they were returning tapes instead of buying them. It shows how far God has brought us, and we are grateful to Him for that growth and development. But we do not think we have arrived. It is our goal to always be climbing.

Dave says, "I don't want us to be a shooting star, one of those ministries that soars like a rocket, then explodes and fizzles." Neither do I. We set ourselves to spend time with God and remain sensitive to His voice so that we can be obedient to His leading. In that way we will continue to minister in the way He desires and reach people with the messages He gives us.

Nobody knows what God is going to do with him or her. I don't know exactly what God is going to do with me. When I was working in that church in St. Louis, I thought I would always be there. But then one day the Lord said to me, "I'm finished with you here." God may have been finished there, but I wasn't. I stayed on for another full year, until the anointing started lifting from me. From that experience I learned when God is finished, He is finished — and so are we!

I once read a book about a man who was an intercessor.[1] Every so often in his life he would be called to go somewhere and start a new work for the Lord. Then later on God would say to him, "I'm finished with you here." The Lord would call him to stop and intercede for a period of time. So the man would leave his work and go off somewhere alone. Nobody would hear from him for months or even years on end, until the Lord called him to do something else.

There are not many of us who are that moldable and pliable in the hands of the Lord, because we get too attached. One of the things the Lord is saying to us today is, "Get detached from your attachments."

We must remember we are stewards of what God has provided us, not owners. The ministry I am involved in is not my ministry; it is God's ministry. If He ever decides He is finished with it, it will be finished. I don't look for that to happen, nor do I plan for it, but I know I must always be prepared to go on with God if it did happen.

We must not get too attached to people or things. We must always be free to move with the Spirit. There is a season in our lives, and when that season is over, we must let it go. Too often we try to hang on to the past, when God is saying, "It's time to move on to something new."

If God is done with something in your life, let it go. Look to the new thing and allow it to "come to pass." Don't live in the past when God has a new season for you. Let go of what lies behind and press on to what lies ahead. (Philippians 3:13,14.) If God is no longer in something, you will no longer be happy in it. Reach out toward that new horizon God has for you. That's what Abraham did — and God blessed him for it.

"THIS IS THAT!"

Now [in Haran] the Lord said to Abram, Go for yourself [for your own advantage] away from your country, from your relatives and your father's house, to the land that I will show you.

And I will make of you a great nation, and I will bless you [with abundant increase of favors] and make your name famous and distinguished, and you will be a blessing [dispensing good to others].

And I will bless those who bless you [who confer prosperity or happiness upon you] and curse him who curses or uses insolent language toward you; in you will all the families and kindred of the earth be blessed [and by you they will bless themselves].

So Abram departed, as the Lord had directed him....

GENESIS 12:1-4

God spoke to Abraham and told him to leave his country, his home, and his relatives and go to a place He would show him. That is what God did to me when He told me to leave that church in St. Louis. The difference is, Abraham obeyed immediately, while I delayed.

God said to me, "Go, and I will show you," and I said, "No, You show me, and I will go." We had an argument for a while because I did not want to leave the job I had at the time. I thought, "There can never be anything better than this — this is *it*." But God was saying to me, "No, this is *that*."

At one time in my life, that job was "it." But now the Lord was telling me it had "come to pass," and it was time for me to move on to something else.

I look back on the people with whom I had such close fellowship in those days and remember all the things we used to do together. They are still there doing those things, but I am no longer a part of them. They still love me, and I still love them, but our relationship is different. Does that mean it was wrong for me to have spent that time there? No, it just means God was finished with that season in my life.

We must remember there are different seasons in our lives and let God do what He wants to do in each of those seasons. We must stop trying to find some "it" that is never going to change. Everything is changing all the time, and so must we.

It is much easier to cast our care when we know that "this too shall pass." Even the good things in life we enjoy so much will not always stay as they are at the moment. I am not being negative or fatalistic. I am just trying to establish the fact that we need to be careful not to become too attached to anybody or anything in this life more than we are to God and His will and plan for us.

ALLOW GOD TO CHANGE YOU

And while He was in Bethany, [a guest] in the house of Simon the leper, as He was reclining [at table], a woman came with an alabaster jar of ointment (perfume) of pure nard, very costly and precious; and she broke the jar and poured [the perfume] over His head.

MARK 14:3

So often we are afraid of brokenness. But if our outer man has things broken off, the powerful things inside us can pour forth. The perfume of the Holy Spirit is within us, but the alabaster box, which is the flesh, has to be broken for that sweet fragrance to be released.

To fully release the power of the Holy Spirit within us, we must allow God to deal with us and do with us as He wills. We must learn to lean on Him and trust in Him completely, knowing that everything in life changes.

In ancient times, whenever a Roman general returned victoriously from war, he would be driven through the streets of Rome which were lined with cheering crowds loudly proclaiming, "Hail the conquering hero!" In the chariot alongside the hero there was always stationed a slave who held over the general's head a gold crown encrusted with precious jewels. But as they rode along, it was the slave's job to constantly whisper in the hero's ear, "Look behind you," or "Remember that you are mortal."[2] This was done to keep him from becoming too proud by reminding him, "This too shall pass."

That is what God does to us. He gives us His Holy Spirit to fill us and empower us and use us as a blessing to others. But He also sends His Spirit to remind us that "this too shall pass."

If you and I are ever going to have stability in our lives, we must quit looking for one thing that will be "it." We must recall that life is a continual process in which everything is constantly changing — including us. We must put our hope not on the things of this world, but on the Lord, because He is the only thing in this world Who does not change. He is the same yesterday, today, and forever. (Hebrews 13:8.)

KEEPING IN BALANCE

...I have learned how to be content (satisfied to the point where I am not disturbed or disquieted) in whatever state I am.

I know how to be abased and live humbly in straitened circumstances, and I know also how to enjoy plenty and live in abundance. I have learned in any and all circumstances the secret of facing every situation, whether well-fed or going hungry, having a sufficiency and enough to spare or going without and being in want.

I have strength for all things in Christ Who empowers me [I am ready for anything and equal to anything through Him Who infuses inner strength into me; I am self-sufficient in Christ's sufficiency].

PHILIPPIANS 4:11-13

Stability is maturity. To grow up in God is to come to the place that we can be content no matter what our situation or circumstances may be, because we are rooted and grounded, not in things, but in the Lord.

Paul was emotionally and spiritually mature because he knew whatever state he may be in at the moment, it too would pass. In verse 12 he said he had learned the secret of facing every situation of life, whether good or bad.

One day as I was reading that verse, the Lord spoke to me and said, "That's how I keep balance in My people." He showed me if we never had to wait for anything, if everything always went just as we wanted it to, when we wanted it to, we would soon become soft and spoiled. We would assume anybody who was not being blessed as much as we were was doing something wrong. We would try to give that individual "victory lessons."

We must be on our guard against spiritual pride. We must not think more highly of ourselves than we should. (Romans 12:3.) We must remember that all blessings come from God and not from our efforts or our holiness. We must never get to thinking we have arrived. We must remember that pride goes before destruction, and a haughty spirit before a fall. (Proverbs 16:18.)

God wants His people to keep in balance. He wants to bless us and be good to us. He wants to use us as vessels through which His Holy Spirit can work. But in order to do that, He must teach us how to handle new realms of blessings without developing a wrong attitude.

That's why we may enjoy wonderful blessings for a time, and then suddenly experience a series of setbacks. God allows that to happen to us occasionally so we will learn to keep things in perspective. He knows if we have too many blessings, we get spoiled and prideful. He also knows if we have too many bad times, we become discouraged and despondent. That's why it is so important to remember that whatever comes our way, "This too shall pass." That's why we must learn to cast it all upon the Lord, knowing that nothing — good or bad — lasts forever.

JUST PASSING THROUGH!

Yes, though I walk *through* the [deep, sunless] valley of the shadow of death, I will fear or dread no evil, for You are with me; Your rod [to protect] and Your staff [to guide], they comfort me.

PSALM 23:4

The psalmist David said he walked *through* the valley of the shadow of death. That's what we must do. In all the situations and circumstances of this life we must remember we are just passing through. Whatever may be happening to us at the moment, in time it too shall pass.

We must be aware of how fast things can change. Even though at times they may seem agonizingly slow, later when we look back at that period, we can see it was not really as long as it seemed.

When the devil tries to whisper to us, "Things will never change, everything will be this way forever; you are trapped!" we should say to him, "Wrong! Things may be this way right now, but whether they change or not makes no difference to me — I'm just passing through!"

In Isaiah 43:2 the Lord has promised us, *When you pass through the waters, I will be with you, and through the rivers, they will not overwhelm you. When you walk through the fire, you will not be burned or scorched, nor will the flame kindle upon you.*

Shadrach, Meshach, and Abednego, the three Hebrew children, were cast into the fiery furnace by King Nebuchadnezzar. But because they trusted themselves to the Lord, they didn't stay there to be consumed by the flames. They came *through* them to victory. (Daniel 3.) Daniel was thrown into the lions' den, but he came *through* that experience unharmed. (Daniel 6.)

In Psalm 91:15 we have seen that the Lord promises the same kind of protection and deliverance to all those who put their faith and trust in Him.

We Are Being Changed

And all of us, as with unveiled face, [because we] continued to behold [in the Word of God] as in a mirror the glory of the Lord, are constantly being *transfigured* into His very

own image in ever increasing splendor and from one degree
of glory to another; [for this comes] from the Lord [Who is]
the Spirit.

2 CORINTHIANS 3:18

One of the things the devil wants us to believe is that we
will never change. But that is not what the Bible tells us. The
King James Version of this verse says that as we behold the glory
of God we *...are changed into the same image from glory to glory,
even as by the Spirit of the Lord.*

The Greek word translated *transfigured* or *changed* in this
verse is *metamorphoo,* meaning "to transform."[3] It is from this
Greek word we get our English word *metamorphosis,* which
means a complete change from one thing to something totally
different, as when a caterpillar enters a cocoon as a worm and
later emerges as a butterfly.[4]

That is the kind of process you and I are going through spiritually, as we change from the old man to the new man. When
the devil tries to tell us we are the same old worm we used to
be, we should say to him, "No, I'm not. I'm in the process of
change. I won't be a worm forever, you just wait and see. One
day I'll be something totally different from what I am right
now. I'll be a beautiful butterfly!"

Before the caterpillar enters the cocoon, to get from one
place to another he has to crawl slowly and laboriously along
on the ground or on a blade or twig. But then he spins a
cocoon and crawls into it for a while. When he emerges from
that cocoon he has been totally changed. He has become a butterfly, one of the freest of God's creatures. He can soar through
the air on beautiful wings. But to emerge from that cocoon is a
struggle, one that is necessary for the butterfly's full transformation and development.

I once read about a man who saw a butterfly struggling to emerge from a cocoon. Moved by misplaced compassion, the man decided to help the poor creature, so he broke open the cocoon and pulled the developing butterfly out. In just a matter of minutes the weakened creature curled up and died.

If we didn't struggle through some things, we would never develop the strength and stamina we need to survive in this world.

I used to complain to God, asking Him why He didn't help me with my ministry. I didn't realize that I was struggling to emerge from my own cocoon. God could have helped me, but if He had done that my ministry would have weakened and died.

God often works through struggle. But He also sometimes works through what I call "suddenlies."

THE "SUDDENLIES"

Behold, I send My messenger, and he shall prepare the way before Me. And the Lord [the Messiah], Whom you seek will *suddenly* come to His temple; the Messenger or Angel of the covenant Whom you desire, behold, He shall come, says the Lord of hosts.

MALACHI 3:1

We all like "suddenlies," and as we draw closer to the end times, the Bible promises us a "season of suddenlies."

For example, in 1 Corinthians 15:51, 52 Paul exhorts us: *Take notice! I tell you a mystery (a secret truth, an event decreed by the hidden purpose or counsel of God). We shall not all fall asleep [in death], but we shall all be changed (transformed) in a* moment, in the twinkling of an eye, at the [sound of the] last trumpet call. For a trumpet will sound, and the dead [in Christ] will be raised imperishable (free and immune from decay), and we shall be changed (transformed).

When Jesus comes back to this earth to take us to Himself, we will be changed or transformed "in a moment, in the twinkling of an eye" — in other words, *suddenly.*

You and I do not have to be discouraged in our walk with God, because no matter what remains to be done in the transformation of our old man into our new man, it will be accomplished *suddenly* — at the appearing of Jesus in the heavenlies. We are not going to stay the way we are forever. If the devil tries to tell us we are, he is lying. God is even now in the process of changing us from glory to glory, and whatever remains to be changed in us He will one day do *suddenly.*

In Acts 2:1, 2 we read: *And when the day of Pentecost had fully come, they were all assembled together in one place, when **suddenly** there came a sound from heaven like the rushing of a violent tempest blast, and it filled the whole house in which they were sitting.*

This passage goes on to describe how all the disciples were filled with the Holy Spirit and began to speak in other tongues. They had been waiting in that upper room for days. Finally, when the time was right, God fulfilled His promise to pour out His Spirit upon them.

God works just as suddenly among us today. In my meetings people are suddenly filled with the Holy Spirit, just as these people were on the Day of Pentecost.

A young woman who was filled with the Spirit in one of my services later wrote me about the experience and the impact it had on her life. She wrote that she had been to many meetings and had stood in many prayer lines before coming to a certain conference I was holding.

"There must have been some kind of curse on me," she explained. "I felt that you were going to call on me and minister to me, and, sure enough, you did. I had been in meetings like yours for years, and I couldn't tell you what the difference was. All I know is, I went home a totally different person."

She went on to write that after that experience her marriage was different, her relationship with her children was different, the way she kept house was different. Even the way she cared for her body was different. She was no longer lazy, but got up every morning and went out to walk for exercise, something she had never done.

What had happened to her? God had suddenly showed up in her life. Now He was at work day by day, changing her from glory to glory.

That's the way God works — sometimes supernaturally and sometimes ordinarily, sometimes suddenly and sometimes over a period of time. That's why we need to get up every day with the hopeful attitude, "Maybe when I go to bed tonight, my circumstances will be totally different because You, Lord, have moved *suddenly* in my life."

In Acts 9 we read about the conversion of Paul on the road to Damascus: *Now as he traveled on, he came near to Damascus, and **suddenly** a light from heaven flashed around him* (v. 3). The account tells how Jesus appeared to Paul and changed him from a persecutor of the Church to a brand-new convert who would later become the leading apostle to the Gentiles.

Sometimes when we pray for others who are not believers or are not living their faith, we get discouraged because we see no evident change in their attitude or behavior. We must remember that if God could suddenly confront and change Paul, He can confront and change anybody. After all, didn't He confront and change us?

We must never get tired of praying for our loved ones, because sometimes God works suddenly, and sometimes He works over a period of time. But He does work in response to prayer and praise, as we see in Acts 16:26 which describes what happened while Paul and Silas were singing praises to the Lord in the Philippian jail: *Suddenly there was a great earthquake, so that the very foundations of the prison were shaken; and at once all the doors were opened and everyone's shackles were unfastened.*

As soon as the jailer heard the noise and saw what had happened, he drew his sword to kill himself, because he thought the prisoners had all surely escaped. But Paul called out to him, "Don't harm yourself, we're all still here!" When the jailer brought Paul and Silas out of the prison cell, his first question to them was, *...Men, what is it necessary for me to do that I may be saved?* (v. 30).

What a change. The same man who had them beaten, chained, and thrown into the innermost dungeon was now asking them for salvation. Once he became a believer, the jailer took them into his own home, bathed their wounds, and served them something to eat. He was so excited he *...leaped much for joy and exulted with all his family that he believed in God [accepting and joyously welcoming what He had made known through Christ]* (v. 34).

Just as God moved in the lives of all these people, He is moving in your life right now. He may be moving in a supernatural way or in an ordinary way. But He is moving on your behalf. Whatever may be going on in your life at the moment — good or bad — cast it all on the Lord so you can retire from care.

9

RETIRING FROM SELF-CARE

...Believe in the Lord Jesus Christ [give yourself up
to Him, take yourself out of your own keeping
and entrust yourself into His keeping]
and you will be saved....

ACTS 16:31

This is what Paul and Silas told the Philippian jailer who asked them, "What must I do to be saved?" This is what salvation really means — giving ourselves up to God, taking ourselves out of our own keeping, and entrusting ourselves into His keeping.

God wants to take care of us. He can do a much better job of that if we will avoid a problem called independence, which is really self-care. The desire to take care of ourselves is based on fear. Basically, it stems from the idea that if *we* do it, we can be sure it will be done right. We are afraid of what might happen if we entrust ourselves totally to God and He doesn't "come through" for us.

The root problem of independence is trusting ourselves more than we trust God.

We love to have a back-up plan. We may pray and ask God to get involved in our lives, but if He is the least bit slow in responding (at least, to our way of thinking), we are quick to take control back into our own hands.

What we fail to realize is, God has a plan for us too — and His plan is much better than ours.

OUR PLAN VERSUS GOD'S PLAN

For I know the thoughts and plans that I have for you, says the Lord, thoughts and plans for welfare and peace and not for evil, to give you hope in your final outcome.

JEREMIAH 29:11

Have you ever wondered why it sometimes seems God will not allow us to help ourselves when we are faced with a problem? The reason this happens is that God wants to help us, but He wants to do it His way and not our way — because our way usually involves a lot of worry, fretfulness, reasoning, anxiety, and excessive plotting and planning.

The Holy Spirit impressed this fact upon me when a lady sent me a letter with a wonderful testimony about the subject of anxiety and self-care. I would like to share it with you because I think it speaks to all of us:

"I recently attended your women's conference in St. Louis on the Holy Spirit. When I came to the conference I was anxious that my life wasn't going to amount to anything for God, and I was afraid that no matter what happened, I was never going to be happy. I had been frustrated and unhappy for about a year and I really needed a breakthrough.

"During the conference I felt God lifting me from many of my worries and cares. I felt a little better after each session. But when I would return home, between the sessions, those same fears and anxious thoughts would attack me all over again.

"During the Saturday session, I gave in the offering, praying that God would deliver me once and for all. I knew God was moving powerfully because several of the women that I sat with received deliverance from their past hurts and pains.

"Finally, after your last session, I decided that I couldn't face another day anxious and fearful. I bought your tapes 'Facing Fear and Finding Freedom,' 'Be Anxious for Nothing,' and 'How To Be Content.'[1] I didn't have the money set aside for them, so then I became worried about how to pay for the other things I had planned to use the money for.

"You also prayed for me after the last session, and you encouraged me to listen to the tapes. Well, I did feel a little tingle in my stomach when you laid hands on me, but that was all. After I left, I put one of your tapes in my car cassette player in hopes that my fears would not attack me before I got home.

"I decided to stop at the Citgo gas station about three minutes from the hotel, and on the way there I realized I didn't have any money. So I decided to use my debit card, which accessed an account containing my rent money, and to transfer some other money into the account later that day to cover the gas.

"When I arrived at the Citgo gas station, I made sure they accepted the type of credit card that I had. I filled my tank and gave [the attendant] the card to pay for the gas. It was denied. The attendant ran the card though three times, and each time my card was denied. I had no other way to pay for the gas. By then I was sweating, hyperventilating, and having visions of myself dressed in the red and orange Citgo uniform, pumping gas to pay for my bill. I thought my life was over.

"But then four women in a van pulled up to the station. One of them got out and asked me if anything was wrong. And, of course, I told her that I was fine and thanked her for asking. I guess the panicked look on my face gave me away, and she insisted on helping me. Finally, I told her that I needed money to pay for my gas, and immediately she and the other three ladies handed me enough money to pay the bill, and they drove off.

"I paid the bill, returned to my car, and sat down in relief. As soon as I started the engine, God spoke to me. As best that I can remember He said the following: 'All your life all you do is plan. You get up in the morning, and you plan out your day. While you brush your teeth, you plan what you're going to wear. During the day, you plan for the evening. You plan what you're going to eat; you plan what you're going to study; you plan when you're going to exercise. All you do all day long is plan, plan, plan....You even planned how you were going to pay for your gas, and look where it got you.'

"Then He paused and said, 'I have a plan.'"

Sometimes we have to lay down our plan to hear God's plan. I believe it is wise to plan our work and work our plan. But we must not become so rooted and grounded in our plan that we argue and resist if God tries to show us a better way.

Obviously we should always have a plan about how we are going to pay our bills. But the woman in this story had such an excessive, elaborate plan that it was confusing. God was trying to make the point with her that she would never enjoy her life until she began trusting God to a much greater degree.

I go to each of my meetings with a definite plan in mind. But many times God changes that plan because He knows better than I do what the people need to hear. If I am not submissive to His will, I am not going to meet the needs of those who have come to hear the Word of God for them.

This woman went on to write: "I was laughing so hard by now I could hardly drive straight down the highway. It is a miracle that I arrived home in one piece. For the rest of the day, God continued to remind me when I would start trying to plan something.

He showed me that by planning all the time, I was trying to figure out my future myself, and that I wasn't fully depending on Him."

The woman who wrote this letter admitted she had a problem with independence. God does not want us to be independent or codependent. He wants us to be dependent upon Him, because He knows that apart from Him we can do nothing. (John 15:5.)

Finally, this woman ended her testimony by writing: "Not only did God deliver me from anxiety, but He completely destroyed the thinking pattern that was fostering the anxiousness. Since then God has given me the opportunity to tell several friends what has happened to me, and God has touched them and me. I am so thankful for the truth that delivered me from this bondage."

This woman's testimony contains the valuable lesson of which we all need to continually remind ourselves: In everything that concerns us, God has a plan, just as He did for Jesus when He sent Him into this world to save us and to serve as our example.

JESUS WAS NOT INDEPENDENT

I am able to do nothing from Myself [independently, of My own accord — but only as I am taught by God and as I get His orders]. Even as I hear, I judge [I decide as I am bidden to decide. As the voice comes to Me, so I give a decision], and My judgment is right (just, righteous), because I do not seek or consult My own will [I have no desire to do what is pleasing to Myself, My own aim, My own purpose] but only the will and pleasure of the Father Who sent Me.

JOHN 5:30

Jesus did not ask Himself what to do, He consulted God. Instead of following His own will, He followed the will of His Father. When He made a decision, it was right because it was not His decision. It was the will of the One Who Sent Him.

Jesus made it clear He was not independent, out on His own trying to do His own thing. We would do well to follow His example.

Sometimes rather than deciding the will of God and then being obedient to it, we figure out what we want and ask God to bless it. Jesus said He had no desire to do what was pleasing to Himself. His aim and purpose were to do the will and pleasure of His heavenly Father. He said to the people of His day, "What you see Me doing is what I see the Father doing. What You hear Me saying is what I hear the Father saying. I do not speak on My own authority, but on His authority."

Jesus did not have a problem with independence, and neither should we. We should realize that anything we do independently, apart from God, will fail to bear any good fruit either for Him or for us.

INDEPENDENCE IS CHILDISH

When I was a child, I talked like a child, I thought like a child, I reasoned like a child; now that I have become a man, I am done with childish ways and have put them aside.

1 CORINTHIANS 13:11

When our son Danny was a teenager, he was a wonderful boy. But in many ways he was still a child in his thoughts, attitude, and behavior. Like many adolescents, he was self-centered. Everything in his life had to revolve around him and benefit him. He would get up in the morning talking about his social life, spend the day talking about his social life, and go to bed talking about his social life. He had a plan for every available minute, and it was all aimed at gratifying his own personal desires. His every thought, word, and deed had to do with himself and what would bless him and make him happy when God is the One Who knows what will truly bless us and make us happy and orders our steps to bring us into what He has for us.

Immature Christians are like young children or teenagers who plan everything according to what *they* think is the best plan for them. If we want to grow up in the Lord, we must learn to seek God's will and plan for our life rather than our own. We must be determined not to go off independently on our own trying to fulfill our own desires or meet our own needs. Instead, we must trust in the Lord with all our heart and mind, and not lean on our own understanding.

OVERCOMING A SPIRIT OF INDEPENDENCE

Lean on, trust in, and be confident in the Lord with all your heart and mind and do not rely on your own insight or understanding.

In all your ways know, recognize, and acknowledge Him, and He will direct and make straight and plain your paths.

Be not wise in your own eyes; reverently fear and worship the Lord and turn [entirely] away from evil.

PROVERBS 3:5-7

This passage does not mean to say we have to seek a divine word from God about every minute decision we make in the course of our daily lives. That would not be possible. God puts wisdom into us in the form of His Holy Spirit, for us to walk by that wisdom step-by-step. But the Lord does want us to know, recognize, and acknowledge Him. He does want us to be aware of His Spirit and to walk in quiet confidence, trust, and obedience to Him.

Some time ago I heard a well-known minister say, "It has been a long, long time since God has said to me, 'Do this.' But that doesn't bother me, because I'm still busy doing the last thing He told me to do years ago."

God expects us to walk by wisdom, but He also expects us to be aware of and care about what we are doing. Acknowledging Him in all our ways is so important because He will direct our paths. If we start to go astray one way or the other, He will nudge us and get us back on the right path, as we read in Isaiah 30:21:

> And your ears will hear a word behind you, saying, This is the way; walk in it, when you turn to the right hand and when you turn to the left.

It is insulting to God when we go through life planning everything without consulting Him or caring what He thinks, yet expecting Him to make everything work out as we envision just because it is what we want.

Like pride, independence is a sin. Independence displays a lack of trust in God. It says, "I want to take care of myself because if I do things my way, I know they will get done right." It doesn't trust God's way of handling something to be better than the person's own plan.

How many of us are like that? We don't want anybody to help us because we don't want to become dependent upon anyone. We would rather do things on our own than ask for help. That's exactly why God gives each of us only a part of the answer, so we will have to work together to accomplish His will in our lives.

If we want to do the will of God, we must be willing to get involved with other people.

For some of us with strong, independent personalities, that is a real problem. Usually the stronger our personality, the more weaknesses and inabilities God has to leave in us so we have no choice but to lean on Him and on others.

In 2 Chronicles 20, we read King Jehoshaphat's prayer to the Lord when Judah was faced with an invasion by enemies who were more powerful than they were. He acknowledged that he and his people had no might to stand against such a great company, adding, "We don't know what to do, Lord, but our eyes are on You." (v. 12.)

That is the statement of a person who is dependent on God, not independent: "I don't know what to do, Lord, and have no ability to do it if I did know, but my eyes are on You."

It pleases our heavenly Father when we acknowledge and confess to Him our inability to run our own lives. That is what we are doing when we say, "Father, help me! I need You!"

God wants us to be dependent upon Him, and He wants us to verbalize that dependence, just as Jesus did. When we come to Him in prayer, He wants us to say: "Father, I need You. Apart from You I can do nothing. Without You, I am hopeless. Unless You lead, guide, strengthen, and uphold me, I will fail every time."

The Incompetent, Competent Twelve

[This is] because the foolish thing [that has its source in] God is wiser than men, and the weak thing [that springs] from God is stronger than men.

For [simply] consider your own call, brethren; not many [of you were considered to be] wise according to human estimates and standards, not many influential and powerful, not many of high and noble birth.

[No] for God selected (deliberately chose) what in the world is foolish to put the wise to shame, and what the world calls weak to put the strong to shame.

And God also selected (deliberately chose) what in the world is lowborn and insignificant and branded and treated with contempt, even the things that are nothing, that He might depose and bring to nothing the things that are,

So that no mortal man should [have pretense for glorying and] boast in the presence of God.

1 CORINTHIANS 1:25-29

We must remember it is not our gifts that matter, it is God's anointing. God usually doesn't call people because of their great wisdom, knowledge, or ability; rather, He calls them because of their foolishness, ignorance, and weakness so that all the glory will go to Him and not to them.

God either calls people with talent then spends years teaching them that without His anointing their talents will do them absolutely no good, or He calls people who are so incapable they know the only way they can ever hope to do anything is by leaning totally on Him every second.

As Paul has written, many of us fall into that second category. In that respect, we are no different from the first disciples Jesus called.

The following is a letter supposedly written to Jesus by the Jordan Management Consultant firm in Jerusalem, which is reporting its findings on the twelve men He has submitted for evaluation:

Dear Sir:

Thank you for submitting the resumes of the twelve men you have picked for management positions in your new organization. All of them have taken our battery of tests; and we have not only run the results through our computer, but also arranged personal interviews for each of them with our psychologist and vocational aptitude consultant....

It is the staff opinion that most of your nominees are lacking in background, education, and vocational aptitude for the type of enterprise you are undertaking. They do not have the team concept. We would recommend that you continue your search for persons of experience in managerial ability and proven capability.

Simon Peter is emotionally unstable and given to fits of temper. Andrew has absolutely no qualities of leadership. The two brothers, James and John, the sons of Zebedee, place personal interest above company loyalty. Thomas demonstrates a questioning attitude that would tend to undermine morale. We feel that it is our duty to tell you that Matthew has been blacklisted by the Greater Jerusalem Better Business Bureau. James, the son of Alphaeus, and Thaddeus definitely have radical leanings, and they both registered a high score on the manic depressive scale.

One of the candidates, however, shows great potential. He is a man of ability and resourcefulness, meets people well, has a keen business mind, and has contacts in high places. He is highly motivated, ambitious, and responsible. We recommend Judas Iscariot as your controller and right hand man. All of the other profiles are self-explanatory.[2]

Basically, what this consulting firm was saying is that the people Jesus chose as His disciples were all losers and that He would get nowhere with them because they would never be of any value to Him.

But as we see in Paul's letter to the Corinthians, God deliberately chooses the nothings of this world so He can use them to confound the wise and powerful. The Lord takes zeros and adds His power to them so that they become great for His glory, as He tells us in Zechariah 4:6: *...Not by might, nor by power, but by My Spirit..., says the Lord of hosts.*

In and of ourselves, you and I are nothing. We must not try to be independent, because if we do we will fail every time. We must recognize and acknowledge our utter dependence on God.

The reason we are so independent-minded may be that we have learned through bitter experience nobody in this world is going to look out for us or have our best interests at heart but us.

If you have been betrayed or mistreated, as I was during my childhood, you may feel everybody is out to harm you, abuse you, or use you. You may think, as I did for so many years, the only way to protect yourself and assure you are not taken advantage of is by keeping total control over every aspect of your life. If so, when God asks you to give up that control to Him, you may find it almost impossible to do so. But you may also fail to realize that your refusal to cast your care upon the Lord and entrust yourself to His keeping is just another form of childish rebellion.

WOE TO THE REBELLIOUS CHILDREN

Woe to the rebellious children, says the Lord, who take counsel and carry out a plan, but not Mine, and who make a league and pour out a drink offering, but not of My Spirit, thus adding sin to sin;

Who set out to go down into Egypt, and have not asked Me — to flee to the stronghold of Pharaoh and to strengthen themselves in his strength and to trust in the shadow of Egypt!

ISAIAH 30:1,2

This is another of those "woe" Scripture passages. In it the Lord pronounces a curse upon those rebellious children who turn from trusting in Him to take counsel of themselves, carry out their own plans, and flee to "the shadow of Egypt" rather than resting under the "shadow of the Almighty."

In this case, fleeing to the "shadow of Egypt" refers to turning to the arm of the flesh rather than leaning on the arm of the Lord. In other words, we are not to trust in ourselves or in others, but only in the Lord. We are not to make rules and regulations about everything, but we are to acknowledge the Lord in all our ways so that He may direct our paths. We are to find our strength in Him, not in ourselves or the world, which is what Egypt always represents in Scripture.

Egypt Is No Help

Therefore shall the strength and protection of Pharaoh turn to your shame, and the refuge in the shadow of Egypt be to your humiliation and confusion....

For Egypt's help is worthless and toward no purpose....

ISAIAH 30:3,7

In this passage, the Lord is saying to us, "Don't turn away from trusting in Me to trusting in your own plans and devices. They won't work, and you will only end up humiliated and confused. Before you do anything, check with Me to see if it is what you should be doing. Don't look to the world for answers, because it has none to give. Salvation and deliverance are with Me, and Me alone."

A Broken Wall

Therefore this iniquity and guilt will be to you like a broken section of a high wall, bulging out and ready [at some distant day] to fall, whose crash will [then] come suddenly and swiftly, in an instant.

And he shall break it as a potter's vessel is broken, breaking it in pieces without sparing so that there cannot be found among its pieces one large enough to carry coals of fire from the hearth or to dip water out of the cistern.

ISAIAH 30:13,14

When you and I make our own plans or run to other people instead of trusting in the Lord, we leave a weak spot in our wall of divine protection. At a time when we least expect it, the enemy will break through that weak spot.

God does not want us to have weak spots in our lives. He wants us to rely on Him and be obedient to Him so our wall will remain strong and thick and our lives will be blessed and full.

The more we depend on God, the more He can do through us. But sometimes we go through a brokenness before we enter into blessings.

Once for about a year and a half I thought I was going mad. All I could do all day long was walk around in my house praying, "Help me, Lord!" I didn't even know what kind of help I needed or for what. Now as I look back on that experience, I know what was happening. The spirit of independence was being broken off of me. God was bringing me to the point that I knew I could do nothing apart from Him.

I remember one night as I was getting ready to go to sleep, I picked up a little book and started reading it. Suddenly I had a visitation from God. For about forty-five minutes I sat there on the edge of my bed and wept. Finally, the Lord spoke to me and said, "Anything good you do has nothing to do with you. I am the One Who is good. When you see yourself doing anything good, it is only because I have wrestled with you to get your flesh under subjection long enough to allow My glory to shine through it."

Sometimes before God can promote us, He has to remind us of our place. In my own case, my ministry was just about to experience a sudden spurt of growth. God was preparing me in advance by telling me, "I'm going to do something marvelous in your life and ministry, and when it happens you must remember that it is I and not you Who is bringing it to pass."

God was teaching me what He is teaching all of us today: The solution to our problems is found in Him and Him alone.

RETURN TO ME, SAYS THE LORD

For thus said the Lord God, the Holy One of Israel: In returning [to Me] and resting [in Me] you shall be saved; in quietness and in [trusting] confidence shall be your strength. But you would not,

And you said, No! We will speed [our own course] on horses! Therefore you will speed [in flight from your enemies]! You said, We will ride upon swift steeds [doing our own way]! Therefore will they who pursue you be swift, [so swift that]

One thousand of you will flee at the threat of one of them; at the threat of five you will flee till you are left like a beacon or a flagpole on the top of a mountain, and like a signal on a hill.

And therefore the Lord [earnestly] waits [expecting, looking, and longing] to be gracious to you; and therefore He lifts

Himself up, that He may have mercy on you and show loving-kindness to you. For the Lord is a God of justice. Blessed (happy, fortunate, to be envied) are all those who [earnestly] wait for Him, who expect and look and long for Him [for His victory, His favor, His love, His peace, His joy, and His matchless, unbroken companionship]!

ISAIAH 30:15-18

What God was telling me that night was the same thing He is telling us today: "Either you are going to depend on Me, or you are going to end up in the biggest mess you have ever seen in your whole life."

We must learn to depend totally upon God. If we don't, we will not be able to do anything of any value. Apart from Him we can do nothing.

When the Lord visited me in my bedroom that night and gave me that message, it was because I had been engaged in a wrestling match with Him for a long time. It had been a battle of wills. I had been doing things the way I wanted them done, according to my plan. He was trying to show me I had to give up all that and submit to His way and plan. He was telling me I had to learn to lean on Him, to trust Him with all my heart and mind and understanding, to acknowledge Him in all my ways. He was warning me not to be wise in my own eyes, because I didn't know half as much as I thought I did.

I thought I had everything figured out, but God had news for me.

OUR WILL OR GOD'S WILL?

I assure you, most solemnly I tell you, when you were young you girded yourself [put on your own belt or girdle] and you walked about wherever you pleased to go. But when you grow old you will stretch out your hands, and someone else will put a girdle around you and carry you where you do not wish to go.

JOHN 21:18

In the Scripture quoted above, I believe that though God was actually speaking to Peter about the type of death he would experience, the Lord was also letting Peter know that he had run his own life for a long time — often walking according to emotions and his own will — but now it was time to grow up. It was time to turn the reins of his life over to God. Father God was also letting him know that he might not like everything that was going to happen, but that it would ultimately end up for the glory of God.

When we were baby Christians, we did our own thing. We made our own decisions and followed our own course. To demonstrate God's providential care, He blessed our plans and let them work. But when we grow up and become mature Christians, we sometimes have to do things we don't particularly want to do in the natural realm, in obedience to God's directions. God no longer blesses and prospers our childish plans and schemes.

For a while, God allows us to "call the shots," so to speak. He lets us do our own thing with His blessing. But through that time, He has begun establishing His way in our individual lives. At a certain point, He starts "wrestling" with us to call us into submission to His will rather than ours. He has begun teaching us to put our trust in Him and not in ourselves.

Jesus asked Peter three times, "Simon Peter, do you love Me?" Three times Peter responded, "Yes, Lord, You know I love You." (John 21:15-17.) Jesus had a reason for asking Peter that question three times. He knew Peter's love was about to be put to the test.

Lately the Lord has been saying to me, "Joyce, do You love Me? If so, will you still love Me and serve Me even if I don't do everything just the way you want or just when you think I should?"

At the time of the Lord's visitation, I had been asking God for a huge ministry. In His visit He said to me, "Joyce, if I asked you to go down to the riverfront here in St. Louis and minister to fifty people for the rest of your life and never be known by anyone, would you do it?"

My response was, "But, Lord, surely You can't really be asking me to do that!"

We always have such grandiose plans for ourselves. If God asks us to do something that isn't prominent, we aren't always sure we are hearing Him correctly, or that it is His will for us!

When God asked me those questions about my ministry, I felt the way I imagined Abraham must have felt when the Lord asked him to sacrifice his son Isaac through whom He had promised to bless him and all nations of the earth. (Genesis 22.) It seemed God was asking me to give up the very work He had given me through which He blessed many others as well as me. But God wasn't asking me to give up that ministry. He was just asking me to lay it on the altar, as Abraham lay Isaac on the altar before the Lord.

We must not let anything — even our work for God — become more important to us than God Himself. To keep that from happening, from time to time God calls upon us to lay it all on the altar as proof of our love and commitment. He tests us by asking us to lay down our most treasured blessing as proof of our love for Him.

In my case, the Lord brought me to the point where I had to say, "Yes, Lord, I'll do it. If that's what You want, I'll go down to the riverfront and minister to fifty people for the rest of my life. I love You enough to do that."

I was weeping when I said it, but I meant it. I fell to my knees and cried out in tears, "Lord, I have nothing to give You but myself, my will, and my love. Your will be done, not mine."

When we get to the place where we can honestly make that kind of commitment, God will begin to honor us and work out His plan for our life.

God had a different plan in mind for Peter than Peter had for himself. Peter was a hothead and a hotshot. He was always going off on tangents and speaking before he thought about what he was saying.

But the Lord loved Peter. He knew the plans He had for him, plans to bless him and do him good, not to harm him or cause him pain. But He also knew He had to deal with Peter because of his tendency to give into the flesh. That's what Jesus was talking about when He told Peter He was praying for him — just as He is praying for you and me right now. (Hebrews 7:25.)

Going Through Times of Testing

Simon, Simon (Peter), listen! Satan has asked excessively that [all of] you be given up to him [out of the power and keeping of God], that he might sift [all of] you like grain,

But I have prayed especially for you [Peter], that your [own] faith may not fail; and when you yourself have turned again, strengthen and establish your brethren.

LUKE 22:31,32

I don't imagine this was very good news to Peter. I am sure he must have wanted to say, "But, Lord, if there is a problem with Satan, why don't You just handle it?"

But that wasn't the answer Jesus gave Peter. He told him He had prayed for him, especially, and that when he had turned he was to strengthen and establish the other disciples. Jesus did not pray that Peter would be delivered from testing. He prayed that Peter's faith would not fail him while he was going *through* that time of testing.

That is the same thing Jesus is praying for you and me right now. He is praying we will come through the times of testing in our lives and emerge from them strengthened and empowered so that we can strengthen and empower others to live in joy, peace, and victory.

It is so important we learn to face the enemy and not always be looking for somebody else to do it for us. If we turn our lives over to the Lord totally and completely, He may not always do everything exactly as we would like it done or just when we would like it to be done. But whatever He does do will be right, the thing that is best in that situation.

But can we *really* trust God to do for us what needs to be done in every situation of life?

GOD WILL PROVIDE

Now after this the Lord chose and appointed seventy others and sent them out ahead of Him, two by two, into every town and place where He Himself was about to come (visit).

And He said to them, The harvest indeed is abundant [there is much ripe grain], but the farmhands are few. Pray therefore the Lord of the harvest to send out laborers into His harvest.

Go your way; behold, I send you out like lambs into the midst of wolves.

Carry no purse, no provisions bag, no [change of] sandals; refrain from [retarding your journey by] saluting and wishing anyone well along the way.

LUKE 10:1-4

When the Lord sent out the seventy to prepare the way for His arrival, He told them, "I am sending you out to do a job for Me, but don't take anything with you to take care of yourselves."

I believe there is a spiritual principle set forth in this passage. The point is not that we are forbidden to take pocketbooks and shoes and clothes with us when we travel from one place to another to minister. The point is that we are to be obedient to do the will of God, trusting Him to meet the needs He knows we will experience.

In Luke 22:35, Jesus asked His disciples, *...When I sent you out with no purse or [provision] bag or sandals, did you lack anything? They answered, Nothing!*

If the Lord has sent us out to do His work, it is His responsibility to make the arrangements necessary to keep us provisioned. He has promised us if we will tend to His harvest, He will tend to our needs.

THE CAMELS ARE COMING!

Now when Jesus was born in Bethlehem of Judea in the days of Herod the king, behold, wise men [astrologers] from the east came to Jerusalem, asking,

Where is He Who has been born King of the Jews? For we have seen His star in the east at its rising and have come to worship Him....

...and behold, the star which had been seen in the east in its rising went before them until it came and stood over the place where the young Child was.

When they saw the star, they were thrilled with ecstatic joy.

And on going into the house, they saw the Child with Mary His mother, and they fell down and worshiped Him. Then opening their treasure bags, they presented to Him gifts — gold and frankincense and myrrh.

MATTHEW 2:1,2,9-11

We all remember the Christmas story: how Jesus was born of Mary in a stable and laid in a manger, how the Wise Men came from the east following a star which led them to the Holy Child, how they came in and worshiped Him, laying before Him precious gifts of gold, frankincense, and myrrh.

In this story we see that Mary and Joseph didn't go out seeking gifts. Although they were forced to spend the night in a cold, dark stable, they didn't send out messages asking for gifts. But because they were in the middle of God's will, He sent them Wise Men from the east mounted on camels loaded down with provisions.

I once heard a sermon preached on this subject in a church in Minnesota. It was titled, "The Camels Are Coming." The basic message was that if we are in the will of God, He will always bring our provision to us. We don't have to try to chase it down; it will seek us out. We don't have to try to make things happen; God will bring them to us.

Let me give you an example.

The church in which this sermon was preached was involved in a building program and needed a great deal of money, so they really grasped the image of God sending camels with their pro-

196

vision. In fact, it was such a vivid image to them, they soon had little camels sitting around on desks and tables to remind them of it. Their theme became, "The Camels Are Coming!"

They needed at least $100,000 to meet an approaching debt payment, but they felt God was telling them not to borrow the money. When the payment came due, they went to the bank and tried to borrow that amount anyway, but their loan application was denied. I am convinced it was denied because it was not God's will for them, so He blocked that avenue.

When an avenue in our life is blocked, before we start trying to kick down the door, we need to back off and consult the Lord. That may not be the way God wants us to go.

This very thing happened to Paul and his ministry team, as we see in Acts 16: *And when they had come opposite Mysia, they tried to go into Bithynia, but the Spirit of Jesus did not permit them* (v. 7). Two verses later, Paul received the vision of the man from Macedonia ...*pleading with him and saying, Come over to Macedonia and help us!* (v. 9). Sometimes God has to block one avenue so we will be open to follow another.

One time our ministry in St. Louis had an eye on a building we thought we needed. We claimed that building by driving around it seven times, saying, "This building is ours in Jesus' name! It will not be sold until we can buy it!"

Not long afterwards, the building was sold — and not to us!

What did that tell us? It told us that was not our building after all. Instead of going down there and standing on the corner rebuking the devil for three hours and reclaiming the building, we simply concluded, "Well, God must have another building in mind for us, because if this one had been it, He would have kept it for us."

Rather than getting all riled up and doing something foolish, we just kept confessing, "The camels are coming!" And eventually they arrived — on God's schedule, not ours.

To the pastor of this church in Minnesota there seemed no way they could meet their debt payment. One Sunday evening a friend of the pastor showed up for services so the pastor asked him to come to the platform and exhort the congregation a bit. The man pulled a sealed envelope out of his pocket and handed it to the pastor, saying, "Here, I want to give you this to spend any way you like. I was praying for you that God would meet your need and provide for you when the Lord said to me, 'Don't pray, do something.'"

The pastor opened the envelope and found in it a check for $100,000! Turning to the church he cried, "Praise God, our camel just came in!"

I believe the camels will come for each of us if we will stay in the will of God. The only way we can expect this kind of provision is by being faithful to stay where God has placed us and do the work He has given us to do for His Kingdom's sake. When we begin to believe this, we are free to cast our care upon Him. We don't have to stay up all night fretting and worrying, trying to figure out what to do to take care of ourselves. We can simply deposit ourselves with God.

DEPOSIT YOURSELF WITH GOD

Therefore, those who are ill-treated and suffer in accordance with God's will must do right and commit their souls [*in charge as a deposit*] to the One Who created [them] and will never fail [them].

1 PETER 4:19

Each pay period when we go to the drive-through bank window, we slide our deposit into the slot and forget about it. We leave our money with the bank officials, trusting them to take care of it for us. In the same way, when we drive by the gates of heaven each morning in prayer, we need to deposit ourselves with God, trusting Him to take care of us.

That is especially true when we are being ill-treated and are suffering because we belong to God and are doing right, being faithful to His will for us. When we give ourselves up to God, we must quit trying to seek justice for ourselves and simply trust Him to justify us and work out everything for the best in accordance with His will and plan. That's what Jesus did.

When He was abused, reviled, and insulted, Jesus did not respond in kind. Instead, He trusted Himself entirely to God Who judges all things and all people fairly and justly.

As followers of Jesus, our Example, we are called to follow His footsteps. Like Him, we are not to try to take matters into our own hands, but instead to commit ourselves to God, trusting Him to work out everything for good to all concerned.

We spend so much time trying to take care of ourselves we have no time left to enjoy our lives. We are too busy with self-care, trying to make sure that nobody takes advantage of us, that everyone treats us right, that we get our fair share.

One time I was invited to preach in a certain church which assured me I would receive a love offering at the end of my series of meetings. Later, just before the meetings were to begin, the church suddenly called and informed me I would receive an honorarium, but no love offering would be taken. Although I didn't say anything to the church, I got upset and began to mouth off to my secretary: "If those people think for one moment they're going to pull that kind of thing on me, they've got another think coming! I won't go! You can just call them back and tell them that!"

In just a few moments the Lord spoke to me and said, "Yes, you will go, and you will not say anything about this matter. You will not be concerned about the money. You will go and minister as you promised, and you will do it sweetly and kindly. You will trust Me to take care of you."

When a love offering is received for a speaker, all the people attending the meeting have an opportunity to give. When an honorarium is given, the church decides what the speaker should have. I felt that the offering would probably be larger if all the people got the opportunity to give. God wanted me to trust Him with the entire matter and believe that He was able to get to me whatever He wanted me to have no matter who He did it through.

Sometimes people do try to take advantage of us and our ministry. But God has taught us not to take matters into our own hands. He has instructed us, "Just keep being faithful to Me, doing what I tell you to do. Sometimes it may appear that people are taking advantage of you, but if you will keep your eyes on Me, nobody can ever take advantage of you, because I am the God of justice. Quit trying to bring justice into your own life, and let Me bring it to you."

This same principle applies to raising money to meet the needs of our ministry. God has told us to cast our care upon Him, and He will provide what we need to carry on His work.

As a minister of the Gospel, my job is not to spend most of my time trying to figure out how to get money to pay bills and erect buildings. My job is to teach and preach, to pray and bless people. It is God's job to bring my provision to me. My part is to share the Word with people concerning giving, let them know our needs, trust God to work in their hearts, and get to us enough to meet every need we have.

If we get so involved in looking out for ourselves, we will fail to do what we are called to do, which is to minister to the needs of others. Whatever happens to us, however we may be treated or mistreated, we must continue to do the work God has set before us. We must deposit ourselves with Him, trusting Him to justify us and vindicate us, to protect us and provide for us, to help us and keep us.

GOD IS OUR HELPER AND KEEPER

I will lift up my eyes to the hills [around Jerusalem, to sacred Mount Zion and Mount Moriah] — From whence shall my help come?

My help comes from the Lord, Who made heaven and earth.

He will not allow your foot to slip or to be moved; He Who keeps you will not slumber.

Behold, He who keeps Israel will neither slumber nor sleep.

The Lord is your keeper; the Lord is your shade on your right hand [the side not carrying a shield].

The sun shall not smite you by day, nor the moon by night.

The Lord will keep you from all evil; He will keep your life.

The Lord will keep your going out and your coming in from this time forth and forevermore.

PSALM 121:1-8

Psalm 121 is a beautiful hymn about God as the Helper and Keeper of those who trust in Him. In the midst of troubled times, we should read and meditate on it constantly.

In Psalm 17:8, the psalmist prayed to God, *Keep and guard me as the pupil of Your eye; hide me in the shadow of Your wings.* We have

201

already seen how God has promised to watch over and protect those who take refuge under the shadow of His wings, but how is the pupil of His eye protected? By the eyelid. The moment danger threatens, the eyelid automatically closes, shutting out anything harmful. That is what God does for us who entrust ourselves to Him.

GOD REWARDS AND RECOMPENSES US

But you shall be called the priests of the Lord; people will speak of you as the ministers of our God. You shall eat the wealth of the nations, and the glory [once that of your captors] shall be yours.

Instead of your [former] shame you shall have a twofold recompense; instead of dishonor and reproach [your people] shall rejoice in their portion. Therefore in their land they shall possess double [what they had forfeited]; everlasting joy shall be theirs.

For I the Lord love justice....

ISAIAH 61:6-8

Hebrews 11:6 says of God, ...*He is the rewarder of those who earnestly and diligently seek Him [out]*. So not only is God our Helper and Keeper, He is also the One Who rewards us and recompenses us. A recompense is a back pay, sort of like Workers' Compensation. (Genesis 15:1.)

One time God spoke to me and said, "Joyce, you work for Me; you are on My payroll. If you get hurt in any way, you don't have to try to get compensation or revenge, because I will take care of you — I will repay, because I am a God of justice."

TRUST THE GOD OF JUSTICE

For we know Him Who said, Vengeance is Mine [retribution and the meting out of full justice rest with Me]; I will repay [I will exact the compensation], says the Lord. And again, The Lord will judge and determine and solve and settle the cause and the cases of His people.

HEBREWS 10:30

Do you know what God means when He says He is the God of justice? He means that sooner or later He will make everything right. He will see we get everything coming to us.

As Christians, it is not our job to seek vengeance, but to pray for our enemies, for those who mistreat us, abuse us, and take advantage of us. If we will do that, God has promised to take care of us.

God is not only our Helper and Keeper and the One Who rewards and recompenses us, He is also the Righteous Judge. He determines and solves and settles the cause and the cases of His people.

You and I need to put the Holy Trinity on our case. With Jesus as our Friend, the Holy Spirit as our Advocate, and the heavenly Father as our Judge, we can retire from self-care, knowing that justice will be done — so that we can be anxious for nothing.

ENDNOTES

Chapter 2

[1] *Webster's II New Riverside Desk Dictionary* (Boston: Houghton Mifflin Company, 1988), s.v. "anxiety."

[2] *Webster's New World College Dictionary*, 3d ed. (New York: Macmillan, 1996), s.v. "anxiety."

[3] Maranatha Music, "He Has Made Me Glad" (Nashville: 1976).

Chapter 6

[1] James E. Strong, "Hebrew and Chaldee Dictionary," in *Strong's Exhaustive Concordance of the Bible* (Nashville: Abingdon, 1890), p. 52, entry #3427, s.v. "dwell," Psalm 91:1.

Chapter 7

[1] Based on definitions from W.E. Vine, Merrill F. Unger, William White Jr., *Vine's Complete Expository Dictionary of Old and New Testament Words* (Nashville: Thomas Nelson, Inc., 1984), "New Testament Section," p. 91, s.v. "CAST," A. Verbs.

[2] Vine, p. 89, s.v. "CARE (noun and verb), CAREFUL, CAREFULLY, CAREFULNESS," A. Nouns, 1.

[3] Footnote to 1 Peter 5:8 written by A.S. Worrell in *The Worrell New Testament* (Springfield, MO: Gospel Publishing House, 1980), p. 352.

[4] Ibid.

Chapter 8

[1] Norman P. Grubb, *Rees Howells Intercessor* (Fort Washington, PA: Christian Literature Crusade, first published 1952, paperback edition 1967, this edition 1980 by special arrangement with the British and American publishers).

[2] Tingay and Badcock, *These Were the Romans* (Chester Springs, PA: Dufour Editions, Inc., 1989).

[3] James E. Strong, "Greek Dictionary of the New Testament," in *Strong's Exhaustive Concordance of the Bible* (Nashville: Abingdon, 1890), p. 47, entry #3339, s.v. "change," 2 Corinthians 3:18.

[4] Based on definition in Webster's 3d, s.v. "metamorphosis": "a marked or complete change of character, appearance, condition, etc."; "the physical transformation, more or less sudden, undergone by various animals during development after the embryonic state...."

Chapter 9

[1] These tapes are available upon request. For a complete listing of teaching tapes on these and other subjects, contact the author at the address in the back of this book.

[2] Robert E. Coleman, Timothy K. Beougher, Tom Phillips, William A. Shell, editors; "Disciple Making: Training Leaders to Make Disciples," The Online Self-Study Course; copyright © 1994 by Billy Graham Center Institute of Evangelism. Available at http://www.wheaton.edu/bgc/ioe/fud/chpt6.html; INTERNET.

Be Anxious for Nothing
Study Guide

Contents

Introduction

*P*eace is available to all who believe in Jesus Christ. It is part of God's plan for our lives through His Son Jesus to be marked by a profound sense of inner peace and serenity. Regardless of our outward circumstances, we are to be enjoying the abundant, joyful, peaceful life that God has intended for us from the beginning. But very few people enjoy this peace as part of the normal condition of their lives.

Many of us have not learned how to entrust ourselves to God and retire from self-care. Like many people in the world, we respond to negative circumstances with restlessness, fear, and apprehension instead of choosing to draw on the peace of God. There are many serious things going on in this world, and we need to be aware of them and prepared for them. But at the same time, we need to learn to relax and take things as they come without getting all nervous and upset about them. God's way is for us to respond with peaceful trust, even when we can't see the way out.

In times of trials, disappointments, and negative circumstances, do you choose trust or torment, anxiety or peace, worry or joy?

I went through a time in my life when I was plagued by worry and anxiety. I lived in a state of turmoil for so many years, I didn't realize how abnormal it really was. In those days I tormented myself with needless worry and apprehension, because I tried to handle everything myself. While I was always a responsible person who took on the responsibility for my life, I also took on the care of it. Once I came to understand 1 Peter 5:7 that says we are to cast our care upon the Lord because He cares for us, I started to apply that principle in my life, and I began to truly enjoy it.

You can be free from anxiety and have a happy, joyful life!

As you work through this study guide, you will learn how to replace the stress, frustration, and worry in your life with victory and peace. I believe that this new knowledge will help you enter the rest of God by taking what the devil tries to give you, turning it over to the Lord, and watching Him turn it into good in accordance with His perfect will and plan for you.[1]

Using This Study Guide

The purpose of this workbook is to reinforce the principles taught in my book, *Be Anxious for Nothing.* You will need a copy of *Be Anxious for Nothing* to work through this book.

This study guide is written in a question and answer format. By reading a chapter in *Be Anxious for Nothing,* studying the designated Scripture verses, and answering the questions in the corresponding chapter of the study guide, you will gain a deeper understanding of the principles and learn more easily how to incorporate them into your daily life.

To use this workbook, look up and read the corresponding chapter in *Be Anxious for Nothing.* Next look up in your Bible the Scriptures designated in the study guide and read them. This is an important step because those Scriptures are the basis of the teaching in that particular chapter and are taken directly from that chapter.

Answer the questions in the study guide by referring to the appropriate chapter in *Be Anxious for Nothing.* Once you have finished answering the questions in each chapter, turn to the answer key in the back of this book to check your answers.

1. Work at a comfortable pace. Don't rush to finish quickly. Stay in each chapter until you have a thorough understanding of the material and how it pertains to your life.

2. Follow these steps with each chapter in this study guide.

3. Use this study guide for individual study or group discussion. When using it in a group, discuss your answers and learn how to apply the principles in a way that may not have occurred to you until you heard the experiences of others.

Consistently and steadily working through this book will empower you to gradually improve the way you respond to difficult times and receive by faith what God desires you to have — His help. Choosing to live in peace and joy rather than to be burdened with worry and anxiety will enable you to change things in your life that you thought you would have to live with forever.

LIVE IN PEACE

Anxiety steals your joy and peace and torments and hinders you from enjoying your life according to God's plan. How happy, joyful and peaceful are you? If you have a problem in this area, I believe the God-directed, God-empowered principles in this guidebook are important tools that will help you to start giving God all your worry, concern, anxiety, and care — and start living in peace as a normal condition.

It is my sincere prayer that working through this study guide, along with the book, *Be Anxious for Nothing,* will help firmly establish in your heart forever that no matter what happens, as you trust God, you will have the privilege of being cared for by the One Who knows and does all things well. When you are secure in that knowledge, you will enjoy a life filled with God's best for you.

1. Read Philippians 4:6,7 NASB; 1 Peter 5:6,7 NASB

   a. As believers in Jesus Christ, what is to be the normal condition for us? _____.

   b. In His Word, what does God tell us to do? _____
   _____
   _____.

   c. Many people are familiar with these Scriptures but _____
   _____ what these Scriptures instruct.

   d. Sometimes we are so accustomed to responding in a natural way to the circumstances we experience in life as unbelievers around us do, how do we spend much of our time?_____
   _____
   _____
   _____.

   e. Instead, what could we be doing? _____
   _____!

   f. In the author's own case, when did she begin to experience the peace of God? _____
   _____
   _____.

   g. If you are not living in the peace of God, you can _____
   _____.

PART 1

Be Anxious for Nothing

Chapter

Jesus and Peace

1

*I*n the original book, *Be Anxious for Nothing,* read Chapter 1, then read in your Bible the Scriptures designated below and answer the questions that follow. When you finish, check your answers in the answer key provided at the end of this book.

As you continue to follow this procedure throughout this workbook, you can be assured that you will gain insight through understanding that will help you integrate these godly principles into your daily life and be free from anxiety!

1. Read John 14:27; Psalm 91; John 10:10; Ephesians 3:20;
    2 Chronicles 16:9; Isaiah 9:6; John 16:33; 14:1; Romans 14:17;
    Luke 17:21; 2 Corinthians 5:21; Galatians 5:22,23

    a. Jesus' statement in John 14:27 is worded as though He _____
        _____ us His peace.

    b. What does it mean that Jesus left us His peace? _____
        _____
        _____
        _____.

    c. What does the Bible show us about the peace Jesus left us?
        _____.

    d. What does Psalm 91 reveal to us about God's protection? __
        _____
        _____
        _____.

e. Based on John 10:10, Ephesians 3:20, and 2 Chronicles 16:9, what does God want to do for us? Why? _____

_____

_____

_____

_____

_____.

f. As Christians, our salvation guarantees us a trouble-free life. True or false? _____.

g. We will still encounter problems. Every one of us at different times in our life go through seasons when things don't work out the way we would like. In John 16:33, what does Jesus, the Prince of Peace, tell us regarding this? _____

_____

_____

_____.

h. In John 14:1 and 27, just before His return to His Father in heaven, what words did Jesus leave us about our hearts? _____

_____

_____.

i. Romans 14:17 tells us that Kingdom living is _____

_____

_____.

j. According to Luke 17:21, where is the Kingdom of God? __

_____.

k. When were we made righteous, or made in rightstanding with God? _____

_____.

l. What are two of the fruit of the Holy Spirit that are inside those of us who believe in Jesus? _____

_____.

m. How do we enter into the joy and peace of God's kingdom?

_____.

2. Read Romans 15:13; Hebrews 4:9-11; Mark 10:15; Luke 10:20; Habakkuk 3:18 KJV; Psalm 16:11; 1 John 4:12-15; John 14:23

a. With what does the passage in Romans 15:13 tell us that God will fill us? Why? _____

_____

_____

_____

_____.

b. According to the writer of Hebrews, who may enter into the blessed Sabbath rest of the Lord? _____

_____.

c. What is required to enter this rest?_____

_____.

d. Why have members of the church sometimes lost the joy of their salvation? _____

_____.

e. In Luke 10:20, Jesus tells us we should rejoice, not because we have power over the demons or circumstances of this life, but because _____

_____.

f. As believers, our joy and peace are not based in doing and achieving, but in _____.

g. Based on Psalm 16:11, 1 John 4:12-15 and John 14:23, how then do joy and peace come? Why? _____

_____

_____

_____

_____

_____

_____.

h. Where do we experience peace? _____

_____

_____

_____.

i. To summarize this section, joy and peace come from _____

_____

_____.

It's OK to Lighten Up!

A s with the previous chapter, before answering the questions below, first read the corresponding chapter in *Be Anxious for Nothing*, then the Scriptures designated below. After you complete the chapter, check the answer key in the back of this book.

To gain the greatest benefit from this workbook, continue using this method throughout.

1. Read Proverbs 12:25

   a. The Bible teaches that anxiety brings _____
   _____ to a person's life.

   b. How does the dictionary define *anxiety?* _____
   _____
   _____
   _____.

   c. Are you ever bothered by this kind of anxiety without know-ing what it is? _____.

2. Read Proverbs 15:15; Song of Solomon 2:15 KJV; review
   John 14:1,27; 16:33; read Mark 4:17

   a. Based on Proverbs 15:15, the author says that once when she went through a period in her life when she was plagued by anxiety, fear, and dread, the Lord told her what was troubling her. What was it? _____
   _____.

b. What does Song of Solomon 2:15 KJV call the things we become upset over that are just not worth becoming upset over? _____
_____.

c. If our life consists of becoming upset over one little thing that really doesn't matter after another, what will be the result?
_____
_____.

d. In other words, what was Jesus saying to us in John 14:1 and 27 about letting our hearts be troubled and afraid?_____
_____.

e. What can we see from John 14:27?_____
_____
_____
_____
_____
_____
_____.

f. Based on Mark 4:17, why will we have persecution? _____
_____.

g. In today's language, what was Jesus' answer for the tribulation we all experience in our daily lives? _____.

h. What gives us plenty of reason to calm down and cheer up?
_____
_____.

    i. If you experience anxiety as a result of deep hurts from the past, although it is not always easy, how can you become free from that emotional bondage?_____

_____!

3. Read 1 Peter 3:4

    a. According to Peter, what kind of spirit does God like?_____

_____

_____.

    b. What does it mean to be "wrought up"? _____

_____.

    c. What does it mean to be "anxious"?_____

_____

_____.

    d. Why does the devil try to make us tense, get us tied up in knots, upset, disturbed, worried, disquieted, and distracted?

_____

_____

_____

_____

_____

_____.

    e. Based on the author's past experience, if we are so tense, worried, and wrought up we blow everything way out of proportion, what do we need to learn to do? _____

_____

_____

_____
_____
_____.

4. Read Psalm 118:24 KJV; 1 Peter 5:8; review John 10:10

   a. What else does *anxiety* mean? _____
   _____
   _____
   _____
   _____.

   b. The author says that the Lord once told her what causes anxiety. What is the cause? _____
   _____
   _____
   _____
   _____
   _____
   _____.

   c. Even though we are to learn to lighten up and enjoy life, what are we also told to do in 1 Peter 5:8? _____
   _____
   _____
   _____
   _____.

   d. Based on John 10:10, what do we need to learn to do?_____
   _____

_____

_____.

e. In spite of all the troubling things going on around us in the world, according to the author, what should be our daily confession? _____

_____

_____.

f. What else do we Christians need to do more of? What would happen if we did so? _____

_____

_____.

g. It is easy to find plenty to worry about. To be happy, we need to _____

_____.

5. Read Philippians 4:4,6,7; 2 Corinthians 3:18; review Psalm 16:11

a. Twice in Philippians 4:6,7 what does the apostle Paul tell us to do? What else does he urge us to do? _____

_____

_____

_____.

b. What is one way we develop spiritual maturity? _____

_____

_____.

c. What does Paul mean when he tells us in 2 Corinthians 3:18 that we are constantly being transformed into the image of God and that we are going "from one degree of glory to another"? _____

_____

_____ .

d. What do we then need to learn? _____

_____

_____ .

e. Instead of postponing being glad until everything is perfect, what do we need to do? _____

_____

_____

_____ .

f. According to the author, the doorway to happiness is expressed in the words of the song to the Lord that says,

_____

_____ .

g. Based on Psalm 16:11, the fullness of joy is found in God's _____ — not in His

_____ !

h. True joy comes from seeking God's _____ .

i. To live in the fullness of the joy of the Lord, what must we do? _____ .

j. Why will we always have opportunities to be anxious, worried, and fretful? _____

_____

_____

_____.

k. When the devil tries to bring anxiety into our heart, what must we do? Why? _____

_____

_____

_____

_____

_____

_____.

6. Read Psalm 34:19

a. Although there are many evils that confront us, how many main categories of anxiety are there? _____.

b. What are they? _____

_____

_____

_____.

7. Read Ecclesiastes 5:1; 2 Corinthians 6:2; Hebrews 3:7,15; 4:7-9; John 8:58; Matthew 6:25-34; 1 Peter 5:7

a. What is the author's personal definition of anxiety? _____

_____

_____.

b. What was the Lord referring to in the Bible when He said, "Today is the day of salvation," when He said that today if we will hear His voice, that today if we will believe, we will enter into His rest? _____
_____.

c. Instead of spending our time in the past or the future, what do we need to do? _____
_____
_____.

d. Why do we find it so hard to give ourselves to one thing at a time? _____
_____
_____
_____.

e. What does the Bible mean when it tells us in Ecclesiastes 5:1 to give our mind to what we are doing, to "keep our foot" — our footing? _____
_____.

f. There is an anointing on _____.

g. Based on what Jesus said in John 8:58, why do we, as His disciples, find life hard for us if we try to live in the past or the future? _____
_____.

h. In Matthew 6:25-34 Jesus plainly told us that _____
_____
_____

_____
_____
_____
_____.

i. Why don't we need to be concerned about tomorrow?_____
_____
_____.

j. What should we do instead? _____
_____.

k. Why do we need to stop wasting our precious "now"?_____
_____.

l. According to 1 Peter 5:7, we are to_____
our responsibility, but we are to _____
our care? Why?_____
_____.

m. We are to _____ from the past and
_____ for the future,
but we are to _____ in the present.

8. Read Mark 13:11,9; Romans 8:28

a. In the passage in Mark 13:11, Jesus was warning His disciples
that _____
_____
_____
_____.

b. How did He finish His remarks? Why? _____
_____
_____
_____
_____
_____
_____
_____.

c. If you are filled with anxiety before a conversation, it may be a sign that _____
_____
_____
_____.

d. Of course, we need to be prepared, but if we excessively rehearse a conversation over and over, it is an indication
_____
_____.

e. In that case, what will be the result? _____
_____
_____!

f. We need to ask the Lord to give us_____ with all those to whom we speak. Why? _____
_____
_____
_____
_____
_____.

9.   Read Luke 10:38-42

    a. In this passage, what difference do we see between one sister, Martha, and the other sister, Mary? _____

_____

_____

_____

_____

_____.

    b. What did the Lord once tell the author about herself? _____

_____

_____.

    c. What did she need to learn? _____

_____

_____

_____

_____

_____!

    d. Is this a lesson you need to learn also? Why or why not?

_____

_____

_____.

The Arm of
the Flesh

1. Read Jeremiah 17:5; John 3:6

   a. What two vastly different arms does the Bible speak of? ___
   _____ .

   b. How do they differ? Explain._____
   _____
   _____
   _____
   _____
   _____
   _____
   _____
   _____ .

   c. Based on John 3:6, what is begun in the flesh must be
   _____ in the flesh, but what
   is begun in the Spirit is _____
   by the Spirit.

   d. What is the difference between trying to operate in the arm of
   the flesh and operating in the arm of the Lord? _____
   _____
   _____
   _____
   _____ .

   e. What is the difference between carrying out our own plans
   and schemes and allowing God to start something? _____

_____
_____
_____
_____
_____.

f. Many times when we face struggles, we assume the devil is causing us problems, so we try to rebuke him, but that does not always work. Explain. _____
_____
_____
_____
_____.

g. No amount of rebuking the devil will do any good when we are _____
_____.

h. If the work was begun by the Lord, how will it get finished?
_____.

2. Read 1 Corinthians 16:9; 1 John 4:4; Deuteronomy 28:7; James 4:7

a. Whenever we do anything for God, what will happen? ____
_____.

b. Based on 1 John 4:4, what do we need to remember when that happens? _____
_____.

c. According to Deuteronomy 28:7, if we are operating in obedience to God's will and plan, what will happen to the enemy? _____

_____.

d. We should not have to spend our lives struggling against the devil. What happens sometimes when we do?_____

_____

_____.

e. In His earthly ministry, why did Jesus not spend a great deal of time fighting against local demons? _____

_____

_____.

f. When we minister in Jesus' name, we have the same power and authority He had. Instead of wearing ourselves out trying to fight spiritual enemies, we should _____

_____

_____.

g. What is the best way to overcome the devil and his demons?

_____

_____

_____.

h. What mistake do many people make in trying to resist the devil? _____

_____!

i. Referring to Christians, what is the difference between a mature individual and immature people?_____

_____
_____
_____
_____
_____.

j. What did the author say happened when she tried to do things her way and in her own power and got out ahead of God? _____
_____.

3. Read Genesis 16:1,2; 15:1-5; 16:3; 17:1-6,15-19; 21:1-14

a. In Genesis 15:1-5, what did the Lord promise Abraham? ____
_____
_____
_____
_____.

b. In Genesis 16:1,2, what plan did Sarah come up with? ____
_____
_____
_____.

c. In Genesis chapter 17, what did the Lord again promise when He appeared to Abraham? _____
_____
_____
_____
_____
_____.

d. Through whom was God's covenant of blessings to be fulfilled? Why? _____

_____

_____

_____

_____

_____

_____ .

e. What happened when Isaac was finally born? _____

_____

_____

_____ .

f. Many times the reason we are having problems is_____

_____

_____

_____

_____

_____

_____ .

g. In such cases, what often happens when things don't turn out the way we expect? _____

_____

_____ .

h. When that happens, what do we often fail to remember?___

_____

_____

_____.

4. Read John 6:63; Romans 7:18,24; Proverbs 21:2

   a. In John 6:63, what did Jesus tell us about the Spirit and the flesh? Why? _____

_____

_____

_____.

   b. If we are to fulfill God's will and plan for us in this life, what has to happen? _____

_____

_____.

   c. It is from _____
that the energy of the soul comes forth to cause us all kinds of problems on_____.

   d. According to Romans 7:18, Paul had the same problem we have in this area. In that passage, how did he describe himself? _____

_____

_____

_____

_____.

   e. In verse 24 of that passage, what did Paul end up crying out in his misery and frustration? _____

_____

_____

_____
_____
_____.

f. When it seems as though no matter how hard we try to make
    things work, everything that can go wrong does go wrong,
    what must we remember? _____
    _____
    _____.

g. What is the purpose of the testing ground? _____
    _____
    _____
    _____
    _____.

h. How can we succeed despite our adversaries and their
    devices? _____
    _____.

i. What is our problem in this area?_____
    _____
    _____
    _____
    _____.

j. What often happens to us if God does not bless our plan? ____
    _____
    _____
    _____.

k. Why are there many frustrated, depressed people in our world who have basically given up on God? Are you one of them?_____

_____.

l. When we plan a work of the flesh, as is often the case, what are we trying to do? _____

_____.

m. What should we do instead? _____

_____

_____

_____

_____.

n. As Christians, we all have a work to do. What is it?_____

_____

_____

_____.

o. If God is not in our work, it will be frustrating and depressing. To avoid that, we must learn to discern between what God is truly_____us to do and what we are _____to do.

p. What great revelation does Proverbs 21:2 give us? _____

_____

_____.

q. What mistake do we make that was also made by the Galatians in Paul's day? _____

_____.

5. Read Galatians 4:22-26; 3:1-7; review Romans 15:13

a. The Bible speaks of two covenants. We know them as the old covenant and the new covenant. What else can they be called? _____

_____.

b. On what is the first covenant based? _____

_____

_____

_____.

c. What is the result of that kind of covenant? _____

_____.

d. On what is the second covenant based? _____

_____

_____.

e. What is the result of that kind of covenant? _____

_____.

f. What does each of these covenants bring? _____

_____.

g. Under the first covenant, we _____
we have to do it all; under the second covenant all we have to
do is _____, and as part of our
believing lifestyle, _____

_____.

h. What is the result of people trying to live by works rather than by God's grace?_____

_____.

i. According to the Word of God, if we will operate in simple, childlike faith, we will _____

_____

_____

_____.

6. Read Galatians 4:27; Isaiah 54:1; review Hebrews 4:10

a. What is the basic message of both Galatians 4:27 and its cross reference, Isaiah 54:1? _____

_____

_____

_____

_____

_____

_____.

b. Why is the Church not seeing the results we want today? __

_____

_____

_____.

c. Based on Galatians 4:27 and Isaiah 54:1, why should a barren woman rejoice?_____

_____

_____.

d. What is the meaning of the statement, "The barren woman is barren of her own works"? _____

_____

_____

_____

_____

_____ .

e. Based on Hebrews 4:10, what is a consequence for those who enter the rest of God?_____

_____

_____

_____ .

7. Read 1 Peter 1:6-8; John 16:7

a. We lack joy because we have problems. True or false? _____

_____ .

b. In 1 Peter 1:6-8, what does the Bible tell us about joy? ____

_____

_____

_____

_____ .

c. What do we need to do if we are not experiencing what the *King James Version* of 1 Peter 1:8 calls "joy unspeakable"?

_____

_____ .

d. The blessings of the second covenant are available to us as believers, yet we are not experiencing them. Why?_____

_____

_____

_____.

e. What will happen as long as we live in ignorance or neglect of the blessings that are ours under the covenant of grace?

_____.

f. The author says that the Lord told her, "Frustration equals

_____.

g. What does that mean? _____

_____

_____

_____

_____

_____

_____.

h. Based on John 16:7, why did God give us His Holy Spirit?

_____.

i. Why then do stubborn, independent people not receive the help they need?_____

_____

_____.

j. How do we receive help — and thus avoid the frustration of works? _____.

    k. Why will only the humble among us do that?_____

_____

_____

_____.

8.   Read 1 Peter 5:5-7; James 4:6,10

    a. Based on 1 Peter 5:5-7, why is humility so important to God?

_____

_____

_____

_____

_____.

    b. God's reasons for asking us to do things in the way He asks are not to take anything away from us. Name two reasons He asks us to do things His way._____

_____

_____

_____

_____.

    c. Why must we always be on our guard against pride? _____

_____

_____.

    d. According to James 4:6, why does God give us more and more grace — power of the Holy Spirit? _____

_____

_____.

e. What does James go on to say in this same verse? _____

_____

_____

_____

_____

_____

_____.

f. In James 4:10, what does James then urge us, just as Peter did? _____

_____

_____

_____

_____.

g. How do we receive the grace of God?_____

_____

_____

_____

_____.

h. Why will proud people not do that?_____

_____

_____.

i. Why will only the humble do that? _____

_____

_____.

9. Read Psalm 127:1,2; Matthew 16:18; 1 Corinthians 3:9; Ephesians 2:20

a. What does Psalm 127:1 say about the building of a house?

_____

_____.

b. What is the first thing we should let God build in our lives?

_____.

c. In Matthew 16:18 Jesus said that He would build His Church. According to what Paul tells us in 1 Corinthians 3:9, who is that Church? _____.

d. Based on Ephesians 2:20, we are the _____, and Jesus is the _____.

e. How are we being built up?_____

_____.

f. The answer to how we get built is found in Paul's letter to the Galatians who needed to be reminded of _____

_____

_____.

10. Read Galatians 3:3-5; Ephesians 2:8,9; 1 Peter 2:5

a. What question do we need to ask ourselves that Paul was asking the "foolish," "senseless," and "silly" Galatians? _____

_____

_____

_____.

b. Just as we are saved by grace (God's unmerited favor) through faith, and not by works of the flesh, how do we need to learn to live?_____

_____

_____.

c. When we were saved, we were in no condition to help ourselves. What kind of condition are we in now that we have
been saved by grace through faith in the finished work of
Jesus Christ? _____

_____!

d. Why then do we keep trying to make things happen that are
never going to happen? _____

_____.

e. What is the only way we are ever going to be ". . . built [into]
a spiritual house, for a holy (dedicated, consecrated) priesthood, to offer up [those] spiritual sacrifices [that are] acceptable and pleasing to God through Jesus Christ"? _____

_____

_____

_____.

f. Since the flesh profits nothing, what causes us to grow up
into the perfection of Christ? _____.

11. Read Ephesians 4:12,13; Philippians 3:10; review Galatians 5:22,23

a. According to Ephesians 4:12, what was God's intention in
regard to the saints, His consecrated people? Why? _____

_____

_____

_____

_____
_____.

b. According to Ephesians 4:13, what does God want the Church of Jesus Christ to arrive at? _____
_____.

c. How is that state defined in verse 13? _____
_____
_____
_____
_____
_____
_____.

d. Are you interested in being perfected? _____.

e. Based on Philippians 3:10 and Galatians 5:22,23, how does the author define being perfected or growing up in the Lord?
_____
_____
_____
_____
_____.

f. Since we cannot do that on our own, or change ourselves from what we are to what we want to be, what is the only thing we can do? _____
_____

_____

_____ .

g. What is the only way that can be done?_____

_____ .

12. Read Colossians 1:4; John 6:28,29

a. According to Colossians 1:4, what is faith? _____

_____

_____

_____

_____ .

b. Based on this verse, what is our only job? _____

_____

_____

_____ .

c. When the Holy Spirit convicts us of our sins, what is the first thing we do? _____

_____

_____ .

d. What is the second thing we do? Why? _____

_____

_____

_____ .

e. According to John 6:29, 'the work that God requires of us is to _____ .

    f.   Believing requires that we _____

        _____

        _____.

    g.   If we truly do that, we will not be_____

        _____. We will

        quit trying to _____ and will

        allow Him to _____

        _____.

13.   Read Hebrews 3:4; Philippians 1:6; 1 John 1:9

    a.   _____ is the Master Builder. _____
is the Chief Cornerstone.

    b.   God is the One Who has to _____
_____ for the work of the Lord Jesus Christ.

    c.   What the apostle Paul was saying to us in Philippians 1:6 is
simply this: _____

        _____

        _____!

    d.   What does that mean to us? _____

        _____.

    e.   Based on 1 John 1:9, what are we to do about our sins and
failures? _____

        _____

        _____

        _____

        _____.

f. What does that do for us? _____

_____

_____

_____.

14. Read 1 Thessalonians 5:22-24

a. What are God's instructions to us for finding peace and joy?

_____

_____

_____

_____.

b. What does the author say that these verses are to us? _____

_____

_____

_____

_____

_____

_____.

c. What then is our part? What is the work that we are to do?
    What does God require of us? _____

_____

_____

_____.

15. Read Acts 20:32

a. In this passage, what has God, the Master Builder, promised
    to do for us if we will allow Him to do so? _____

_____.

b. We have already discussed the first area in our lives in which we need to allow God to build. What is it? _____

_____.

c. What is the second area in our lives in which we need to allow God to build?_____.

d. What is the third area in our lives in which we need to allow God to build? _____.

16. Read Galatians 1:10; Philippians 2:7 KJV; Galatians 5:1; John 12:42,43

a. What choice made by the apostle Paul in his ministry must each of us make? _____

_____.

b. In Philippians 2:7 KJV we read that Jesus made Himself of no reputation. What does that mean to us?_____

_____

_____.

c. What will happen if it is our goal to try to build a name for ourselves? _____

_____

_____

_____.

d. If we are to be truly free in the Lord, we must do as Paul has told us in Galatians 5:1:_____

_____.

_____

_____.

e. There is nothing the devil uses more to keep people out of the
   will of God than _____

   _____.

f. The followers of Jesus have faced the choice between pleasing people and pleasing God since the very beginning. In the
   same way, what decision are we faced with today? _____

   _____

   _____

   _____

   _____

   _____

   _____

   _____.

1. Read John 12:38; Romans 12:1

    a. Explain how the arm of the Lord is in direct contrast to the arm of the flesh. _____
    _____
    _____
    _____.

    b. On what does each one of the two covenants depend?_____
    _____.

    c. What do we do under each one of the two covenants?_____
    _____
    _____
    _____
    _____
    _____
    _____.

    d. In Romans 12:1 what are we told to do? _____
    _____
    _____
    _____
    _____.

    e. According to the author, the Lord revealed three things to her that we must be in order to be filled with His Spirit and be pleasing to Him. What are they? _____
    _____.

f. How do we apply these three things to our lives? _____

_____

_____

_____

_____.

g. Name three things we must do to be pleasing to God. _____

_____

_____

_____

_____

_____

_____

_____

_____

_____

_____.

h. In summary, to be pleasing to God, we must _____

_____

_____

_____.

2. Read Acts 7:9

a. What mistake did Joseph make in regard to the dream he had in which he saw himself being honored by all the members of his family, and why was what he did a mistake? _____

_____

_____

_____

_____

_____.

b. Why did God have to spend several years doing a work in Joseph before He could use him to fulfill His plan to bless him and his family and many, many others? _____

_____

_____.

c. What mistake do we make that young Joseph also made? __

_____

_____

_____

_____

_____

_____.

d. What was the result of the rashness of Joseph and his brothers?

_____

_____

_____.

e. What must we go through if we are going to enjoy the fullness of God in our lives? _____

_____.

f. What happens when all of the people and things we have been leaning on are stripped away from us? _____

_____

_____.

g. As in the case of Joseph, God wants us to depend upon ____
_____ and not
_____.

h. If it is not wrong to ever seek advice from others, why must
we be careful when we do so? _____
_____
_____.

i. What is the difference between most birds and eagles? ____
_____
_____.

j. What must each of us decide in reference to birds and eagles?
_____
_____
_____
_____.

k. If we want to be an eagle, we must_____
_____.

l. Joseph had to face hard, lonely times in his life, especially
during the period he spent in prison in a foreign country.
Despite all the adversity that came against him, what do the
Scriptures say about his situation? _____.

3. Read Acts 7:10; Psalm 75:6; Romans 8:31

a. Based on Acts 7:10, what did God do for Joseph, just as He
will do for us?_____
_____

_____
_____
_____.

b. Based on Psalm 75:6, how do we overcome adversity and opposition and gain favor and promotion? _____
_____
_____.

c. Based on Romans 8:31, why can no devil or person on earth prevent us from receiving favor and promotion?_____
_____
_____
_____.

d. If God's criteria for using people is not their talents, gifts, and abilities, what kind of people is He looking for? _____
_____.

e. If that is true, what then should you do to become successful in your life?_____
_____
_____
_____
_____
_____.

4. Read Genesis 50:18-20; review Romans 8:28

a. Based on Romans 8:28, whatever may have happened to us in the past, it does not have to dictate our future. Why? _____
_____

_____
_____.

b. Joseph's brothers meant evil to him, but God _____
    _____.

c. Despite what others — even his own brothers — did to him,
    what two things did Joseph know that kept him from allow-
    ing himself to be filled with bitterness, resentment, and
    unforgiveness? _____
    _____
    _____
    _____
    _____
    _____.

d. What did Joseph do that we need to do? _____
    _____
    _____.

5. Read Isaiah 40:6-8

a. The author says that when God called her into the ministry
    she did not have the kind of personality needed to minister,
    but what happened? _____
    _____
    _____.

b. Why should that be an encouragement to you? _____
    _____
    _____.

6. Read Philippians 3:3; review Isaiah 40:6-8

   a. Based on Philippians 3:3, we are going to either lean on the arm of the flesh or on the arm of the Lord. Explain. _____

   _____

   _____

   _____

   _____.

   b. Why has the Lord told us through the prophet Isaiah not to trust in the flesh? _____

   _____

   _____.

   c. Since we can put no confidence in the flesh, and apart from the Lord we can do nothing, what then must we do? _____

   _____

   _____

   _____.

7. Read Proverbs 3:6; review Philippians 3:10; read Psalm 27:4; review Psalm 16:11; Ephesians 4:13; read Ephesians 6:4 KJV; Proverbs 22:6 KJV

   a. Based on Proverbs 3:6, what does it mean to acknowledge the Lord in all our ways? _____

   _____

   _____

   _____.

   b. Based on Philippians 3:10, what does God want for us?____

   _____

_____

_____.

c. Based on Psalm 27:4 and 16:11, what one thing should we seek after? Why? _____

_____

_____.

d. What happens when we seek God's face (His Presence) to get to know our wonderful, loving heavenly Father better? ____

_____

_____.

e. Based on Ephesians 4:13, what is God waiting for us to do as His children?_____

_____.

f. Based on Ephesians 6:4 KJV and Proverbs 22:6 KJV, God is training us up, His children, in the way we _____ go — not the way we_____to go, but the way we _____ go.

8. Read James 4:13-15; Proverbs 16:18

a. According to James 4:13-15, instead of talking about our own plans, what should we say? _____

_____

_____.

b. What should we learn to want more than our own will? ___

_____.

c. If we want something and God says no, although it may hurt our feelings and be hard for us to accept, it will be_____

_____.

d. What is wrong with making our own plans and expecting God to bless them?_____

_____

_____

_____.

e. What does Proverbs 16:18 say about pride and a haughty spirit?

_____.

f. What is the key to the abundant, joyful, peaceful life Jesus died to give us? _____.

g. Why do we need to learn to humble ourselves under the mighty hand of God? _____

_____.

h. What is one way we humble ourselves? _____

_____

_____.

i. It honors God when we _____
Him. When we honor Him, He _____
us — and frequently gives us _____

_____!

j. The real issue here is _____.

9. Read 2 Kings 4:1-7; Galatians 2:20; review Philippians 1:6

   a. What is the key to value and worth? _____
      _____.

   b. Like the poor widow in 2 Kings 4:1-7, what is the first step to
      fullness? _____.

   c. We are empty vessels. What then is the only thing of value
      any of us has in us? _____
      _____
      _____
      _____.

   d. What do we have to offer God? _____.

   e. What value do we have? _____
      _____.

   f. Why is there nothing of value or worth in our flesh? _____
      _____
      _____.

   g. In Galatians 2:20, what did the apostle Paul say about the life
      he lived in the body? _____
      _____
      _____
      _____.

   h. Although it may seem as though reaching the place you
      desire is taking forever, what does Philippians 1:6 say about
      the good work that the Lord has begun in us? _____
      _____

_____
_____
_____
_____.

i. What will we be like if we press on and are sincere about spir-
    itual maturity? _____
    _____
    _____
    _____
    _____.

j. What must we do to know and experience what God can do?
    _____
    _____
    _____
    _____
    _____.

10. Read 2 Chronicles 20:1,4-6,10-12

a. In verse 12 of this passage, what three important statements
    do we see that apply to us today as much as they did to the
    people of Judah who faced overpowering enemies? _____
    _____
    _____
    _____
    _____.

b. When is the Lord free to move on our behalf, as He did for
    the people in this story?_____

_____

_____

_____

_____.

c. Why does it sometimes seem that God is not moving in our lives? _____

_____.

d. What is the reason that God may not be taking control of our situation? _____.

11. Read 2 Chronicles 20:13-18; review 20:12; Psalm 46:10 KJV; read Isaiah 40:31; Numbers 10:35; Philippians 2:10,11

a. According to 2 Chronicles 20:12, what three things must we do before we begin to shout what we read in verse 15, "O God, the battle is not mine, but Yours"? _____

_____

_____

_____

_____

_____.

b. When will God begin to give us His instructions for what to do? _____

_____.

c. Often His instructions to us will be what He told the people in the passage in 2 Chronicles 20:17: _____

_____.

d. Based on Numbers 10:35, what does the author say should be our war cry? _____
_____ !

e. Based on Philippians 2:10,11, what do we need to remember about the Lord? _____
_____
_____
_____
_____ .

f. In verse 17 of the passage in 2 Chronicles 20, what directions did God begin to give to His people through His prophet?
_____
_____
_____ .

g. Why were they not to be afraid or dismayed? _____
_____ .

h. Faced with their enemies, what position did the people of God take in their situation that should be our position today?
_____
_____
_____ .

i. We need to spend more time in worship and praise and less time in _____, _____,
and _____ .

j. We need to remember that God _____
the proud, but _____ to the humble.

12. Review 1 Peter 5:5; read 2 Corinthians 4:4

   a. The world says,_____
      _____but that
      statement is totally _____.

   b. The Bible tells us God helps those who _____
      _____ in the sense
      that we are to _____
      _____
      _____
      _____, but on Him.

   c. Saying that God helps those who help themselves is not only
      unscriptural, but misleading. Why? _____
      _____
      _____
      _____
      _____.

   d. Satan, the god of this world's system, would like nothing bet-
      ter than for us to_____
      _____
      _____
      _____.

   e. If God does not help those who help themselves, who does
      He help? _____
      _____
      _____.

13. Read Deuteronomy 33:27

    a. Based on this verse, what does the author say that we should feel when we sing that old hymn, "Leaning on the Everlasting Arms"?_____
_____
_____.

    b. What should we experience? What decision should we make? _____
_____
_____.

14. Read 2 Chronicles 32:7,8; Jeremiah 17:5-8

    a. Based on 2 Chronicles 32:7,8, rather than looking at our past failures, our present fallacies, or our future fears, we should be _____
_____
_____.

    b. We should be reminding ourselves that no matter how many problems may be facing us, _____
_____
_____.

    c. In Jeremiah 17:5-8 we read that those who put their trust in the arm of the flesh are cursed with great evil. Explain.____
_____
_____
_____.

d. According to that passage, those who put their trust in the arm of the Lord are blessed. Explain. _____

_____

_____

_____

_____

_____

_____

_____.

e. As we have already seen, we are not to lean on the arm of flesh, but on the arm of the Lord. To review, what does that mean? _____

_____.

f. Like Jesus, we need to _____ people, but not _____ourselves to them.

15. Read John 2:23-25

a. Although Jesus loved people, especially His disciples, why did He not put His trust in them?_____

_____.

b. That does not mean He had no trust in His relationship with them. What does that mean?_____

_____

_____

_____

_____.

c. Many times why do we become devastated when we form relationships with people? Explain. _____

_____

_____

_____

_____

_____

_____

_____ .

d. Even in the best of human relationships we sometimes say and do things that hurt one another. Why does that happen?

_____ .

e. Instead of placing our trust in the weak arm of the flesh, we should place it only in _____

_____ .

f. What happens when we expect things from people they are not able to give us?_____

_____ .

The Warfare of Rest

1. Read Hebrews 4:3; 2 Timothy 3:1-5,11-14; 4:2-5

   a. What does Hebrews 4:3 say about those of us ". . . who have believed (adhered to and trusted in and relied on God). . ."?

   _____

   _____.

   b. In the warfare of rest, how do we defeat what the devil is trying to do in our life? _____

   _____.

   c. Believers operate from a different world than that of unbelievers. Explain. _____

   _____.

   d. Based on 2 Timothy 3:1, what kind of times are we in? _____

   _____

   _____.

   e. What do verses 2 through 5 of 2 Timothy chapter 3 describe?

   _____

   _____.

   f. In verse 11 of that chapter, after describing the persecutions and sufferings he endured, what does Paul then state about them?_____

   _____.

   g. In chapter 4, what does Paul start to explain that is based on the passage in 2 Timothy chapter 3?_____

_____
_____
_____.

h. People who have "itching ears" in the church today won't listen to teaching that doesn't suit them. What do they do
   instead? _____

   _____
   _____
   _____.

i. It is very dangerous to not listen to _____ —
   to _____ and _____ based
   on God's Word!

j. In verse 5 of 2 Timothy chapter 4, Paul tells us what our
   response is to be to all the trouble in the world, all the trouble in our lives, the people that are hard to deal with or hard
   to bear. Based on that Scripture, our response to trouble is to
   be, _____

   _____!

k. When trouble starts in someone's life, and they react immediately in the flesh instead of seeking the Lord for direction, the
   author calls this _____

   _____.

l. When trouble starts, sometimes God has us do such things as
   rebuke devils, fast, get people from church to pray with us
   and pull strongholds down, but what should we do first?

_____
_____
_____ .

m. What must we remember in times of trouble? _____
_____
_____
_____ .

2. Read Ephesians 6:13; Mark 8:22-25; John 9:1-7; Mark 10:46-52

   a. Based on Ephesians 6:13, what things are we to do when faced with challenges? _____
   _____
   _____ .

   b. But what must we realize about crises? _____
   _____
   _____
   _____ .

   c. What is the reason that the solution to one crisis may not work the second time? _____
   _____
   _____
   _____
   _____ .

   d. The passages in Mark chapter 8, John chapter 9, and Mark chapter 10 show how God uses _____methods for _____ people and in _____situations.

    e. It was not any of the methods Jesus used that opened the blind eyes of these men in these passages so they could see. The thing that brought their healing was _____

       _____.

    f. The different methods were simply the different means used by Jesus to_____

       _____.

    g. The key to unleashing the power of God is _____.

3. Read Hebrews 4:2,3; 11:6; review Psalm 91:1

    a. According to Hebrews 4:2, why didn't the message of glad tidings the Israelites heard benefit them? _____

       _____

       _____

       _____

       _____

       _____

       _____

       _____.

    b. Whatever the Lord may lead us to do in order to release our faith and activate the power of God on our behalf, it will do us no good if we do not remain in the rest of God. Why?

       _____

       _____

       _____.

    c. What does Hebrews 11:6 tell us? _____

       _____.

    d. According to Hebrews 4:2,3, rest is a _____.
The author believes that it is the_____
_____ spoken of in Psalm 91:1. That
secret place is _____

_____.

    e. Why can we relax and be secure when we are in that secret
place?_____

_____

_____.

4.   Read Exodus 33:12-14; review Psalm 91:1

    a. When Moses complained to God that He had not let him
know whom He was going to send with him on his mission,
he asked Him to show him His way so He could get to know
Him better. According to this passage, what did the Lord do?

_____

_____.

    b. This was considered by God to be a great privilege. To Him,
it was _____.

    c. What was true for Moses is true for us. As much as we would
like to know God's plans and ways for us, all we really need
to know is that _____

_____.

    d. What should we do if things don't work out the way we want
them to? _____

_____.

e. What must we remember if our plan is ruined? _____

_____

_____

_____

_____

_____

_____.

f. What do we often do when things don't work out just as we want them to? _____.

g. Too often in the midst of our troubles what do we do wrong?

_____.

h. Instead of getting all upset and rebuking the devil every time something goes wrong, what does the author suggest we should do?_____

_____

_____

_____

_____.

5. Review Psalm 91; read Exodus 15:26

a. Of whom do verses 1 and 2 of Psalm 91 speak? _____

_____

_____

_____

_____

_____.

b. What is listed in the rest of the psalm? _____

_____

_____ .

c. In *The Amplified Bible* there is a footnote at the bottom of the page on which Psalm 91 appears, which says that the promises of this whole psalm are dependent upon meeting exactly the conditions of the first two verses. Basically, what are the conditions of these first two verses? _____

_____ .

d. According to the author, from what do we need to be delivered? _____

_____

_____

_____

_____

_____ .

e. We need to remember that the _____
of the Lord depend upon the_____
of the Lord, which is always accompanied by the _____
_____ of the Lord.

6. Review John 14:27; read John 20:19,21,26; Psalm 42:5,11

a. What was the gift Jesus said He was leaving His disciples just before He was to go to the cross? _____

_____ .

b. After His resurrection, what was the first thing He said to them each time He appeared to them? _____
_____!

c. Obviously, what does Jesus intend for His followers to do despite what may be going on around them at the time? ___
_____.

d. Simply stated, what was He saying to His disciples — and to us? _____
_____
_____.

e. According to Psalm 42:5 and 11, what do we need to do when we begin to become cast down and disquieted within? ____
_____
_____
_____.

f. When we begin to lose our_____,
we need to remember our_____.

7. Read Ephesians 2:4-6; 1:20; Colossians 3:1; Hebrews 1:3,13; 8:1; 10:12; 12:2; 1 Peter 3:22; Revelation 4:2

a. Our place is in Christ. Where is He according to Ephesians 1:20? _____
_____.

b. If we are in Him, and He is seated, then where should we be?
_____.

8. Review Hebrews 1:3,13

   a. In this passage, we not only see the nature of Jesus as _____
      _____, and the role of Jesus as
      _____,
      we also see the place of Jesus — _____
      _____.

   b. It was _____Who made the devil into a
      _____.

9. Read Revelation 20:10

   a. How do we vocalize authority over the devil? _____
      _____.

   b. But at the same time, what do we need to recognize?_____
      _____
      _____
      _____.

   c. We are the Body of Christ, which includes His feet. What
      does that mean? _____
      _____
      _____
      _____
      _____
      _____
      _____
      _____
      _____.

10. Read Hebrews 10:12,13; 9:24; Exodus 28:35

   a. As we have already seen, Christ is seated in heavenly places and we are seated there with Him. According to Hebrews 10:12,13, what is He waiting for? _____ _____ _____.

   b. Under the old covenant, why were there no chairs in the earthly Holy of Holies?_____ _____ _____.

   c. Based on Hebrews 9:24, when would the Sabbath rest for God's people be instituted? _____ _____ _____ _____.

   d. What did the Jewish high priest have to be doing all the time he was in the earthly Holy of Holies? _____ _____.

   e. Under the old covenant, the covenant of works, the high priest had to keep moving while in the Holy of Holies; he was not allowed to sit down and rest. But once Jesus (our High Priest) had finished the work of salvation through His shed blood, when He entered into heaven what did His Father say to Him? _____ _____.

f. That is the same message God is giving us today. What does He want us to know that is part of our inheritance as saints of the Lord?_____

_____

_____.

g. Now instead of running around trying to please God and win His favor through works of the flesh, what can we do? ____

_____

_____.

11. Read Matthew 11:28,29; Mark 4:39 KJV

a. Based on this passage in Matthew 11, how does God want us to enter His rest? _____

_____

_____.

b. What does finding rest, relief, ease, refreshment, recreation, and blessed quiet for the soul mean? _____

_____

_____

_____

_____

_____

_____

_____

_____.

c. Based on Mark 4:39 KJV, when something goes wrong, instead of getting all upset and just rebuking the devil, what can we do? _____

_____

_____

_____

_____.

d. The author says that the Lord has taught her in trying times we can possess our soul. In doing this what are we actually doing? _____

_____.

12. Read Luke 21:19; review Psalm 91:11; read Psalm 37:23 KJV

a. According to Luke 21:19, how will we win the true life of our souls?_____

_____.

b. The author says that all of us need to learn not to _____

_____

_____

_____.

c. If we have done our best, God will_____

_____.

d. We often become so upset over what happened, we fail to realize _____

_____.

e. To summarize, we need to refuse to get wild. We need to refuse to allow our mind, will, and emotions to rule our spirit. In our patience we need to _____ _____ _____ .

13. Read Ephesians 4:26,27

a. As we saw happen to the author, what sometimes happens when someone we love wants us to do something we don't want to do? _____ _____ .

b. Why do we need to learn to "go with the flow" and not cause so many problems over things that don't really matter? ____ _____ _____ _____ .

c. Instead of making mountains out of molehills, blowing things up all out of proportion, and making major issues out of minor situations that are of no real importance whatsoever, what do we need to learn to do? _____ _____ _____ _____ _____ .

d. What happens when we get all upset about unimportant things? _____

_____

_____.

e. It is amazing what the Lord would deliver us from, sovereignly and supernaturally, if we would _____

_____.

f. Does learning to control our emotions instead of letting them control us mean that we are to have no feelings? Explain. __

_____

_____

_____.

14. Read Philippians 1:28; Romans 4:21

a. According to Philippians 1:28, what is the clear sign, proof, seal, token, and evidence to our enemies of their defeat and destruction and of our deliverance and salvation? _____

_____.

b. What is the sign to the devil that he cannot control us?____

_____

_____.

c. Why then does our deliverance sometimes seem to take so long? _____

_____.

d. The devil does not want us to think we can relax, rest, and enjoy life while we are having problems. He wants us to ___

_____

_____

_____

_____.

e. The author says that when the devil sends people to ask us what we are going to do in times of adversity, our answer should be_____

_____

_____

_____

_____.

15. Read Psalm 94:12,13

a. How does God use the events and people of our lives? ____

_____

_____.

b. For what purpose and goal do we think God wants to empower us?_____

_____.

c. The Lord has a much greater goal and purpose in mind for empowering us. What is it?_____

_____

_____

_____

_____

_____.

d. Why is God working in our lives to discipline, instruct, and teach us? _____
_____.

e. With that power, what are we able to do? _____
_____
_____
_____
_____.

f. In review: Seated with Christ at the right hand of God in heavenly places, trusting not in the arm of the flesh but in the arm of the Lord, what can we truly be? _____
_____.

PART 2

Cast All Your Care

Introduction

"Casting the whole of your care [all your anxieties, all your worries, all your concerns, once and for all] on Him, for He cares for you affectionately and cares about you watchfully."

1 Peter 5:7

*A*re you enjoying the peace that results from casting all your care on God? You may be in the habit of taking on those cares and trying to handle them yourself. As long as that is true, you will be frantic, erratic, and frenzied in your approach to life.

Cares and concerns seem to be a part of life. You can triumph in the midst of them by remaining calm.

God wants to bless you with peace, but His hands are tied until you make some adjustments. You cannot handle your own problems; no one can. We are not built for it. The devil wants you to be weighed down and burdened with care. He wants you to think about your problems, worry about them, try to reason them out and solve them yourself. God wants you to cast all of your care on Him and enter into a lifestyle of peace and joy.

God doesn't want you to be anxious because it prevents you from receiving and doing all He has planned for you. He loves you and wants to bless you and has provided ways for you to be carefree.

I believe this next section of the guidebook will give you the insight you need to help you deal with several issues relating to your care. Every day is a wonderful gift from God in which He has exciting things in store for you. All you have to do is trust Him. He is faithful, and you can depend on Him to take care of you. As you give your care to Him, He will give you something in return — the full and abundant life that He wills for us through His Son Jesus Christ.

1. Review 1 Peter 5:7

   a. Based on 1 Peter 5:7, why does the Bible say we can cast all our care on God? _____
   _____.

   b. What does that mean? _____
   _____.

   c. In order for Him to do that, what must we do? _____
   _____
   _____.

   d. In His Word, what does the Lord promise us if we will give Him our care? _____
   _____.

2. Read Isaiah 61:1-3

   a. In this passage, what does God promise us? _____
   _____
   _____
   _____.

   b. What is one of the positive exchanges God promises to make?
   _____.

   c. What happens if we do not give God our ashes? _____
   _____.

    d. What must we do if we are to receive the blessings God wants to bestow upon us? _____

_____.

    e. _____ for

_____ — that's quite an exchange!

3.   Review John 10:10

    a. What did we learn in Part 1 of this book? _____

_____

_____

_____

_____

_____.

    b. In Part 2 we are going to deal with_____

_____.

Chapter
6

He Careth for You

1. Review Psalm 91; read John 15:4

   a. As we have seen, what do verses 3 through 16 of this psalm contain?_____
   _____.

   b. What must we do to receive the blessings promised us in this psalm? _____
   _____
   _____
   _____
   _____.

   c. There are three aspects of Psalm 91:1,2 that determine our ability to receive God's richest blessings. What is the first one and what does it mean? _____
   _____
   _____
   _____.

   d. What is the second one and what does it mean? _____
   _____
   _____
   _____
   _____
   _____
   _____
   _____.

e. What is the third one and what does it mean? _____

_____

_____

_____

_____

_____

_____ .

2. Review Psalm 91:3-8; 91:1,2

What are the wonderful promises the Lord will fulfill for us when we do the things required of us in verses 1 and 2? _____

_____

_____

_____

_____

_____

_____

_____ .

3. Review Psalm 91:9-16; read Luke 10:19

a. What does *The Amplified Bible* version make very clear about this passage of Psalm 91?_____

_____

_____

_____ .

b. Luke 10:19 describes our place in God. We believers are___

_____

_____

_____.

c. We are also in a position of _____

and _____with God.

d. Saying we have angelic protection does not mean we will
never have any trials or afflictions. What does it mean?____

_____

_____

_____

_____.

e. What is one important thing we must learn about this angelic protection and deliverance?_____

_____.

f. In verses 15 and 16 of Psalm 91, what does the Lord promise?

_____

_____

_____

_____

_____.

g. Based on what the Lord promises, what is the pattern? ____

_____

_____

_____

_____.

4. Read Psalm 27:4-6

   a. Based on this passage, what does the author do that we should do when things start to go wrong in our life? _____
   _____
   _____
   _____
   _____
   _____
   _____
   _____.

   b. If we worship and seek God, what does He do? _____
   _____.

5. Read Psalm 63:1-7

   a. Based on this passage, how does the author describe a shadow? _____
   _____
   _____
   _____.

   b. In the same way how does that relate to us if we are to remain under the shadow of God's wings? _____
   _____
   _____
   _____
   _____.

   c. Why should we choose to remain under the shadow of God's wings rather than to walk out from under them? _____

_____

_____

_____

_____.

d. The wise thing is not only to choose to stay under the shadow of the Almighty, but to _____

_____.

e. The dividing lines between lanes and the signposts along the road are put there for our benefit and protection. In the spiritual realm, what are the "lines and signs" that keep us on the way of the Lord and out of danger? _____

_____.

f. What will happen as long as we place our trust and confidence in the Lord? _____

_____

_____.

6. Review Philippians 4:6,7

a. In this passage the apostle Paul does not say, "Pray and worry." Instead, he says,_____

_____.

b. Why are we to pray and not worry? _____

_____

_____.

c. What are we supposed to do when the devil tries to give us care? _____

_____.

d. How do we do that? Why? _____

_____

_____

_____

_____.

e. What are we doing if we pray about something and then keep on worrying about it?_____

_____

_____

_____

_____.

f. Why do many people operate at zero power level spiritually?

_____

_____

_____

_____.

g. Why should we not worry? _____

_____

_____

_____

_____

_____.

7. Review Hebrews 4:3

   a. Based on this verse, if we are not at rest, we are not _____
      _____ . Why? _____
      _____ .

   b. If we are truly believing God and trusting the Lord, what has
      happened to us? _____
      _____ .

   c. If we have entered into God's rest, we have prayed and cast
      our care upon the Lord and are now _____
      _____
      _____ .

8. Read Romans 5:2-4

   a. It is easy to say, "Don't worry." What does it require to actu-
      ally do that? _____ .

   b. What does it take for a person to fully overcome the habit of
      worry, anxiety, and fear and develop the habit of peace, rest,
      and hope? _____
      _____ .

   c. That's why it is so important to continue to have faith and
      trust in God in the very midst of trials and tribulations, to
      resist the temptation to give up and quit when the going gets
      rough — and keeps on getting rougher over a long period of
      time. What is the Lord building in us in those hard, trying
      times? _____
      _____

_____

_____

_____.

d. When we are in the midst of battle against our spiritual enemy, every round we go through produces valuable _____ and _____. Each time we endure an attack, we become _____

_____.

e. If we hang in there and refuse to give up, what will be the result? _____

_____.

f. When that happens, we will have reached _____

_____.

g. We should learn to pray to God and cast our care upon Him — _____. We need to learn to endure our personal suffering _____.

h. There is a time to share what we are going through, and there is a time to keep things between us and God. Often we talk so much about "what we are going through" that_____

_____

_____.

i. What does God do with things that Satan intends for our harm? _____.

9. Read Isaiah 53:7

    a. In the Old Testament, what did the prophet Isaiah foretell about what would happen when the Messiah was led away to be sacrificed for the sins of the world? _____

    _____

    _____

    _____.

    b. What happens to us in trying times? _____

    _____

    _____

    _____.

10. Read Philippians 4:11

    a. As he stated in Philippians 4:11, what ability did Paul have?

    _____

    _____.

    b. What did he know how to do that gave him that ability?

    _____

    _____

    _____.

    c. In spite of all the challenges he faced and all the hardships he had to go through, what did Paul know? _____

    _____

    _____.

    d. If that is not true of you, what did Paul say that will keep you from becoming discouraged?_____

_____

_____.

e. If we do not have it yet, sooner or later we can begin to develop the ability to be content in whatever state we may find ourselves. How? _____

_____

_____

_____

_____.

11. Read Proverbs 3:5,6

a. As we travel down the road of life, how will the devil try to distract us to keep us from making progress toward our goal?

_____

_____

_____.

b. But what can happen if we keep within the lines and obey the signs along the way? _____

_____

_____.

c. Instead of trying to figure out everything for ourselves, what should we do?_____

_____

_____.

d. How can we tell when we have begun to cross over the boundary? _____

_____.

e. Whatever the problem may be that is causing us to lose our peace, what should we do about it? _____

_____

_____

_____

_____.

f. In the passage from Proverbs 3:5,6 what are we told to do?

_____

_____.

g. As we have seen, faith is the leaning of the _____

_____

on God in absolute_____

and_____in His power,

wisdom, and goodness.

h. What does God mean when He says that we are to lean on Him? _____

_____

_____.

i. What is always a sign we are getting over the line and headed for trouble? _____

_____.

12. Review Matthew 6:25-33

a. What does Jesus talk to us directly about in this passage?

_____

_____.

b. What should we do every time we are tempted to worry or be anxious about anything in life? _____ _____.

c. In verse 25 what does Jesus command us specifically to do? _____ _____ _____.

d. Why should we quit torturing ourselves with negative thoughts and feelings? _____ _____ _____.

e. In verse 26 Jesus commands us to look at the birds of the air. What does He want us to see and understand? _____ _____ _____ _____ _____.

f. In verse 32 Jesus assure us_____ _____ _____ _____ _____.

g. Finally, in verse 33 Jesus gives us the key to living in the peace of the Lord. What is it? _____ _____ _____

_____
_____.

h. What is the reason that we worry and fret and live in anxiety
and fear? _____

_____
_____
_____.

i. As the Body of Christ, we are supposed to seek God, not the
answer to our problems. What are we promised if we will
seek Him and His righteousness? _____

_____.

j. Instead of spending all our time seeking the perfect mate or a
happy home or a successful career or ministry, what are we
told to do in the Word of God? _____

_____
_____
_____
_____.

13. Read 1 Peter 5:6,7 KJV; review Psalm 27:4-6; 91; Matthew 6:25-34;
read Psalm 37

*Let's take a moment to review some of the things we have learned
so far.*

a. In Psalm 27 we saw the psalmist had the right idea when he
wrote the one thing he asked of the Lord was _____

_____
_____.

b. What did we see in Psalm 91?_____
_____
_____
_____
_____
_____.

c. What did we see in Matthew 6:25-33 that we are not to seek
after? _____
_____
_____
_____.

d. What did we see in verse 34 of that passage? _____
_____
_____
_____
_____
_____.

e. What are we told in the passage in 1 Peter 5:6,7 KJV?_____
_____
_____
_____
_____.

f. What are we told several times in Psalm 37? What are we to
do instead? _____
_____
_____
_____

_____

_____

_____

_____.

14. Read Psalm 18:1-3; 61:2; 62:2; Ephesians 6:10-17; Psalm 125:1,2; review Psalm 37:17.

   a. In Psalm 18:1-3, 61:2 and 62:2, David said God only was his Rock and Fortress. That should be our testimony also. In that case, Who should our Rock of security be? _____

   _____.

   b. A rock is a type of a sure foundation. When the waters of trial threaten to rise up and overwhelm us, what should we do?

   _____

   _____.

   c. David also called the Lord his Fortress. What is a fortress?

   _____

   _____

   _____

   _____

   _____

   _____

   _____.

   d. What else did David also call the Lord? _____

   _____

   _____

   _____

_____

_____.

e. What do Psalm 125:1,2 and Psalm 37:17 tell us about where God is? _____

_____

_____.

f. Based on those passages, what is God doing for us? _____

_____

_____

_____

_____.

g. The devil is against us, but God is _____us, and _____ us, and _____ us, and_____us.

h. Because He cares for us, what does God do for us?_____

_____

_____

_____

_____.

*Cast Your Care,
Not Your Responsibility*

1. Read 1 Peter 5:6,7; review John 6:28,29

    a. It is important that we learn to cast our _____, but
        not our _____.

    b. So often what do we do instead?_____
        _____
        _____.

    c. There is a difference between _____
        _____ and _____
        _____.

    d. As Jesus told us in John 6:28,29, what is our first responsi-
        bility as believers? _____.

    e. Why should that not be a struggle for us? _____
        _____
        _____
        _____.

    f. To summarize, what is one thing God has told us to do? ___
        _____
        _____.

2. Read Matthew 11:12; Philippians 3:12

    a. Why does the author say that *casting* is a violent word?____
        _____
        _____
        _____

_____

_____.

b. In Matthew 11:12, what did Jesus say about the Kingdom of God? _____

_____

_____

_____.

c. In what way, then, and about what are we going to have to get violent? _____

_____

_____

_____

_____.

d. Where is part of that violence expressed? _____

_____

_____

_____

_____.

e. In Philippians 3:12, what did the apostle Paul say he did?

_____

_____

_____.

f. Sometimes we have to get angry enough to _____

_____

_____

_____ that try to keep us from enjoying

_____

_____

_____.

g. Often we get mad at other people when we should be mad at

_____.

h. Just as anger at Satan can be a form of righteous violence, so can be casting our care on the Lord. Explain. _____

_____

_____

_____

_____.

i. What can we do when Satan tries to force us to carry a burden of care?_____

_____

_____

_____!

j. Everyone has their own set of problems, but has become very good at hiding them. How can we be free of that kind of charade? _____

_____

_____

_____

_____.

k. What do we need to do to settle once and for all the spiritual issues that are keeping us from walking in the fullness of joy, peace, and rest the Lord intends for us? _____

_____

_____.

l. The Bible says we are to cast all our care upon God. What does the Greek word translated *care* in 1 Peter 5:7 mean?

_____

_____

_____

_____.

m. Why does the devil try to give us care? _____

_____.

n. What do we need to know in order to cast our care, but not our responsibility? _____

_____.

3. Read 1 Peter 5:7 WORRELL

a. According to the footnote in the *Worrell New Testament*, what does the Greek tense of 1 Peter 5:7 indicate?_____

_____

_____.

b. The footnote continues, "This, in a sense, is done when ___

_____

_____

_____

_____.

c. Then the footnote tells us, "When one puts the whole management of his life in God's hands, he may _____

_____

_____

_____

_____.

d. What sin are we often guilty of, which causes many problems? _____.

e. A desire for independence is a sign of _____

_____.

f. Why do we sometimes not want our heavenly Father's help when He tries to help us? What is the result? _____

_____

_____

_____.

g. If we want to experience the peace of the Lord, what must we do?_____

_____.

h. Based on Worrell's study notes, what is the way we overcome a spirit of independence?_____

_____

_____

_____.

i. So what is our first responsibility? What is our second responsibility?_____

_____

_____

_____

_____.

4. Read John 16:7,8

    a. We must learn to distinguish between _____ part
        and _____ part — and then leave _____
        _____ to Him, refusing to _____
        _____.

    b. People cannot change people. Only _____
        can change people.

    c. According to the Bible, Who convicts and convinces of sin
        and of righteousness? _____.

    d. Like the author, when we try to convict others of what we
        think are their sins and try to convince them of our right-
        eousness, why are we always in such a struggle?_____
        _____
        _____.

    e. In addition to submitting ourselves entirely to the Lord, trust-
        ing Him to work out things for us as He knows best, what else
        must we do? _____
        _____
        _____
        _____.

5. Read 1 Corinthians 2:16; Isaiah 55:8,9

    a. Based on these passages, it is not our job to give God _____
        _____, _____ or
        _____.

    b. In His Word, He makes it clear that He doesn't need us to
        _____ or tell Him _____
        _____.

    c. What is our job concerning this? _____
        _____
        _____
        _____
        _____
        _____.

    d. God is God — and we aren't. Why do we need to simply rec-
        ognize that truth and trust ourselves to Him? _____
        _____
        _____.

    e. We are created in God's image, but He is still above us and
        beyond us. Since His thoughts and ways are higher than ours,
        what will He do if we will listen to Him and be obedient to
        Him?_____.

6. Read Romans 9:20,21

    a. It is not our place to cross-examine God. Why not?_____
        _____
        _____.

b. What may be the reason God does not answer our prayers?

_____

_____.

c. What has been noted as the biggest problem for most Christians? _____

_____

_____.

d. What makes us think that what we are asking is God's will?

_____

_____

_____

_____.

e. Since many things in this life are not clearly laid out in Scripture, what must we have from the Lord to know whether they are His will for us or not? _____

_____.

f. Even if something is God's will for us, what must we also consider? What does that take on our part?_____

_____.

g. Like the author, why do we often struggle with these matters?

_____

_____

_____

_____

_____.

     h. As the author realized about her prayers, too often what are our prayers, and what do we try to do through them? _____

       _____

       _____

       _____.

     i. According to the author, the Lord showed her in His Word what the problem was that kept Him from answering her prayers as He promised. Like her, even though we are asking, what is our problem? _____

       _____

       _____.

7. Read James 4:1-3

     a. Based on this passage, why do we often get into struggles and strife? _____

       _____

       _____

       _____.

     b. Based on the second part of this passage, as we already discussed, why do we not get our prayers answered even when we do ask?_____

       _____

       _____.

     c. Like the author, when we ask the Lord for something and we don't get it, it's not because He doesn't want to bless us or because He is holding out on us. What is the reason? _____

       _____

_____

_____

_____.

8. Review Psalm 37:3-5; read Deuteronomy 8:19

   a. What has the author learned since the Lord spoke to her about what was wrong with the way she was praying? _____

   _____

   _____.

   b. How did she say that she prays if she is not sure what God's will is in a situation? _____

   _____

   _____

   _____

   _____

   _____

   _____

   _____.

   c. According to what she has learned about prayer, what should we seek first? _____

   _____

   _____

   _____

   _____

   _____.

d. What will happen if we seek God for money or things without seeking Him? _____

_____.

e. If our _____ does not go as deep as our _____, we only get in trouble.

f. What must happen in our lives for anything else to work properly? _____

_____.

g. Literally any blessing of the Lord can get us in trouble if we don't keep our lives in balance and turn the blessing into a god. What must we do regularly to keep that from happening? _____

_____

_____.

h. It is such a deliverance to turn the management of our life over to God. Does that mean we are to become passive and stop resisting the enemy Satan when he attacks us? Explain.

_____

_____

_____.

i. What will happen if we wait on the Lord and listen to Him?

_____

_____

_____

_____

_____

_____

_____.

j. Although it is God's will to bless us, why does He not neces-
    sarily bless us on our terms? _____

    _____

    _____.

k. In all our seeking, struggling, and striving — even in prayer
    — why must we be careful not to give birth to Ishmaels?

    _____

    _____.

l. What should we do instead? Why?_____

    _____

    _____

    _____

    _____.

9. Read Isaiah 45:9-11; review Romans 9:20,21; read Ephesians
    2:10; 1 Corinthians 13:12

    a. We see that the passage in Isaiah 45:9-11 talks against ques-
        tioning God, and in Romans 9:20,21 we saw we are not to

        _____

        _____

        _____.

    b. Who can say why God puts us together the way He does? But
        He is the _____, and we are the

        _____.

c. Not only do we question God about why He made us the way
   He did, we also question Him about_____
   _____.

d. As long as we argue with God and strive with our Maker,
   what will be the result? _____
   _____.

e. Once we accept God's will, what will be the result? _____
   _____
   _____.

f. In Romans 9:21, when Paul asks whether the potter has the
   right to make one vessel for honorable use and another vessel for dishonorable use, does that mean dishonorable in
   God's eyes? Explain._____
   _____
   _____
   _____
   _____
   _____.

g. We are where we are because God Himself has placed us
   there. Wherever He has placed us, what must we do? _____
   _____
   _____
   _____
   _____.

h. As long as we function in the position God has created us for,
   His _____. But

the moment we get out of our God-ordained role, we are

_____

_____.

i. Based on 1 Corinthians 13:12, what is the best answer to the question of why God does anything the way He does?_____

_____.

j. It is not our job to question God, or even try to explain Him. It is our job to_____and

_____ Him and to

_____

_____upon Him.

10. Read 2 Timothy 4:5

a. As ministers of the Gospel of Jesus Christ, which is what we are all called to be, what are our basic duties or responsibilities? _____

_____

_____

_____

_____.

b. When there is something that greatly concerns us, like the salvation of our spouse or children, what can happen? ____

_____

_____.

c. Excessive prayer, especially in the area of spiritual warfare, can become _____

_____.

    d. In our prayers, as in every other aspect of our Christian life, we need not be afraid of_____

_____.

    e. It is our responsibility to trust, to pray without worry, and to avoid works of the flesh. What happens when we go beyond that responsibility and start to pray and worry? _____

_____

_____

_____

_____.

11. Read Galatians 2:21 KJV

    a. God is not against work. He is against _____.

    b. What is the difference? _____

_____

_____

_____

_____

_____

_____

_____

_____

_____.

    c. What happens when we do the work God has called us to do?

_____.

d. Physically we may be tired, but spiritually we are renewed and refreshed by the Spirit of the Lord. That is a good example of _____ _____ and _____ _____.

e. What works of the flesh are one of the biggest problems among God's people today? _____ _____ _____ _____.

f. As we have seen, what is the opposite of works? _____.

g. As long as we are trying to live the Christian life by works of the flesh, we are never going to be _____ _____.

h. Why does the devil try to use works of the flesh against us? _____ _____ _____ _____ _____.

i. Instead of trusting in the Lord and waiting for Him to move in His own way and timing, what does the devil want us to do? _____ _____ _____.

12. Read Genesis 16:5,6; 3:12

    a. In Part 1, we read how Sarah, despairing of ever having a child of her own in her old age, suggested to Abraham that he take her Egyptian maid Hagar as his "secondary wife" and have a child by her. What was Abraham's response? _____

       _____

       _____

       _____.

    b. In Genesis 16:5,6, what immediate consequences of that action do we see? _____

       _____

       _____

       _____.

    c. What did Sarah do in reaction to this situation? _____

       _____

       _____!

    d. In what way was Abraham to blame for this situation? ____

       _____

       _____

       _____.

    e. Instead of waiting for the Lord to supernaturally produce the promised heir, what was the result of Abraham and Sarah's foolish attempt to produce an heir on their own through totally human effort? _____

       _____

_____

_____.

f. What was the reason that Abraham failed to fulfill his responsibility? _____

_____

_____

_____

_____.

g. How is that often our problem? _____

_____

_____

_____

_____

_____

_____

_____.

h. When Hagar became pregnant and treated Sarah cruelly, how did Abraham again shift his responsibility? _____

_____

_____.

i. In both cases, how did Abraham avoid his God-given responsibility? _____

_____.

j. Based on Genesis 3:12, the same kind of thing happened with Adam in the Garden of Eden. Explain. _____

_____

_____

_____

_____

_____

_____

_____ .

k. What job has the devil done on many men today? _____

_____

_____

_____

_____ .

l. What change in this situation are we seeing? _____

_____

_____

_____

_____ .

13. Read Colossians 4:17 NIV

a. In review, what are our first three duties or responsibilities?

_____

_____

_____ .

b. What are our three final duties or responsibilities? _____

_____

_____

_____

_____ .

14. Read John 2:5; 2:1-11; Galatians 6:9

    a. Based on the passage in John 1-11, the first rule of miracles is

    _____.

    b. If you are looking for a miracle in your life, what should you
       do? Based on Galatians 6:9, why should you do so? _____

       _____

       _____

       _____

       _____

       _____.

    c. Sometimes when things are not working out the way we
       think they should, or we are not receiving the answers to our
       prayers as quickly as we would like, we get the idea, "Well,
       since God's not doing anything, why should I? Why should I
       be obedient if it isn't producing results?" In such times we
       must realize that _____

       _____

       _____.

15. Read Psalm 139:15,16; John 5:17; Matthew 9:29 KJV

    a. In Psalm 139:15,16, the psalmist wrote that long before his
       actual appearance in this world, he was _____

       _____.

    b. What kind of work did God put together in the form of King
       David of Israel, just as He is putting together in our lives?

       _____.

c. David did not make his appearance in this world until ____
   _____.

d. In the same way, when will God bring forth His perfect work
   in us? _____
   _____.

e. Even though it may seem God is doing nothing, He is _____
   _____
   _____. We may not
   be able to hear it or see it, but we can accept it_____
   _____.

f. Based on Matthew 9:29 KJV, at this very moment while you
   are reading this book, God is at work in your life and in your
   present situation, if you _____.

g. If you have cast your care upon the Lord and left it with Him
   to handle, what is He doing right now? _____
   _____
   _____.

h. What does He want you to do? _____
   _____
   _____
   _____.

i. How do you do that? _____
   _____
   _____
   _____
   _____.

16. Read Jeremiah 17:7,8; Ephesians 3:17; review Galatians 5:22,23;
James 4:6

    a. What should we be doing while we are waiting on the Lord?

    _____.

    b. What should we be like? Why?_____

    _____

    _____

    _____

    _____

    _____.

    c. If we are firmly planted in Jesus Christ and deeply rooted in
His love, what will we still do even though we may have all
kinds of problems in our lives? _____

    _____

    _____

    _____.

    d. Why should we not think we have a license to be miserable
and ugly when we are going through hard times?_____

    _____

    _____.

    e. In James 4:6 what does the Bible teach us about such "evil
tendencies"? _____

    _____

    _____

    _____

    _____.

17. Read Hebrews 13:15; review Psalm 139:13-16

    a. In Psalm 139:15,16, what did we see that David acknowledged about God?_____

    _____

    _____.

    b. In verses 13 and 14 of that Psalm, for what did he praise the Lord? _____

    _____

    _____.

    c. Like David, what are we to do in the midst of our problems?

    _____

    _____

    _____

    _____

    _____

    _____.

    d. In summary, it is not our responsibility to worry and fret or try to play God by taking into our own hands things that should be left to Him alone. Instead, it is our responsibility to

    _____

    _____

    _____

    _____

    _____

    _____.

This Too Shall Pass

1. Read Genesis 4:14 KJV; Genesis 39 KJV; Revelation 1:1 KJV

    a. What prophetic word do we see in the beginning chapters of
        the book of Genesis? _____
        _____.

    b. In fulfillment of this word, the expression "it came to pass" is
        used hundreds of times throughout the *King James Version* of
        the Bible. What should that tell us? _____
        _____
        _____
        _____.

    c. Life is a continual process in which everything is constantly
        changing. If we can grasp that truth, how will it help us?
        _____
        _____
        _____
        _____
        _____
        _____
        _____.

    d. What does God want us to enjoy? _____
        _____.

2. Read Ecclesiastes 5:18

    a. Based on this verse, do you find enjoyment in your labor?
        Why or why not? _____

_____

_____ .

b. The author says that the Lord showed her in our lives we are always going to be _____

_____ . As soon as we finish one,

_____

_____ .

c. She says the Lord was teaching her that since we are going to spend our entire lives waiting for something, we should ___

_____

_____ .

d. What will happen if we don't do that? _____

_____ .

3. Read Zecharaiah 4:10

a. Like the author, we may have hated the "day of small things" and the hardships of early times while they were going on, but now we see their value. Why were they important? ____

_____

_____

_____ .

b. Why is it sad that today many times people give up in the hard times? _____

_____ .

c. It is easy to start something, but it is much harder to_____

_____ .

d. In the beginning, we are filled with emotion, and usually have all kinds of enthusiastic support. Everybody cheers us on. But as the days go by and the great and glorious cause becomes a matter of daily, consistent hard work, what often happens to us? _____

_____

_____

_____.

e. That's when we have to decide if we are going to _____

_____.

That's when we have to realize _____

_____

_____.

f. In the meantime, what should we do? _____

_____.

4. Read Mark 9:2-6

a. In the Gospels we never find Jesus saying, "This is it!" Instead, what do we often find Him saying? _____

_____

_____.

b. Then what does He do? _____.

c. What is one of our problems in this area? _____

_____.

d. We like to think that things, especially pleasant things, are never going to change. When we win a victory, we like to think that is the end of our troubles, and we will never have to fight another battle. Why does the Lord try to tell us that is not so? _____

_____.

e. One season always leads to_____.

f. If the situation we are in at the moment is not very pleasant, it will at least _____

_____.

g. In the same way, a pleasant situation may have to change for a while so _____

_____.

h. What do trying times do for us? _____

_____

_____

_____

_____

_____.

i. We have to grow and develop. Like all of God's children, we have to go through some _____

_____.

5. Read Hebrews 12:7-11

In verse 11 of this passage, what does the phrase "but afterwards" mean? _____

_____

_____

_____

_____.

6.   Review Psalm 91:14-16

   a.   What three things does God promise us in this passage if we
        are in trouble?_____

        _____

        _____

        _____.

   b.   The author believes the message the Lord is giving us in these
        verses is simply this:_____

        _____

        _____

        _____

        _____

        _____.

7.   Read Mark 13:31

   a.   God doesn't always change those people we want Him to
        change; instead, He often uses them to _____.

   b.   What we believe to be our worst enemy often, in actuality, is
        our _____.

   c.   What things does God use to change us?_____

        _____.

    d. Sometimes we need to look ahead with the eye of faith to __

    _____

    _____.

    e. When God is dealing with you, instead of looking at the training, correction, and discipline you are going through for the moment, what should you look at? _____

    _____

    _____.

    f. When you don't see the manifestation of your prayers, what should you do? _____

    _____

    _____

    _____

    _____.

    g. To review, when you are going through trying times, what should be your message to yourself? _____

    _____.

8. Read Ecclesiastes 3:1; Psalm 62:10; Proverbs 27:24; Philippians 3:13,14

    a. What two lies does the devil offer us? _____

    _____.

    b. Why are both of these lies untrue? _____

    _____.

c. What happens if we continue to believe God and place our trust in Him?_____

_____.

d. When we do have good things going on in our lives, does that mean that they will stay exactly the same forever? Explain.

_____

_____

_____

_____

_____.

e. The devil wants you to feel that things will never change, and if you believe his lies,_____

_____

_____.

f. Sometimes changes are exciting — sometimes they're hard. But Jesus never changes — and as long as we _____

_____, we will

_____ the changes

in our life and continue _____

_____.

g. When the Bible tells us that we are not to set our hearts on the things of this world, what does it mean? _____

_____

_____.

h. As believers, to what is our attachment supposed to be? ___
_____
_____.

i. We are to enjoy what we have while we have it, but we are never to get to the point where we _____
_____.

j. According to the author, what is one of the things the Lord is saying to us today?_____
_____.

k. We must remember that we are_____
of what God has provided us, not _____.

l. Why must we not get attached to people or to things?_____
_____
_____.

m. There is a season in our lives, and when that season is over, what must we do? _____.

n. Too often what mistake do we make in this area? _____
_____
_____
_____.

o. If God is done with something in your life, what should you do?_____
_____
_____
_____

_____

_____.

p. If God is no longer in something, you will no longer be happy in it. What then should you do? Why? _____

_____

_____

_____.

9. Read Genesis 12:1-4

a. In this passage, what did God tell Abraham to do? _____

_____

_____.

b. The author says that is what God did to her when He told her to leave a certain job. At one time in her life, that job was "it," but now the Lord was telling her _____

_____

_____.

c. Does that mean it was wrong for her to have spent that time there?_____

_____.

d. We must remember there are different seasons in our lives and let God _____

_____.

e. Why must we stop trying to find some "it" that is never going to change? _____

_____.

    f. It is much easier to cast our care when we know that _____
_____.

    g. We need to be careful not to become too attached to anybody or anything in this life more than we are to _____
_____.

10.   Read Mark 14:3; Hebrews 13:8

    a. Based on the verse in Mark 14:3, why should we not be afraid of brokenness? _____
_____
_____.

    b. The perfume of the Holy Spirit is within us, but what has to be done for that sweet fragrance to be released? _____
_____
_____.

    c. To fully release the power of the Holy Spirit within us, what must we do? What must we learn? _____
_____
_____
_____
_____
_____.

    d. In ancient times, whenever a Roman general returned victoriously from war, why was a slave stationed to ride in a chariot alongside the hero's chariot and given the job of constantly whispering in the hero's ear, "Look behind you," or "Remember that you are mortal"?[1] _____

_____
_____.

e. That is what God does to us. Explain. _____
_____
_____
_____
_____
_____.

f. If we are ever going to have stability in our lives, what must
we do? What must we recall? _____
_____
_____
_____
_____
_____.

g. Why must we put our hope not on the things of this world,
but on the Lord? _____
_____
_____
_____.

11. Read Philippians 4:11-13; Romans 12:3; review Proverbs 16:18

a. Stability is_____.

b. What does it mean to grow up in God? _____
_____
_____
_____

_____

_____

_____.

c. Why was Paul emotionally and spiritually mature? _____

_____

_____

_____.

d. In verse 12 of Philippians chapter 4, what did Paul say on this subject? _____

_____

_____.

e. According to the author, the Lord showed her what would happen if we never had to wait for anything, if everything always went just as we wanted it to, when we wanted it to. Explain. _____

_____

_____

_____

_____

_____

_____.

f. Based on Romans 12:3 and Proverbs 16:18, what must we be on our guard against? _____.

g. God wants to keep His people in balance. He wants to bless us and be good to us. He wants to use us as His vessels through which His Holy Spirit can work. But in order to do that, what must He teach us? _____

_____
_____.

h. Why does God allow us to enjoy wonderful blessings for a time, and then suddenly experience a series of setbacks?

_____
_____
_____.

i. What does God know will happen if we have too many blessings? _____
_____.

j. What does He also know will happen if we have too many bad times? _____
_____.

k. That's why it is so important to remember that whatever comes our way, _____.

l. That's why we must learn to cast it all upon the Lord, knowing that _____
_____.

12. Read Psalm 23:4; Isaiah 43:2; Daniel 3; Daniel 6; review Psalm 91:15

a. In Psalm 23:4, the psalmist David said he _____ the valley of the shadow of death.

b. That's what we must do. In all the situations and circumstances of this life, what must we remember? _____

_____
_____
_____.

c. What must we be aware of?_____
_____.

d. When the devil tries to whisper to us, "Things will never
change, everything will be the same forever; you are
trapped!" we should say to him _____
_____
_____
_____!

e. What has the Lord promised us in Isaiah 43:2?_____
_____
_____
_____
_____
_____
_____.

f. What happened when the three Hebrew children were cast
into the fiery furnace by King Nebuchadnezzar?_____
_____
_____
_____.

g. What happened when Daniel was thrown into the lions' den?
_____
_____.

h. As we have seen, what does the Lord promise in Psalm 91:15?

_____

_____

_____.

13. Review 2 Corinthians 3:18

a. What is one thing the devil wants us to believe about ourselves? _____.

b. But what does the Bible tell us in the *King James Version* of this verse? _____

_____

_____

_____.

c. The Greek word translated "transfigured" or "changed" in this verse is *metamorphoo*, meaning "to transform."[2] It is from this Greek word we get our English word *metamorphosis*, which means_____

_____

_____

_____

_____

_____.

d. How does that relate to us spiritually? _____

_____

_____

_____.

e. What should we say to the devil when he tries to tell us we are the same old worm we used to be? _____

_____

_____

_____

_____

_____

_____!

f. Like the caterpillar and the butterfly, what would happen to us if we didn't struggle through some things? _____

_____

_____.

g. God often works through struggle. But He also sometimes works through _____.

14. Read Malachi 3:1; 1 Corinthians 15:51,52; Acts 2:1,2; Acts 9; 16:26-34

a. We all like "suddenlies." What does the Bible promise us as we draw closer to the end times? _____

_____.

b. According to 1 Corinthians 15:51,52, when Jesus comes back to this earth to take us to Himself, we will be changed or transformed_____

_____

_____.

c. Why do we not have to be discouraged in our walk with God?

_____

_____

_____

_____

_____

_____

_____.

d. God is even now in the process of _____
   _____, and whatever

   He will one day do _____.

e. Just as God worked among the disciples in Acts 2:1,2, how
   does He work among us today? _____.

f. In the story of the young woman who was filled with the
   Holy Spirit in one of the author's services, she wrote of how
   God had suddenly showed up in her life and now He was at
   work day by day, changing her from glory to glory. That's the
   way God works — sometimes_____
   and sometimes_____,
   sometimes _____and sometimes

   _____

   _____.

g. In Acts 9, we read about the conversion of Paul on the road
   to Damascus. What does the account tell us? _____

   _____

   _____

   _____

_____

_____.

h. From this incident, what should we remember to keep from getting discouraged when we pray for others who are not believers or are not living their faith, and we see no evident change in their attitude or behavior? _____

_____

_____.

i. Why should we never get tired of praying for our loved ones?

_____

_____

_____

_____.

j. As we see in Acts 16:26, how does God work? _____

_____.

k. Just as God moved in the lives of all these people in this passage, He is moving in your life right now. As we have seen, how may He be moving? _____

_____

_____.

l. Whatever may be going on in your life at the moment — good or bad — what should you do? _____

_____

_____.

Retiring From Self-Care

1. Read Acts 16:31

    a. Based on this verse, what does salvation really mean? _____
    _____
    _____
    _____
    _____.

    b. God wants to take care of us. He can do a much better job of
    that if we will avoid a problem called independence, which is
    really_____.

    c. Explain the author's statement, "The desire to take care of
    ourselves is based on fear." _____
    _____
    _____
    _____
    _____
    _____.

    d. The root problem of independence is _____
    _____
    _____.

    e. We love to have a back-up plan. We may pray and ask God to
    get involved in our lives, but if He is the least bit slow in
    responding (at least, to our way of thinking), we are quick to
    take control back into our own hands. When we do that,

what do we fail to realize? _____

_____

_____.

2. Read Jeremiah 29:11; John 15:5

a. It sometimes seems that God refuses to help us when we are faced with a problem. Yet, although He will not help us to meet our own need, He will help us meet someone else's need. What is the reason this happens? _____

_____

_____

_____

_____

_____

_____.

b. Why do we sometimes have to lay down our plan? _____

_____.

c. Although it is wise to plan our work and work our plan, what must we not do? _____

_____

_____

_____.

d. What point was God trying to make in the story of the woman at the gas station who had such an excessive, elaborate plan about how she was going to pay for her gas that her plan was confusing? _____

_____
_____.

e. God does not want us to be independent or codependent. He wants us to be dependent upon Him. Why? _____
_____
_____.

f. What valuable lesson does the woman's testimony contain of which we all need to continually remind ourselves? _____
_____
_____
_____
_____.

3. Read John 5:30

a. Jesus did not ask Himself what to do, He_____
_____. Instead of following His own will, He followed_____
_____. When He made a decision, it was right because _____
_____
_____.

b. What example did Jesus make clear that we would do well to follow?_____
_____.

c. Sometimes rather than deciding the will of God and then being obedient to it, what do we do instead?_____
_____.

    d. Jesus said He had no desire to do what was pleasing to Himself. His aim and purpose were _____ _____.

    e. What did He say to the people of His day? _____ _____ _____ _____ _____.

    f. Jesus did not have a problem with independence, and neither should we. Why? What should we realize? _____ _____ _____ _____ _____.

4. Read 1 Corinthians 13:11

    a. In describing her son Danny as a teenager, the author says that like many adolescents, he was self-centered. His every thought, word, and deed had to do with himself and what would bless him and make him happy, when God is the One Who_____ _____ _____ _____.

    b. How are immature Christians like young children or teenagers? _____

_____
_____.

c. If we want to grow up in the Lord, what must we learn? ___

_____
_____.

d. What must we be determined not to do? _____

_____
_____
_____.

e. Instead, what must we do? _____

_____
_____
_____.

5. Read Proverbs 3:5-7; Isaiah 30:21; 2 Chronicles 20:12

a. Does the passage in Proverbs 3:5-7 mean that we have to seek a divine word from God about every minute decision we make in the course of our daily lives? _____

_____.

b. How does God put wisdom into us and for what reason? ____

_____
_____.

c. But the Lord does want us to _____,
_____, and_____Him. He does want us to be aware of_____
_____ and to walk in _____

_____, _____,

and _____ to Him.

d. God expects us to walk by wisdom, but what does He also
    expect us to do? _____
    _____.

e. Why is acknowledging God in all our ways so important? ___
    _____.

f. Based on Isaiah 30:21, what will God do for us if we start to
    go astray one way or the other? _____
    _____
    _____.

g. It is_____to God when we
    go through life planning everything without _____
    _____Him or caring what He thinks, yet expecting
    Him to make everything work out as we envision just because
    it is _____.

h. Like pride, independence is a sin. Why? _____
    _____.

i. Why don't we want anybody to help us? _____
    _____
    _____.

j. Why does God give each of us only a part of the answer? __
    _____
    _____.

k. If we want to do the will of God, we must be willing to ____

_____.

l. Usually the stronger our personality, the more weaknesses and inabilities God has to leave in us. Why? _____

_____

_____.

m. In 2 Chronicles 20:12, we read King Jehoshaphat's prayer to the Lord when Judah was faced with an invasion by enemies who were more powerful than they were. What did he acknowledge? _____

_____

_____

_____

_____

_____.

n. What kind of statement is that? _____

_____

_____.

6. Read 1 Corinthians 1:25-29; Zechariah 4:6

a. We must remember it is not our gifts that matter, it is God's

_____.

b. Why does God call people because of their foolishness, ignorance, and weakness rather than their great wisdom, knowledge, or ability? _____

_____.

c. What two kinds of people does God usually call? _____

_____

_____

_____

_____

_____

_____

_____.

d. Many of us fall into that second category. In that respect, we are no different from _____

_____.

e. In the story about the consulting firm, what was the firm basically saying about the people Jesus chose as His disciples?

_____

_____

_____.

f. Based on Paul's letter to the Corinthians, why does God deliberately choose the nothings of this world? _____

_____

_____.

g. Based on Zechariah 4:6, God takes _____ and adds His _____ to them so that they become _____.

h. Since in and of ourselves we are nothing, why must we not try to be independent? _____

_____.

i. What must we do instead?_____

_____.

j. What may be the reason we are so independent-minded? __

_____

_____

_____

_____.

k. If you have been betrayed or mistreated, you may think the only way to protect yourself and assure you are not taken advantage of is by _____

_____.

l. If so, when God asks you to give up that control to Him, you may find it_____

_____.

m. What may you also fail to realize is just another form of childish rebellion?_____

_____.

7. Read Isaiah 30:1,2

a. In this "woe" Scripture passage, upon whom does the Lord pronounce a curse? _____

_____

_____

_____
_____
_____
_____.

b. In this case, to what does fleeing to the "shadow of Egypt"
    refer? _____
    _____
    _____.

c. In other words, we are not to trust in ourselves or in others,
    but only in _____.

d. We are not to make rules and regulations about everything,
    but, as we have already seen, we are to _____
    _____
    _____.

e. We are to find our strength in_____, not in
    _____ or _____,
    which is what Egypt always represents in Scripture.

8. Read Isaiah 30:3,7

    a. According to the author, in this passage, what is the Lord say-
        ing to us and why?_____
        _____
        _____
        _____.

b. What does the Lord then say to do before we do anything?

    _____

    _____

    _____

    _____

    _____

    _____ .

9. Read Isaiah 30:13,14

    a. What happens when we make our own plans or run to other people instead of trusting in the Lord?_____

    _____

    _____ .

    b. Then what will happen at a time when we least expect it?__

    _____

    _____ .

    c. God does not want us to have weak spots in our lives. What does He want us to do? Why?_____

    _____

    _____

    _____

    _____ .

    d. The more we depend on God, the more_____

    _____. But sometimes we go through a _____ before we enter into _____ .

   e. Sometimes before God can promote us, what must He do to
      us? _____.

   f. What did God teach the author that He is teaching all of us
      today? _____
      _____.

10. Read Isaiah 30:15-18

   a. According to the author, what is God telling us today? ____
      _____
      _____
      _____
      _____.

   b. What will happen to us if we don't learn to depend totally
      upon God? Why? _____
      _____
      _____
      _____.

11. Read John 21:18; 21:15-17; Genesis 22; Hebrews 7:25

   a. In the Scripture in John 21:18, the author believes that
      though God was actually speaking to Peter about the type of
      death he would experience, the Lord was also letting Peter
      know something else. What was it? _____
      _____
      _____
      _____
      _____

_____
_____.

b. What was another thing that Father God was also letting him
    know? _____

    _____
    _____
    _____
    _____.

c. When we were baby Christians, we did our own thing. We
    made our own decisions and followed our own course. To
    demonstrate God's providential care, what did He do for us?

    _____
    _____.

d. But when we grow up and become mature Christians, we
    sometimes have to do things we don't particularly want to do
    in the natural realm, in obedience to God's directions. What
    does He no longer do for us?_____

    _____
    _____
    _____.

e. For a while, God allows us to "call the shots," so to speak. He
    lets us do our own thing with His blessing. But what has He
    been doing to us through that time?_____

    _____
    _____.

f. At a certain point, God starts "wrestling" with us to call us into submission to His will rather than ours. What has He begun teaching us?_____

_____

_____.

g. In John 21:15-17, what was the reason Jesus had for asking Peter three times, "Simon Peter, do you love Me?" _____

_____

_____.

h. Like the author, when it seems God is asking us to give up the very work He has given us, is He really asking us to give it up?_____

_____

_____

_____.

i. Why does God ask us to do that? _____

_____

_____

_____.

j. How does God test us?_____

_____

_____

_____.

k. What will happen when we get to the place where we can honestly make the kind of commitment the author made, to give God ourselves, our will, and our love and say, "Your will be done, not mine"? _____

_____.

l. If the Lord loved Peter and knew the plans He had for him, plans to bless him and do him good, not to harm him or cause him pain, why did He have to deal with him?_____

_____

_____.

m. What did Jesus tell Peter and how does that relate to us?

_____

_____.

12. Read Luke 22:31,32

a. In this passage, Jesus did not pray that Peter would be delivered from testing. He prayed that _____

_____

_____

_____.

b. What is Jesus praying for us right now?_____

_____

_____

_____

_____

_____

_____.

c. It is so important we learn to _____

_____ and not always

be looking for somebody else to do it for us.

d. What will happen if we turn our lives over to the Lord totally and completely? _____

_____

_____

_____

_____

_____.

13. Read Luke 10:1-4; Luke 22:35

a. In the passage in Luke 10:1-4, when the Lord sent out the seventy to prepare the way for His arrival, what did He tell them?_____

_____

_____

_____.

b. What is the spiritual principle that the author believes is set forth in this passage? _____

_____

_____

_____

_____

_____

_____

_____.

c. Based on Luke 22:35, if the Lord has sent us out to do His work, it is His responsibility to _____

_____

_____.

d. What has He promised us? _____

_____

_____.

14. Read Matthew 2:1,2,9-11

a. In the Christmas story in this passage, what do we see about Mary and Joseph? _____

_____.

b. If they didn't send out messages asking for gifts, how were their needs met? _____

_____

_____

_____

_____.

c. Explain the basic message of a sermon titled, "The Camels Are Coming" that the author heard preached on this subject in a church in Minnesota. _____

_____

_____

_____

_____

_____

_____.

d. When an avenue in our life is blocked, before we start trying to kick down the door, what do we need to do? Why?_____

_____

_____

_____.

e. Based on Acts 16:7,9, why does God sometimes have to block one avenue? _____

_____.

f. Like the author, rather than getting all riled up and doing something foolish when something we think we need doesn't become ours, what should we do? _____

_____

_____

_____.

g. According to the author, the camels will come for each of us if we will _____

_____.

h. The only way we can expect this kind of provision is by ___

_____

_____

_____.

i. What happens when we begin to believe this? _____

_____

_____

_____

_____

_____

_____.

15. Read 1 Peter 4:19

   a. Based on this passage, in the same way we leave our money
      with bank officials, trusting them to take care of it for us,
      what do we need to do each morning in prayer?_____

      _____

      _____.

   b. When is that especially true?_____

      _____

      _____

      _____

      _____.

   c. When we give ourselves up to God, what must we do? Why?

      _____

      _____

      _____

      _____

      _____.

   d. How did Jesus react when He was abused, reviled, and insult-
      ed? _____

      _____

      _____

      _____

      _____.

e. As followers of Jesus, our Example, we are called to follow His footsteps. Explain. _____
_____
_____
_____
_____
_____.

f. Why do we have no time left to enjoy our lives?_____
_____
_____
_____
_____
_____.

g. What will happen if we get so involved in looking out for ourselves? _____
_____.

h. Whatever happens to us, however we may be treated or mistreated, what must we do?_____
_____
_____
_____
_____.

16. Read Psalm 121:1-8; 17:8

    a. How does the author describe Psalm 121? _____

       _____

       _____

       _____.

    b. According to the author, what should we do with it in the midst of troubled times? _____

       _____.

    c. We have already seen how God has promised to watch over and protect those who take refuge under the shadow of His wings, but how is the pupil of His eye protected, and how does that relate to us? _____

       _____

       _____

       _____

       _____.

17. Read Isaiah 61:6-8; review Hebrews 11:6; read Genesis 15:1

    a. Isaiah 61:6-8 lists some of the rewards God promises His people, and Hebrews 11:6 tells us how we receive those rewards. What does Hebrews 11:6 say of God? _____

       _____

       _____.

    b. So not only is God our Helper and Keeper, He is also the One Who _____ us and _____ us.

     c. Based on Genesis 15:1, what is a recompense? _____

_____

_____.

18.   Read Hebrews 10:30

     a. What does God mean when He says He is the God of justice?

_____

_____

_____

_____.

     b. As Christians, it is not our job to seek vengeance, but to

_____

_____

_____.

     c. If we will do that, God has promised to _____

_____

_____.

     d. God is not only our Helper and Keeper and the One Who rewards and recompenses us, He is also the Righteous Judge. What does He do? _____

_____

_____.

     e. Why do we need to put the Holy Trinity on our case? _____

_____

_____

_____

_____.

Prayer for a
Personal Relationship
With the Lord

God wants you to receive His free gift of salvation. Jesus wants to save you and fill you with the Holy Spirit more than anything. If you have never invited Jesus, the Prince of Peace, to be your Lord and Savior, I invite you to do so now. Pray the following prayer, and if you are really sincere about it, you will experience a new life in Christ.

Father,

You loved the world so much, You gave Your only begotten Son to die for our sins so that whoever believes in Him will not perish, but have eternal life.

Your Word says we are saved by grace through faith as a gift from You. There is nothing we can do to earn salvation.

I believe and confess with my mouth that Jesus Christ is Your Son, the Savior of the world. I believe He died on the cross for me and bore all of my sins, paying the price for them. I believe in my heart that You raised Jesus from the dead.

I ask You to forgive my sins. I confess Jesus as my Lord. According to Your Word, I am saved and will spend eternity with You! Thank You, Father. I am so grateful! In Jesus' name, amen.

See John 3:16; Ephesians 2:8,9; Romans 10:9,10; 1 Corinthians 15:3,4; 1 John 1:9; 4:14-16; 5:1,12,13.

Answers

Introduction

1a. Peace.

1b. To be anxious for nothing and to cast our care on Him.

1c. Don't know how to do.

1d. Muddling along in worry or confusion.

1e. Enjoying the abundant life and peace God has for us!

1f. When she began to study the Word of God and apply it to her life.

1g. Live in His peace as a normal condition.

Part 1: Be Anxious for Nothing

Chapter 1

1a. Willed.

1b. That living in turmoil, worry, anxiety, fear, and frustration for a believer is abnormal.

1c. How to receive and live in it.

1d. That as believers, we have a tremendous amount of His protection on us and around us.

1e. God wants to bless us abundantly and is always looking for ways to bless and reach us with His love so that we will be more open to receiving His blessings.

1f. False.

1g. ". . . For I have overcome the world. [I have deprived it of power to harm you and have conquered it for you]."

1h. "Do not let your hearts be troubled. . . ."

1i. Righteousness, peace, and joy in the Holy Spirit.

1j. It is within us.

1k. When we entered into a personal relationship with Jesus.

1l. Joy and peace.

1m. Through believing.

2a. The God of hope will fill us with all joy and peace as we believe, so that we may abound and be overflowing — bubbling over — with hope.

2b. We who truly believe.

2c. A childlike attitude of faith.

2d. Because the basis of their joy has been misplaced.

2e. Our names are enrolled in heaven.

2f. Believing.

2g. They come as a result of building our relationship with the Lord. Because in His presence is fullness of joy; if we have received Jesus as our Savior and Lord, He, the Prince of Peace lives inside us.

2h. We experience peace in the Lord's presence, receiving from Him and acting in response to His direction.

2i. Knowing, believing — trusting in the Lord with simple childlike faith.

Chapter 2

1a. A heaviness.

1b. As ". . . a state of uneasiness; worry . . . Abnormal fear that lacks a specific cause."[1]

1c. (Your answer.)

2a. "Evil forebodings."

2b. "Little foxes, that spoil the vines."

2c. We won't have much peace or joy.

2d. "Stop it!"

2e. We can see that we can control the way we respond to something that might trouble us. We can choose peace or trouble. We can choose to stay calm or to calm down if we start becoming agitated.

2f. For the Word's sake.

2g. "Cheer up!"

2h. Jesus, Who lives inside those of us who believe in Him, has overcome the world.

2i. By letting the Holy Spirit lead you step-by-step on a path that will take you into freedom!

3a. A peaceful spirit that is not anxious or wrought up.

3b. To be tense, tied in a knot, upset and disturbed.

3c. To be worried, disquieted, or distracted.

3d. He wants to keep us from focusing our attention on the good things God has given us. He wants to keep us from enjoying our relationship with the Lord and the abundant life Jesus died to provide for us.

3e. We need to learn to relax, lighten up, and let things go. We need to learn that even if everything does not always work out exactly as we want it to, it will not be the end of the world.

4a. To take thought or being ". . . apprehensive, or worried about what may happen; concern about a possible future event."[2]

4b. "Anxiety is caused by trying to mentally and emotionally get into things that are not here yet or things that have already been" — mentally leaving where you are and getting into an area of the past or the future.

4c. To be sober-minded, vigilant, and cautious, on our guard against our enemy, the devil, who is out to devour us.

4d. To enjoy the good life God has provided for us through the death and resurrection of His Son Jesus Christ.

4e. "This is the day the Lord has made; I will rejoice and be glad in it."

4f. Laugh. If we would just laugh a little more — "be of good cheer," "cheer up" — we would find that a little bit of laughter makes that load much lighter.

4g. Work on it a little. We need to laugh and have a good time.

5a. To rejoice. Not to fret or have any anxiety about anything but to pray and give thanks to God in everything — not after everything is over.

5b. By learning to enjoy life even in the midst of trying circumstances.

5c. There are many stages we must go through in the course of our spiritual growth.

5d. How to enjoy the glory we are experiencing at each level of our development.

5e. We need to learn to rejoice and be glad in the Lord this day and every day along the way toward our goal.

5f. "He has made me glad; He has made me glad; I will rejoice for He has made me glad."

5g. Presence; presents.

5h. Face.

5i. Find something to be glad about besides our current circumstances.

5j. The devil will see to that because he knows that anxiety in a man's heart weighs it down.

5k. Give that anxiety to the Lord in prayer with thanksgiving, making our requests known to Him. Then the peace that passes all understanding will keep our hearts and minds in Christ Jesus.

6a. Three.

6b. 1. The past and the future. 2. Confrontations and conversations. 3. Duties and obligations of the day.

7a. Mentally leaving where you are and getting into an area of the past or the future.

7b. That God wants us to learn to be "now people."

7c. Learn to live now — mentally as well as physically and spiritually.

7d. Because we are more occupied with the past or the future than we are with the present.

7e. We are to keep a balance in life.

7f. Today.

7g. Because Jesus is always in the present.

7h. We don't need to worry about anything. All we need to do is seek the Kingdom of God, and He will add to us whatever we need, whether it is food or clothing or shelter or spiritual growth.

7i. Because tomorrow will have problems of its own.

7j. Concentrate our full attention on today and stop being so intense and wrought up.

7k. Because it will never come again.

7l. Handle; cast. Because the Lord cares for us.

7m. Learn; prepare; live.

8a. When they went out into the world to preach the Gospel to every creature, as He was commanding them to do, they would run into opposition.

8b. By instructing His disciples not to worry about what to say or even try to figure out or meditate upon it, because when they opened their mouths to speak, it would not be them speaking but the Holy Spirit within them.

8c. You think the outcome of that conversation depends upon you and your ability rather than upon the Holy Spirit and His ability.

8d. We are not trusting in the anointing of God but in ourselves.

8e. We will not do as well as if we were depending completely on God!

8f. Favor. Then we can be confident that whatever the results of our conversation or confrontation, it is the will of God, and it will work out for the best for all concerned.

9a. Martha is upset and distracted because she is overly occupied and too busy, while Mary is happily seated at the feet of Jesus enjoying His presence and fellowship.

9b. That she could not enjoy life because she was too complicated.

9c. She needed to learn to be more like Mary and less like Martha. Instead of worrying and fretting, she needed to learn to simplify her plans, lighten up, and enjoy life!

9d. (Your answers.)

Chapter 3

1a. The arm of the flesh and the arm of the Lord.

1b. One of these is "our deal," the other is "God's deal"; that is, one is based on human ideas and effort, the other is based on God's plan and power. One is of the flesh, the other is of the Spirit.

1c. Maintained; maintained.

1d. When we try to operate in the arm of the flesh we end up frustrated, but when we operate in the arm of the Lord we end up victorious.

1e. It is hard work to carry out the plans and schemes we ourselves have devised. But when God starts something, He carries it through to completion without any struggle on our part.

1f. Often the problem is not the devil but ourselves. We are trying to accomplish our will and plan, not the will and plan of God.

1g. Operating in the arm of the flesh rather than the arm of the Lord.

1h. He will finish it.

2a. The adversary will oppose us.

2b. That greater is He Who is in us than he who is in the world.

2c. Although he may come at us one way, he will have to flee from us seven ways.

2d. Sometimes we spend more time talking about Satan than we do talking about God.

2e. When He appeared on the scene, they either fled in terror or were driven out by Him with a word.

2f. Stand strong in the authority given us by Jesus.

2g. Stay in God's will and plan by operating in the arm of the Lord and not the arm of the flesh.

2h. They try to resist the devil without submitting themselves to God!

2i. A mature individual is patient and waits on the Lord to work out things according to His perfect will and timing. Immature people rush ahead of God and end up frustrated.

2j. She give birth to Ishmaels instead of Isaacs.

3a. That He would bless him and give him an heir from his own body so that his descendants would be as numerous as the stars in the heavens.

3b. A plan to produce an heir for Abraham by having him take her handmaid Hagar as his "secondary wife."

3c. The Lord appeared to Abraham and again promised to bless him and make him the father of many nations. He then went on to bless Sarah and promised to give Abraham a son by her in their old age.

3d. It was through this promised son, Isaac, and not through the natural son, Ishmael. Isaac was God's idea and plan; Ishmael was Sarah's idea and plan. One was the child of promise, the child of the Spirit; the other was the child of human effort, the child of the flesh.

3e. Ishmael caused problems in the household, so Abraham had to send Ishmael and his mother Hagar away.

3f. Because we have produced Ishmaels rather than Isaacs. We are reaping the consequences of trying to carry out our own ideas and plans rather than waiting for God to bring forth His ideas and plans.

3g. We get angry at God because He is not making everything work out as we want it to.

3h. That what is born of the Spirit is spirit, and what is born of the flesh is flesh.

4a. He told us that it is the Spirit Who is important, not the flesh. Because the Spirit gives life while the flesh profits nothing.

4b. The flesh — the selfish, rebellious sin nature within us — has to die.

4c. Within us; the outside.

4d. He described how miserable he was because he failed to practice the good deeds he desired to do, but succeeded in doing the evil deeds he did not want to do.

4e. He cried out, "O unhappy and pitiable and wretched man that I am! Who will release and deliver me from [the shackles of] this body of death?"

4f. All of that is a testing ground, one which we must all go through.

4g. To teach us to deny the flesh and depend on the Spirit in order to build character in us as we go through the hard times and refuse to give up.

4h. If we are committed to doing what God has told us to do.

4i. Instead of getting God's plan and being obedient to Him as He works it out, we try to make up our own plan and get Him to bless it.

4j. We get angry at Him; we get confused and often very negative in our emotions and conversations.

4k. Because He didn't make their plan work. (Your answer.)

4l. We are trying to kick doors open and make our own way.

4m. We should wait on the Lord, believe and trust in Him, and enjoy where we are and what we are doing until He opens the doors for us.

4n. To believe, not to cook up all kinds of plans and schemes to try to make things happen.

4o. Leading; "trying."

4p. The discovery that we are all wrong sometimes.

4q. We try to live by the flesh, by works, rather than by the Spirit.

5a. The covenant of works and the covenant of grace.

5b. On man's doing everything on his own, struggling, striving, and laboring to be acceptable to God.

5c. It steals joy and peace.

5d. It is based not on what man can do, but on what Christ has already done.

5e. It takes the pressure off of us to perform.

5f. One brings bondage; the other brings liberty.

5g. Believe; believe; act on what God tells us to do.

5h. They have no hope, peace, or joy.

5i. Be bubbling over with joy. We will also see much more positive results in our lives.

6a. Those who do not labor to bring forth their own results but who depend entirely upon the grace of God will enjoy more results than those who wear themselves out trying to produce by their own efforts.

6b. Because God's people are trying to do with the arm of flesh what can only be done by the arm of the Lord.

6c. Because the writers of these Scriptures are talking about spiritual, not natural, children.

6d. It means that she has given up trying to give birth the natural way. Instead, she has learned to put her faith and trust in God to give birth spiritually. She has ceased from her labor and has entered the rest of God.

6e. They end up having more children — enjoying more and better results — than those who try to produce by their own works.

7a. False.

7b. That we can have inexpressible, glorious, triumphant, heavenly joy right in the very midst of our trials and temptations.

7c. We need to ask why not.

7d. Something can be available to us yet never be of any benefit to us because we never avail ourselves of it.

7e. We will live in the frustration of works.

7f. "Works of the flesh."

7g. We only benefit from the blessings of the covenant of grace by living under grace. As long as we live under works, we will be frustrated and depressed because we are trying to do God's job.

7h. To be our Helper in life.

7i. Because they don't want any help. They want to do everything for themselves.

7j. By simply asking for it.

7k. Because asking for help is an acknowledgment that we are not able to do everything for ourselves.

8a. If we are full of pride and doing things our own way without listening to Him, we will end up in situations that will result in anxiety and stress.

8b. He is trying to set us up for a blessing. Or He may be trying to protect us from something we don't know about.

8c. Because it will keep us from experiencing peace and joy in this life.

8d. To overcome all of our evil tendencies.

8e. Exactly what Peter said in his first letter to the believers: ". . . God sets Himself against the proud and haughty, but gives grace [continually] to the lowly (those who are humble enough to receive it)."

8f. "Humble yourselves [feeling very insignificant] in the presence of the Lord, and He will exalt you [He will lift you up and make your lives significant]."

8g. By humbling ourselves before Him, casting all our cares upon Him, and trusting Him to take care of them as He has promised in His Word.

8h. Because they think they can handle everything for themselves.

8i. Because they know they can't handle everything — only God can.

9a. "Except the Lord builds the house, they labor in vain who build it. . . ."

9b. Us.

9c. We are.

9d. Building; Chief Cornerstone.

9e. One brick at a time, day by day, from glory to glory.

9f. The difference between works and faith.

10a. Having begun our new lives in Christ by dependence on the Spirit, are we now trying to live them in the flesh?

10b. By grace (God's unmerited favor) through faith, and not by works of the flesh.

10c. We are still in no condition to help ourselves!

10d. (Your answer.)

10e. By submitting ourselves to God and letting Him do the work in us that needs to be done.

10f. Only the Spirit.

11a. ". . . the perfecting and the full equipping of the saints (His consecrated people), [that they should do] the work of ministering toward building up Christ's body (the church). . . ."

11b. ". . . really mature manhood. . . ."

11c. ". . . (the completeness of personality which is nothing less than the standard height of Christ's own perfection), the measure of the stature of the fullness of the Christ and the completeness found in Him."

11d. (Your answer.)

11e. To mature and be Christlike in our attitude and behavior, to know Jesus and the power of His resurrection, to measure up to His stature and operate in the fruit of His Spirit.

11f. Be willing to be changed and humbly submit ourselves to the Lord, allowing Him to build us into the people He wants us to be.

11g. Through faith.

12a. The leaning of the entire human personality on God in absolute trust and confidence in His power, wisdom, and goodness.

12b. To abide in the Lord, to lean on Him totally and completely, to put our trust and confidence in Him.

12c. Confess those sins. We get into agreement with God about them.

12d. Acknowledge our inability to do anything about our sins. The more we try to change ourselves, the worse we get.

12e. Believe.

12f. Cleave to, trust in, rely on, and have faith in Him and His Son Jesus Christ.

12g. Anxious or worried. Build ourselves; build us and equip us.

13a. God; Jesus.

13b. Build us and equip us.

13c. "It was God Who started this work in you, and it is God Who will finish it!"

13d. That means we should leave God alone to do His work.

13e. We are to confess our sins and failures to the Lord, confident that He will forgive us of those sins and failures and cleanse us from all unrighteousness, as He has promised in His Word.

13f. That takes the pressure off of us, which relieves us of the worry and anxiety we feel so often as we try to perfect ourselves.

14a. Stay away from wrong behavior and allow the Lord of peace Himself to sanctify us, preserve us, complete us, hallow us, and keep us.

14b. They are our call from God to a certain kind of holy living. They are also our assurance that it is not we who bring about this holy life, but God Himself, Who can be trusted utterly to do the work in and for us.

14c. Our part is to believe. Our work is to trust the Lord. His requirement is that we let go and let God.

15a. To build us.

15b. Ourselves.

15c. Our ministry.

15d. Our reputation.

16a. The choice between pleasing men and pleasing God.

16b. Our Lord did not set out to make a name for Himself, and neither should we.

16c. It will cause us to live in fear of man rather than in fear of God. We will try to win favor with people rather than with the Lord.

16d. ". . . stand fast then, and do not be hampered and held ensnared and submit again to a yoke of slavery [which you have once put off]."

16e. The threat of rejection.

16f. Are we going to go on trying to build ourselves, our ministries, and our reputations, or are we willing to give up all our human efforts and simply trust God? Are we ready to stop operating in the arm of the flesh and start operating in the arm of the Lord?

Chapter 4

1a. While the arm of the flesh is based on the covenant of works, the arm of the Lord is based on the covenant of grace.

1b. The first depends upon law, the second depends upon faith.

1c. Under the first covenant we wear ourselves out trying to make things happen on our own. Under the second covenant we enter into the rest of God and depend upon Him to do for us what we cannot do for ourselves.

1d. To present our bodies as a living sacrifice, holy and well pleasing to God, which is our reasonable service and spiritual worship.

1e. 1) Willing, 2) yielded, and 3) empty.

1f. We must be willing for God to use us as He sees fit. We must be willing to follow His plans rather than our own. We must be empty of ourselves.

1g. Give up all our human efforts to build ourselves, our ministries, and our careers and allow the Lord to build them for us according to His will and plan for us. Learn to be satisfied where we are and with what we are doing. Quit worrying and fretting and simply allow the Lord to do the work in us and through us that He knows needs to be done.

1h. Quit looking to the arm of the flesh and start looking to the arm of the Lord.

2a. The mistake he made was telling that dream, because it was one of the things that made his brothers so hateful, envious, and angry that they tried to get rid of him by selling him into slavery.

2b. Joseph was a little overly exuberant.

2c. When God reveals to us His dream and vision for our life, we share it with others who are not as thrilled about it as we are and who may even cause us problems, just as Joseph's brothers did for him.

2d. Joseph ended up alone in a prison cell in Egypt far from home and family with no one to turn to but the Lord.

2e. Periods in which we have to stand alone.

2f. We are forced to place our entire faith and trust in God.

2g. The arm of the Lord; the arm of the flesh.

2h. We may follow the advice people give us instead of seeking God's direction.

2i. Most birds fly in flocks, but eagles fly alone.

2j. We must decide whether we want to fly along as one of the many birds in a flock or be an eagle.

2k. Learn to fly alone.

2l. But God was with him.

3a. He built his reputation and career. He put him in the right place at the right time. He gave him favor with the right people and promoted him when the time was right.

3b. When God is ready to move in our lives, He will give us favor and promotion.

3c. ". . . If God is for us, who [can be] against us? [Who can be our foe, if God is on our side?]"

3d. People who are willing, yielded, and empty.

3e. Let God build you, your ministry, and your reputation and career. When the time is right, He will deliver you just as He delivered Joseph. Then you will see the fulfillment of your dream, just as Joseph did.

4a. Regardless of what people may have tried to do to us, God can take it and turn it for good.

4b. Meant good to him.

4c. He knew it didn't matter who was against him, because God was for him and would eventually work out everything for the best for all concerned. He knew that whatever happened, God was on his side.

4d. He let God build his life, his reputation, and his career.

5a. God went to work on her and began to change her.

5b. He will do the same for you, if you will keep your eyes on Him and not on yourself.

6a. Either we will spend our lives trying to take care of ourselves or we will let go and let God take care of us as we put our faith and trust in Him.

6b. Because all flesh is as frail as grass. Like the flowers of the field, it is here today and gone tomorrow.

6c. We must humble ourselves under His mighty hand and wait upon Him to exalt us in His good time.

7a. It means to submit all our plans to Him to work them out according to His will and desire for us.

7b. What He wants is for us to come to know Him in the power of His resurrection and to behold Him in all His beauty and glory.

7c. To dwell in God's presence. Because only there can we experience the fullness of joy.

7d. His hand is always open to us.

7e. To grow up in all things unto the stature of His Son Jesus Christ.

7f. Should; want; should.

8a. ". . . If the Lord is willing, we shall live and we shall do this or that [thing]."

8b. What God wants.

8c. Better for us in the long run.

8d. When we do that, we are showing Him disrespect by not acknowledging Him in our plans.

8e. It says, "Pride goes before destruction, and a haughty spirit before a fall."

8f. Humility.

8g. So that He may exalt us in due time.

8h. By waiting on the Lord, refusing to move in the energy of the flesh.

8i. Acknowledge; honors; our heart's desire!

8j. Attitude.

9a. Knowing who we are in Jesus.

9b. To recognize we are empty.

9c. The power of God that is resident there to flow out of us.

9d. Nothing.

9e. Only the value the Lord assigns to us because of the blood of His Son Jesus Christ.

9f. What is born of flesh is flesh, and it profits us nothing.

9g. He said, ". . . the life I now live in the body I live by faith in (by adherence to and reliance on and complete trust in) the Son of God. . . ."

9h. The Lord ". . . will continue until the day of Jesus Christ [right up to the time of His return], developing [that good work] and perfecting and bringing it to full completion . . . ."

9i. We will all eventually be like the woman in 2 Kings 4:1-7 — empty of ourselves and ready to be used by God to fill other empty people.

9j. We must realize and acknowledge what we cannot do. We must get our eyes off of ourselves and our limited ability, and totally onto Him and His infinite power.

10a. 1) "We have no might to stand against this great company that is coming against us," 2) "We do not know what to do," and 3) "But our eyes are on You."

10b. When we reach the place of being able to make these three statements to the Lord in total honesty and complete dependence upon Him.

10c. The answer may be that we are still too full of ourselves.

10d. We won't let go of it.

11a. 1) Acknowledge we have no power to save ourselves, 2) admit we do not know what to do about our situation, and 3) turn our eyes upon the Lord, placing our faith and trust in Him to deliver us.

11b. Once we stop looking to the arm of flesh for our solution.

11c. "Be still."

11d. "Let God arise and His enemies be scattered!"

11e. That when He rises up, every knee shall bow and every tongue shall confess that Jesus Christ is Lord, to the glory of God the Father.

11f. He told them to take up their positions, stand still, and see the deliverance of the Lord.

11g. Because God was with them.

11h. All the people bowed their faces to the ground and worshipped the Lord.

11i. Planning; scheming; trying to tell God what He needs to do.

11j. Resists; gives grace.

12a. "God helps those who help themselves"; unscriptural.

12b. Cannot help themselves; depend not upon our own efforts, plans, and schemes to get us through this life and solve all our problems.

12c. This statement tends to make people feel as though they need to do all they possibly can for themselves before ever asking God to help.

12d. Believe that lie and spend our lives in frustration trying to take care of ourselves rather than leaning on God.

12e. Those who know they cannot help themselves, those who, like King Jehoshaphat and the people of Judah, realize that they are totally dependent upon Him for their deliverance.

13a. The everlasting arms of the Lord coming down and lifting us up.

13b. We should experience the manifest presence of God with us as we make the conscious decision to no longer lean on the arm of the flesh, but on the arm of the Lord.

14a. Looking to the Lord and trusting in His wisdom, strength, and power.

14b. The One Who is with us is greater than all those who oppose us.

14c. They are like a plant in the desert that is dry and destitute. They will not see any good come.

14d. They are like a tree planted by a river. They do not cease to produce fruit even in the midst of a drought. No matter what comes, they will flourish and ". . . shall not be anxious and full of care. . . ."

14e. We are not to lean on ourselves or on other people, but on God.

14f. Love; trust.

15a. Because He knew what was in human nature.

15b. He just didn't open Himself up to them and give Himself to them in the same way He trusted God and opened Himself up to His heavenly Father.

15c. Because we form relationships with people we should not be involved with. We become too familiar with them, start depending upon then idolizing them, and looking to them when we should be looking to God.

15d. It happens because we are not perfect.

15e. The strong arm of the Lord.

15f. We always end up disappointed and hurt.

Chapter 5

1a. We ". . . do enter that [God's] rest. . . ."

1b. Simply by refusing to become upset.

1c. We are in this world, but not of it.

1d. Hard times: "hard to deal with and hard to bear."

1e. The times we are living in today and one action we are to take.

1f. ". . . out of them all the Lord delivered me."

1g. What our response to living in this kind of atmosphere and situation should be.

1h. Instead of stopping to check with their heart to see if it is right, they find someone who teaches what they want to hear and go there.

1i. Truth; teaching; counsel.

1j. "I am to be calm, cool, and collected"!

1k. "A wild spirit."

1l. Make sure we are acting in obedience to the leading of the Lord and not just reacting out of emotion.

1m. That works not energized by God are "dead works" and do not produce any good result.

2a. We are to take a stand, after having done all in our power that God has led us to do.

2b. What we do to overcome one crisis may not be what we are to do to handle the next crisis that arises.

2c. Because the solution to the problem is not in the procedure, it is in the power — which God gives us to accomplish what He directs us to do.

2d. Different; different; different.

2e. The power of God flowing through Jesus.

2f. Release the faith within each person to whom He ministered.

2g. Faith.

3a. ". . . because it was not mixed with faith (with the leaning of the entire personality on God in absolute trust and confidence in His power, wisdom, and goodness) by those who heard it. . . ."

3b. Because if we are not abiding in His rest, we are not operating in true faith.

3c. That without faith it is impossible to please God.

3d. Place. Secret place. The presence of the Lord.

3e. Because we know that in the presence of the Lord there is joy, peace, and rest.

4a. He assured Moses His presence would be with him and give him rest.

4b. All that Moses needed.

4c. His presence will be with us wherever He sends us and in whatever He gives us to do.

4d. Stay relaxed and trust God to show us what to do.

4e. If it was God Who ruined our plan, we had the wrong plan to begin with. If it was the devil who ruined our plan, the Lord will give us another plan, one that will be ten times better than the one that failed.

4f. We start rebuking the devil.

4g. We talk to the wrong person.

4h. Learn to turn to the Lord and say, "Father, You are my Refuge and my Fortress, my God; on You I lean and rely, and in You I confidently trust."

5a. Of the person who dwells in the secret place of the Most High, who claims the Lord as his Refuge and Fortress, and who leans, relies, and confidently trusts in Him.

5b. All the promises of God's provision and protection.

5c. Basically, they are that we stay in rest.

5d. The "wild spirit" that so often motivates us to lose our self-control so that we say and do things that cause pain and problems for us as well as for others.

5e. Promises; presence; peace.

6a. His peace.

6b. ". . . Peace to you!"

6c. To live in peace.

6d. "Stop allowing yourselves to be anxious, worried, and upset."

6e. We need to hope in God and wait expectantly for Him, Who is our Help and our God.

6f. Peace; place.

7a. Seated at the right hand of God the Father in heavenly places.

7b. Seated also.

8a. The Word of God; the Upholder, Sustainer, and Redeemer of the universe; at the right hand of God on high.

8b. God; footstool.

9a. By speaking forth the Word of God in faith.

9b. That we are not the ones who exercise ultimate power and authority over the enemy.

9c. It means that although Jesus has given us power and authority over the devil and his demons on this earth, in the end it is God Himself Who is ultimately going to take away from Satan every bit of his power and send him to his final place of eternal punishment.

10a. He is waiting ". . . until His enemies should be made a stool beneath His feet."

10b. Because under the covenant of works the people were not allowed to sit down and rest.

10c. After Jesus had gone into the true Holy of Holies and sprinkled His own blood on the heavenly altar.

10d. He had to be ministering to the Lord.

10e. He said to Him, "Well done. Your work is finished. Sit here at My right hand until I make your enemies Your footstool."

10f. He wants us to know we are seated at His right hand with His Son Jesus Christ.

10g. We can enter into His throne room and find rest for our souls.

11a. God wants us not only to enter into His rest in our body, He also wants us to enter into His rest in our soul.

11b. It means finding freedom from mental activity. It means not having to constantly try to figure out what we should do about everything in our life. It means not having to live in torment of reasoning, always trying to come up with an answer we don't have. We don't have to worry; instead we can remain calm in a place of quiet peace and rest.

11c. Speak to our raging soul and tortured mind just as Jesus spoke to the wind and waves by simply saying: "Peace, be still."

11d. We are walking in authority over Satan.

12a. By our ". . . steadfastness and patient endurance. . . ."

12b. Let our mind and emotions get the best of us, especially when it involves things we have no control over.

12c. Do the rest.

12d. What God protected us from.

12e. Learn to possess our souls and not give the devil a foothold in our lives.

13a. Our soul rises up and causes strife.

13b. Because many times the thing we think we don't want is the best thing for us.

13c. We need to learn to adapt, to let things go, to quit allowing our souls to rule our lives. We need to learn to walk by the Spirit and not by the flesh.

13d. We throw open the door for the devil. We give him an opportunity to come in and wreak havoc.

13e. Choose to honor Him by staying in peace.

13f. No. It just means we need to manage our feelings and not let them manage us.

14a. Our constancy and fearlessness.

14b. Our constancy and fearlessness in the face of his onset.

14c. Often it is because God is waiting to see if we really trust Him or not.

14d. Think we have to be up and running around doing something, like the Old Testament priests in the Holy of Holies.

14e. "I'm going to stay seated in Christ and enjoy the rest of the Lord while He handles this situation and uses it to bless me."

15a. To build our spiritual character as well as our spiritual power.

15b. To overcome every problem of life by rebuking the devil.

15c. He is working to get us to the point where, no matter what is going on around us, we remain the same, rooted and grounded in Christ and His love, standing firm on the Rock of our salvation.

15d. So He can give us power to keep ourselves calm in the days of adversity.

15e. Wait patiently and confidently for our promised deliverance and salvation, and for the impending destruction of all our enemies.

15f. Anxious for nothing.

Part 2: Cast All Your Care

Introduction

1a. Because He cares for us.

1b. God wants to take care of us.

1c. We must stop taking the care upon ourselves and start casting it upon Him.

1d. He will give us something in return.

2a. To give us several positive things in exchange for the negative things in our lives.

2b. To give us beauty for ashes.

2c. He cannot give us His beauty.

2d. Be willing to give Him the messes in our lives.

2e. Blessings; messes.

3a. Not to be anxious about anything but to turn from the arm of the flesh and depend upon the arm of the Lord as we remain calm — quietly and confidently seated with Christ in heavenly places.

3b. Several issues relating to our care.

Chapter 6

1a. Many of the blessings offered us by the Lord in exchange for our "messes."

1b. Meet the conditions of the first two verses, which is that we dwell in the secret place of the Most High, remaining stable and fixed under the shadow of the Almighty.

1c. First, we must *dwell,* which means "to remain . . . to settle . . . continue . . . sit (-down)."[1]

1d. Second, we must dwell in the "secret place" of the Most High, meaning a hiding place, a place of protection, a place with a covering over it so we will be kept safe from all our enemies.

1e. Third, we must remain under the "shadow" of the Almighty, meaning we must make the Lord our Refuge and our Fortress, leaning and relying on Him and confidently trusting in Him.

2. He will deliver us, cover us, keep us from fear and terror, and protect us against evil plots and slander so that we have no fear of pestilence, destruction, or sudden death, even though others may be falling from these things all around us.

3a. God promises angelic protection and deliverance to those who are serving Him and walking in obedience to Him.

3b. In a position of power and authority over Satan and his demons and devices.

3c. Favor; influence.

3d. It means we are protected from what Satan ultimately has planned for us as long as we keep our trust in God and say the right things of Him.

3e. We must learn it is a process.

3f. The Lord promises us that when we call upon Him, He will answer us and be with us in our troubles and will strengthen us and accompany us through them to victory, deliverance, and honor.

3g. God is with us in our trials and troubles, then He begins to deliver us out of them, and afterwards He honors us.

4a. Instead of getting all anxious and upset and weeping and wailing, go into the secret place of the Lord and lift up shouts of joy while the devil is trying to destroy us. Find refuge and remain stable and fixed under the shadow of the Almighty.

4b. He fights our battles.

5a. A shadow is a shade, a protection from the heat or the sun. It is also a border between light and dark.

5b. There are definite borders or limits within which we must stay if we are to remain under the shadow of God's wings — that is, under His protection against the world or the devil.

5c. We will be much more comfortable and much better protected against danger than when we choose to walk out from under those wings.

5d. Take up permanent residence there.

5e. Trust and confidence.

5f. He will keep us under the shadow of His wings and protect us from all danger and harm.

6a. "Pray and don't worry."

6b. Because prayer is supposed to be the way we cast our care upon the Lord.

6c. Turn and give that care to God.

6d. In prayer. That's what prayer is, our acknowledgment to the Lord that we cannot carry our burden of care, so we lay it all on Him.

6e. We are mixing a positive and a negative. The two cancel each other out so that we end up right back where we started — at zero.

6f. They cancel out their positive prayer power by giving in to the negative power of worry.

6g. As long as we are worrying, we are not trusting God. It is only by trusting, by having faith and confidence in the Lord, that we are able to enter into His rest and enjoy the peace that transcends all understanding.

7a. Believing. Because the fruit of believing is rest.

7b. We have entered into His rest.

7c. Abiding in the perfect peace of His holy presence.

8a. Experience with God.

8b. Years of experience.

8c. The patience, endurance, and character that will eventually produce the habit of joyful and confident hope.

8d. Experience; strength. Stronger.

8e. Sooner or later we will be more than the devil can handle.

8f. Spiritual maturity.

8g. In secret. Privately.

8h. The intended work never gets accomplished.

8i. He works them out for our good.

9a. That He would be silent and submissive, a sign of His inner strength and stability.

9b. We get to know the Lord and, like the apostle Paul, learn to be quiet and confident in whatever circumstances we may find ourselves.

10a. The ability to be content in whatever state he found himself.

10b. He knew how to cast his cares upon the Lord and remain in the secret place under the shadow of His wings.

10c. He knew how to live day by day without being disturbed or disquieted.

10d. He said it was something he had learned to do — and that takes time and experience.

10e. If we keep following the Lord, being faithful and obedient to Him regardless of what may happen to us.

11a. He will continually tempt us to "take the road of worry" so he can lead us off into destruction.

11b. We can remain within the boundaries of God's guidance and protection.

11c. Trust the Lord to lead us in the way we should go and get us safely to our final destination.

11d. When we begin to lose our peace.

11e. Be sensitive to our lack of peace and find the reason for it so we can correct the problem and move back into the way of the Lord.

11f. To trust in the Lord not just with our heart, but with our heart and our mind.

11g. Entire human personality; trust; confidence.

11h. He means totally, completely. He means we are to trust Him mentally and emotionally as well as spiritually.

11i. Being in constant turmoil and confusion.

12a. About the futility of worry and anxiety.

12b. Read these verses out loud.

12c. To stop being perpetually uneasy, worried, and anxious.

12d. Because when we do that we are not only harming ourselves, we are also being disobedient to God.

12e. Just as God feeds the birds and animals and even clothes the grass and flowers of the field, so He will feed and clothe those of us who put our faith and trust in Him.

12f. Our heavenly Father knows all the things we have need of and that He has promised to provide them for us.

12g. We are to seek first God's Kingdom and His righteousness, and then all these other things will be given to us as well.

12h. Simply because we have the wrong priorities. We are seeking security in the things of this world rather than in the Creator of this world.

12i. He has promised to provide all the answers we need.

12j. We are told to seek God and His righteousness, trusting Him to provide all these other things He knows we need in accordance with His divine plan and timing.

13a. That he might dwell in the presence of the Lord and behold His beauty all the days of his life.

13b. If we seek to dwell in the secret place of the Most High, leaning and relying on Him in confidence and trust, He will add to us all the blessings He has promised in the rest of that psalm.

13c. We are not to seek after the things of this life, but to seek first God's Kingdom and His righteousness.

13d. We are not to be worried or anxious about tomorrow, because tomorrow will have worries and anxieties of its own; it is enough for us to deal with each day's cares as they arise.

13e. How we are to deal with each day's cares — by casting them all on the Lord Who cares for us affectionately and cares about us watchfully.

13f. We are told to fret not ourselves and to avoid anxious thoughts, which can quickly become irritating. Instead, we are to place our faith and confidence in the Lord, Who is our Refuge and our Fortress.

14a. Not God plus something else, but God only.

14b. We should do as David did and climb up on the rock that is higher than we are.

14c. A castle, a fort, a defense, a place into which we go when we are being hunted or attacked. It is not a hiding place in which our enemy cannot find us. It is a place of protection in which we can see and be seen but cannot be reached because we are safe in God's protection.

14d. His High Tower — another lofty and inaccessible place — and his Shield and Buckler — which are part of the protective armor that surrounds the believer.

14e. He is not just above us and around us, He is even underneath us.

14f. He is holding us up by His powerful right hand and is surrounding us as the mountains surround the holy city of Jerusalem.

14g. For; over; with; in.

14h. He watches over us and keeps us so we can find rest and peace under the shadow of His wings as we cast all our care upon Him.

Chapter 7

1a. Care; responsibility.

1b. We do just the opposite; we cast our responsibility, but keep our care.

1c. Casting our care; being passive.

1d. To believe.

1e. Because if God has told us something, we should have no problem believing it and doing what He says for us to do.

1f. To cast all of our care upon Him, which itself can be something of a violent matter.

2a. Because it refers to throwing, hurling, arising, sending, striking, thrusting, driving out, or expelling — all rather forceful terms.[1]

2b. He said that since the days of John the Baptist, the Kingdom of God has endured violent assault, and violent men have seized it by force.

2c. We are going to have to get violent — spiritually violent — about casting our care upon the Lord and abiding in the secret place of the Most High, under the shadow of the Almighty.

2d. In our absolute refusal to live any longer under guilt and condemnation, which can actually be worry about past mistakes.

2e. He pressed on to take hold of those things for which Christ Jesus had laid hold on him.

2f. Rise up against the principalities, powers, and wickedness in high places; all the blessings bought for us by Jesus Christ.

2g. The devil and his demons.

2h. We can resist and resist Satan and the guilt, condemnation, worry, and anxiety he tries to place on us, until we get so fed up we react with a holy anger.

2i. We can stop and violently take back what Satan is trying to take from us by saying, "No! I will not carry that care. I am casting it upon the Lord!"

2j. We need to engage in some holy violence. When we feel the devil starting to lay any kind of guilt, condemnation, and care upon us, we need to take it and cast it upon the Lord.

2k. We need to cast them upon the Lord.

2l. "'To draw in different directions, distract' hence signifies 'that which causes this, a care, especially an anxious care.'"[2]

2m. To distract us from our fellowship with God.

2n. What our responsibility is and what it is not.

3a. ". . . a momentary and complete casting of one's anxiety, once for all, upon God. . . . "[3]

3b. ". . . one makes a complete surrender of himself and his all to God for Him to manage at His will. . . . "[4]

3c. ". . . reach the place where all anxiety leaves him, regardless of the outward testings that may fall to his lot."[5]

3d. The sin of independence.

3e. An immature Christian.

3f. We want to do everything for ourselves — and we end up making a terrible mess of things.

3g. Learn to cast all our care upon Him permanently.

3h. By placing ourselves totally into God's hands and allowing Him to be the Manager of our life.

3i. Our first responsibility is to trust God. The second is not to try to take His place.

4a. Our; God's; His part; "play God."

4b. God.

4c. The Holy Spirit.

4d. We are trying to do the work of the Holy Spirit.

4e. We must stop trying to play God in our own life and in the lives of other people. We must let God be God.

5a. Guidance; counsel; direction.

5b. Inform Him of what is going on; what He needs to do about it.

5c. It is our job to listen to God and let Him tell us what is going on and what we are to do about it — leaving the rest to Him to work out according to His knowledge and will, not ours.

5d. Because He is greater than we are in every aspect and area.

5e. He will teach us His ways.

6a. He is not on trial.

6b. We may be praying out of the will of God.

6c. Their inability to distinguish between God's will and personal ambition.

6d. Usually it's because what we are asking is what we want, so we assume it must be what God wants too.

6e. Some discernment.

6f. His timing. Patience and trust.

6g. Because we already have our mind made up about the way things are supposed to be, even before we go to God in prayer about them.

6h. They are really just PR sessions in which we try to manipulate God to get what we want from Him.

6i. Although we are asking, we are doing so with the wrong purpose and motives.

7a. Because we try to make things happen on our own instead of simply asking that God's will be done.

7b. Because we ask with the wrong purpose or with the wrong motives.

7c. It's because He has something better in mind for us, but we are not yet spiritually mature enough to know how to ask Him for it.

8a. She has learned not to ask Him for anything out of His will.

8b. She always prays for what she wants to have or would like to see happen, but she follows her request with this statement: "Lord, if what I am asking for is not Your will, please don't give it to me. I want Your will more than I want my own."

8c. Seek first His will and His righteousness, trusting Him to add to us all the things He knows we really need, the things that will bless us and not be a burden to us or draw us away from Him.

8d. Even if He gives them to us, having them will only cause us to sin.

8e. Spiritual life; outward blessings.

8f. God must become and always remain first in our lives.

8g. We must regularly examine our priorities and be sure they are in proper order.

8h. No, not at all. It simply means we are to trust in the Lord and put our confidence in Him.

8i. He will show us when we need to rise up against the evil spirits that come to deceive us and destroy us. If we listen to Him, we will not be so quick to start rebuking every situation that arises or every circumstance in which we find ourselves.

8j. Because sometimes what we think would be a wonderful blessing would not bless us at all.

8k. If we do, we will have to spend the rest of our days taking care of them.

8l. We need to learn to wait for God to bring forth the Isaacs in our life. They will be a blessing to us for as long as we live.

9a. Criticize, contradict, or answer back to God. We are not to ask God, "Why did You make me this way?"

9b. Potter; clay.

9c. Why He made others as they are.

9d. We are going to be unhappy.

9e. We can be used and blessed by Him as He sees fit.

9f. No. It means dishonorable in the eyes of those who do not understand God's purpose, those who think some people are more honorable and some work more important than others.

9g. We must each accept the role God has assigned us and submit ourselves to Him to mold and make us after His will and plan, and not ours.

9h. Grace is with us. Operating outside of His anointing.

9i. Now we know only in part.

9j. Trust; obey; cast our care.

10a. Our first responsibility is to trust God. Our second responsibility is to pray without worry. Our third responsibility is to avoid works of the flesh.

10b. We can be so intense we become obsessive about it, even in our prayer life.

10c. Just another work of the flesh.

10d. Being led by the Spirit.

10e. We cancel out our prayers. They become nothing more than a work of the flesh, an attempt to change things by our own energy and effort.

11a. Works.

11b. "Work" is doing by the grace of God what He has called us to do. It is the expending of our energy and effort to see the will of God come to pass in our life. But "works" is doing by our own strength and ability what we want done. It is the expending of our energy and effort to try to make happen what only God can make happen.

11c. He gives us superhuman energy.

11d. The difference between works of the flesh; the work of the Spirit.

11e. Worry, reasoning, and trying to figure out what to do to make things happen according to our will and timing.

11f. Grace.

11g. Really, truly happy.

11h. To rob us of our joy. Satan doesn't want us to be filled with contentment, peace, and rest. He wants us to be worried, confused, and upset.

11i. To take things into our own hands, as Abraham and Sarah did in the Old Testament.

12a. Abraham agreed and did as Sarah suggested.

12b. As soon as Hagar saw she was pregnant with Abraham's child, she despised Sarah and began to treat her with contempt.

12c. Sarah complained to Abraham saying, "May the responsibility for this terrible situation be upon you!"

12d. Because by agreeing with Sarah's suggestion, he failed to fulfill his God-given responsibility.

12e. Trouble and unhappiness for all concerned: Sarah, Abraham, Hagar, Ishmael, and Isaac.

12f. He was passive. Instead of truly casting his care upon the Lord and trusting Him to work out His divine plan, Abraham went along with his wife's misguided scheme.

12g. Instead of casting our care on the Lord, we cast our responsibility. We become passive, often due to laziness. It just seems to be too much trouble to take a stand on the Word of God and wait for Him to act on our behalf as we confidently trust in Him.

12h. By telling Sarah, "Well, she's your maid, do whatever you want to with her."

12i. By trying to shift it to his wife.

12j. When God questioned Adam about eating from the forbidden tree of the knowledge of good and evil, like Abraham, he tried to shift his responsibility from himself to his wife. He even went so far as to imply it was God's fault for giving Eve to him in the first place.

12k. The job of getting men to be spiritually passive and leave the responsibility for spiritual matters to the women in their lives.

12l. More and more men are beginning to seek God and become the spiritual leaders in their marriages and families.

13a. To trust God, to pray without worry, and to avoid works of the flesh.

13b. To continue in obedience during the time of waiting, to continue to bear good fruit, and to offer God a sacrifice of praise.

14a. Obedience.

14b. Make sure you are sowing seeds of obedience. Because the Lord has promised us that if we do so in patient confidence and trust in Him, we will eventually reap.

14c. God is always working. We just may not be able to see it, because He usually works in secret.

15a. Being formed in secret by the Lord.

15b. A perfect work.

15c. The Lord determined the time was right.

15d. When He knows everything is right for us.

15e. Secretly working behind the scenes. By faith.

15f. Believe He is.

15g. He is working on your behalf right now.

15h. He wants you to untie His hands.

15i. By refusing to worry and by dwelling in the secret place of the Most High, hidden away safe and secure under the shadow of His wings.

16a. Bearing good fruit.

16b. We should be like a tree planted by the water, drawing strength and life from its source because its roots go down deep into the ground. Even in times of drought, such a tree will continue to bear good fruit.

16c. We will still bear the fruit of the Spirit described in Galatians 5:22,23.

16d. Because that kind of attitude and behavior will not bring our answer.

16e. We are not to give in to them, but rather to continue to bear fruit, giving thanks and praise to God even in the midst of negative circumstances.

17a. He acknowledged God had been working secretly in his life from before his birth.

17b. For Who He is and for His wonderful works on his behalf.

17c. While we are waiting to see the fulfillment of our prayers, we are to be continually offering up to God the fruit of lips that thankfully acknowledge and confess and glorify His name.

17d. Cast our care upon the Lord, trusting Him, praying without worry, avoiding works of the flesh, continuing in obedience, bearing good fruit, and offering Him the sacrifice of praise.

Chapter 8

1a. That things will "come to pass."

1b. That in this life whatever exists now, or will exist in the future, is not permanent, but temporary.

1c. It will help us make it through the difficult times in which we find ourselves. It will also help us not to hold on too tightly to the good times, thinking, "If I ever lose all this, I just can't make it."

1d. All of life — not just its destination, but also the trip itself.

2a. (Your answers.)

2b. Moving toward some goal or objective. Another will be there.

2c. Learn to enjoy life as it unfolds.

2d. Life will pass us up and we will never enjoy where we are right now.

3a. Because they were times of preparation for the greater days the Lord knew lay ahead.

3b. Because they never get to enjoy the fruit of all their labor.

3c. Finish it.

3d. Often we are left with nobody to support us and urge us on but ourselves and God.

3e. See it through to the finish. Everything we are going through at the moment will one day pass and we will enjoy the fruit of our labor.

3f. Enjoy where we are on the way to where we are going.

4a. "This is that which was prophesied and has now come to pass."

4b. Then He moves on.

4c. We get caught up in the "This is it" mentality.

4d. Because as soon as we overcome one problem, we will have another one to overcome.

4e. Another.

4f. Prepare us for the next situation, which may be more to our liking.

4g. We can be prepared for something even better.

4h. They help us get more deeply rooted in God. They work humility in us and cause us to be very thankful when the blessings come.

4i. Training, correction, and discipline.

5. No training, correction, or discipline seems pleasant at the time it is being administered to us, "but afterwards" we come to appreciate it.

6a. 1) He will be with us, 2) He will deliver us and honor us, and 3) He will grant us long life and will show us His salvation.

6b. "No matter what you are going through at the moment, sooner or later it will pass. Someday it will all be over and done. In the meantime, cast your care upon Me and trust Me to work out everything for the best."

7a. Change us.

7b. Best friend.

7c. Things that we think are absolutely too difficult to endure.

7d. The time when the situation will be over.

7e. The fruit you are going to bear "afterwards."

7f. Realize that God is building faith in you, and "afterwards" that faith will be used to bring you into a greater realm of blessing.

7g. "This too shall pass."

8a. The forever lie and the never lie.

8b. Because sooner or later, everything changes.

8c. Bad things ultimately give way to better things.

8d. No. We might go through another hard time, but eventually through Christ, the difficulty will be changed into even better times than the ones we had previously.

8e. Then you won't be ready for the changes that surely will come.

8f. Keep our eyes on Him; make it through; growing from glory to glory.

8g. We are not to get too wrapped up in anything in this life.

8h. To the Lord alone and not to anyone or anything else.

8i. Think we could not live without it.

8j. "Get detached from your attachments."

8k. Stewards; owners.

8l. We must always be free to move with the Spirit.

8m. Let it go.

8n. We try to hang on to the past, when God is saying, "It's time to move on to something new."

8o. Let it go. Look to the new thing and allow it to "come to pass." Don't live in the past when God has a new season for you. Let go of what lies behind and press on to what lies ahead.

8p. Reach out toward that new horizon God has for you. That's what Abraham did — and God blessed him for it.

9a. To leave his country, his home, and his relatives and go to a place He would show him.

9b. It had "come to pass," and it was time for her to move on to something else.

9c. No, it just means God was finished with that season in her life.

9d. Do what He wants to do in each of those seasons.

9e. Because everything is changing all the time, and so must we.

9f. "This too shall pass."

9g. God and His will and plan for us.

10a. Because if our outer man has things broken off, the powerful things inside us can pour forth.

10b. The alabaster box, which is the flesh, has to be broken.

10c. We must allow God to deal with us and do with us as He wills. We must learn to lean on Him and trust in Him completely, knowing that everything in life changes.

10d. This was done to keep him from becoming too proud by reminding him, "This too shall pass."

10e. He gives us His Holy Spirit to fill us and empower us and use us as a blessing to others. But He also sends His Holy Spirit to remind us that "this too shall pass."

10f. We must quit looking for one thing that will be "it." We must recall that life is a continual process in which everything is constantly changing — including us.

10g. He is the only thing in this world Who does not change. He is the same yesterday, today, and forever.

11a. Maturity.

11b. To come to the place that we can be content no matter what our situation or circumstances may be, because we are rooted and grounded, not in things, but in the Lord.

11c. Because he knew whatever state he may be in at the moment, it too would pass.

11d. He said he had learned the secret of facing every situation of life, whether good or bad.

11e. We would soon become soft and spoiled. We would assume anybody who was not being blessed as much as we were was doing something wrong. We would try to give that individual "victory lessons."

11f. Spiritual pride.

11g. How to handle new realms of blessings without developing a wrong attitude.

11h. God allows that to happen occasionally so we will learn to keep things in perspective.

11i. We get spoiled and prideful.

11j. We become discouraged and despondent.

11k. "This too shall pass."

11l. Nothing — good or bad — lasts forever.

12a. Walked through.

12b. We are just passing through. Whatever may be happening to us at the moment, in time it too shall pass.

12c. How fast things can change.

12d. "Wrong! Things may be this way right now, but whether they change or not makes no difference to me — I'm just passing through!"

12e. "When you pass through the waters, I will be with you, and through the rivers, they will not overwhelm you. When you walk through the fire, you will not be burned or scorched, nor will the flame kindle upon you."

12f. Because they trusted themselves to the Lord, they didn't stay there to be consumed by the flames. They came through them to victory.

12g. Daniel came through that experience unharmed.

12h. The same kind of protection and deliverance to all those who put their faith and trust in Him.

13a. That we will never change.

13b. That as we behold the glory of God we ". . . are changed into the same image from glory to glory, even as by the Spirit of the Lord."

13c. A complete change from one thing to something totally different, as when a caterpillar enters a cocoon as a worm and later emerges as a butterfly.[3]

13d. It is the kind of process we are going through spiritually, as we change from the old man to the new man.

13e. "No, I'm not. I'm in the process of change. I won't be a worm forever, you just wait and see. One day I'll be something totally different from what I am right now. I'll be a beautiful butterfly!"

13f. We would never develop the strength and stamina we need to survive in this world.

13g. "Suddenlies."

14a. A "season of suddenlies."

14b. "In a moment, in the twinkling of an eye" — in other words, suddenly.

14c. Because no matter what remains to be done in the transformation of our old man into our new man, it will be accomplished suddenly — at the appearing of Jesus in the heavenlies.

14d. Changing us from glory to glory; remains to be changed in us; suddenly.

14e. Just as suddenly.

14f. Supernaturally; ordinarily; suddenly; over a period of time.

14g. How Jesus appeared to Paul and changed him from a persecutor of the Church to a brand-new convert who would later become the leading apostle to the Gentiles.

14h. If God could suddenly confront and change Paul, He can confront and change anybody.

14i. Because sometimes God works suddenly, and sometimes He works over a period of time.

14j. He works in response to prayer and praise.

14k. In a supernatural way or in an ordinary way. But He is moving on your behalf.

14l. Cast it all on the Lord so you can retire from care.

Chapter 9

1a. Giving ourselves up to God, taking ourselves out of our own keeping, and entrusting ourselves into His keeping.

1b. Self-care.

1c. Basically, it stems from the idea that if we do it, we can be sure it will be done right. We are afraid of what might happen if we entrust ourselves totally to God and He doesn't "come through" for us.

1d. Trusting ourselves more than we trust God.

1e. God has a plan for us too — and His plan is much better than ours.

2a. God wants to help us, but He wants to do it His way and not our way — because our way usually involves a lot of worry, fretfulness, reasoning, anxiety, and excessive plotting and planning.

2b. To hear God's plan.

2c. Become so rooted and grounded in our plan that we argue and resist if God tries to show us a better way.

2d. That she would never enjoy her life until she began trusting God to a much greater degree.

2e. Because He knows that apart from Him we can do nothing.

2f. In everything that concerns us, God has a plan, just as He did for Jesus when He sent Him into this world to save us and to serve as our example.

3a. Consulted God. The will of His Father. It was not His decision. It was the will of the One Who Sent Him.

3b. He was not independent, out on His own trying to do His own thing.

3c. We figure out what we want and ask God to bless it.

3d. To do the will and pleasure of His heavenly Father.

3e. "What you see Me doing is what I see the Father doing. What you hear Me saying is what I hear the Father saying. I do not speak on My own authority, but on His authority."

3f. We should realize that anything we do independently, apart from God, will fail to bear any good fruit either for Him or for us.

4a. Knows what will truly bless us and make us happy and orders our steps to bring us into what He has for us.

4b. They plan everything according to what they think is the best plan for them.

4c. To seek God's will and plan for our life rather than our own.

4d. Go off independently on our own trying to fulfill our own desires or meet our own needs.

4e. Trust in the Lord with all our heart and mind, and not lean on our own understanding.

5a. No, that would not be possible.

5b. God puts wisdom into us in the form of His Holy Spirit, for us to walk by that wisdom step-by-step.

5c. Know, recognize, and acknowledge. His Spirit; quiet confidence, trust, and obedience.

5d. To be aware of and care about what we are doing.

5e. Because He will direct our paths.

5f. He will nudge us and get us back on the right path.

5g. Insulting; consulting; what we want.

5h. It displays a lack of trust in God.

5i. Because we don't want to become dependent upon anyone.

5j. So we will have to work together to accomplish His will in our lives.

5k. Get involved with other people.

5l. So we have no choice but to lean on Him and on others.

5m. He acknowledged that he and his people had no might to stand against such a great company, adding, "We don't know what to do, Lord, but our eyes are on You."

5n. That is the statement of a person who is dependent on God, not independent.

6a. Anointing.

6b. So that all the glory will go to Him and not to them.

6c. God either calls people with talent then spends years teaching them that without His anointing their talents will do them absolutely no good, or He calls people who are so incapable they know the only way they can ever hope to do anything is by leaning totally on Him every second.

6d. The first disciples Jesus called.

6e. That they were all losers and that He would get nowhere with them because they would never be of any value to Him.

6f. So He can use them to confound the wise and powerful.

6g. Zeros; power; great for His glory.

6h. Because if we do we will fail every time.

6i. Recognize and acknowledge our utter dependence on God.

6j. We have learned through bitter experience nobody in this world is going to look out for us or have our best interests at heart but us.

6k. Keeping total control over every aspect of your life.

6l. Almost impossible to do so.

6m. Your refusal to cast your care upon the Lord and entrust yourself to His keeping.

7a. Upon those rebellious children who turn from trusting in Him to take counsel of themselves, carry out their own plans, and flee to "the shadow of Egypt" rather than resting under the "shadow of the Almighty."

7b. Turning to the arm of the flesh rather than leaning on the arm of the Lord.

7c. The Lord.

7d. Acknowledge the Lord in all our ways so that He may direct our paths.

7e. Him; ourselves; the world.

8a. "Don't turn away from trusting in Me to trusting in your own plans and devices. They won't work, and you will only end up humiliated and confused."

8b. "Before you do anything, check with Me to see if it is what you should be doing. Don't look to the world for answers, because it has none to give. Salvation and deliverance are with Me, and Me alone."

9a. We leave a weak spot in our wall of divine protection.

9b. The enemy will break through that weak spot.

9c. He wants us to rely on Him and be obedient to Him so our wall will remain strong and thick and our lives will be blessed and full.

9d. He can do through us. Brokenness; blessings.

9e. Remind us of our place.

9f. The solution to our problems is found in Him and Him alone.

10a. "Either you are going to depend on Me, or you are going to end up in the biggest mess you have ever seen in your whole life."

10b. If we don't, we will not be able to do anything of any value. Apart from Him we can do nothing.

11a. That he had run his own life for a long time — often walking according to emotions and his own will — but now it was time to grow up. It was time to turn the reins of his life over to God.

11b. That he might not like everything that was going to happen, but that it would ultimately end up for the glory of God.

11c. He blessed our plans and let them work.

11d. God no longer blesses and prospers our childish plans and schemes.

11e. He has begun establishing His way in our individual lives.

11f. To put our trust in Him and not in ourselves.

11g. He knew Peter's love was about to be put to the test.

11h. No, He is just asking us to lay it on the altar, as Abraham lay Isaac on the altar before the Lord.

11i. Because we must not let anything — even our work for God — become more important to us than God Himself.

11j. By asking us to lay down our most treasured blessing as proof of our love for Him.

11k. He will begin to honor us and work out His plan for our life.

11l. Because of his tendency to give into the flesh.

11m. He told Peter He was praying for him — just as He is praying for us right now.

12a. Peter's faith would not fail him while he was going through that time of testing.

12b. He is praying we will come through the times of testing in our lives and emerge from them strengthened and empowered so that we can strengthen and empower others to live in joy, peace, and victory.

12c. Face the enemy.

12d. He may not always do everything exactly as we would like it done or just when we would like it to be done. But whatever He does do will be right, the thing that is best in that situation.

13a. "I am sending you out to do a job for Me, but don't take anything with you to take care of yourselves."

13b. The point is not that we are forbidden to take pocketbooks and shoes and clothes with us when we travel from one place to another to minister. The point is that we are to be obedient to do the will of God, trusting Him to meet the needs He knows we will experience.

13c. Make the arrangements necessary to keep us provisioned.

13d. If we will tend to His harvest, He will tend to our needs.

14a. They didn't go out seeking gifts.

14b. Because they were in the middle of God's will, He sent them Wise Men from the east mounted on camels loaded down with provisions.

14c. If we are in the will of God, He will always bring our provision to us. We don't have to chase it down; it will seek us out. We don't have to try to make things happen; God will bring them to us.

14d. We need to back off and consult the Lord. That may not be the way God wants us to go.

14e. So we will be open to follow another.

14f. Just keep confessing, "The camels are coming!" And eventually they will arrive — on God's schedule, not ours.

14g. Stay in the will of God.

14h. Being faithful to stay where God has placed us and do the work He has given us to do for His Kingdom's sake.

14i. We are free to cast our care upon Him. We don't have to stay up all night fretting and worrying, trying to figure out what to do to take care of ourselves. We can simply deposit ourselves with God.

15a. Deposit ourselves with God, trusting Him to take care of us.

15b. When we are being ill-treated and are suffering because we belong to God and are doing right, being faithful to His will for us.

15c. We must quit trying to seek justice for ourselves and simply trust Him to justify us and work out everything for the best in accordance with His will and plan. That's what Jesus did.

15d. Jesus did not respond in kind. Instead, He trusted Himself entirely to God Who judges all things and all people fairly and justly.

15e. Like Him, we are not to try to take matters into our own hands, but instead to commit ourselves to God, trusting Him to work out everything for good to all concerned.

15f. We spend so much time trying to take care of ourselves. We are too busy with self-care, trying to make sure that nobody takes advantage of us, that everyone treats us right, that we get our fair share.

15g. We will fail to do what we are called to do, which is to minister to the needs of others.

15h. We must continue to do the work God has set before us. We must deposit ourselves with Him, trusting Him to justify us and vindicate us, to protect us and provide for us, to help us and keep us.

16a. A beautiful hymn about God as the Helper and Keeper of those who trust in Him.

16b. Read and meditate on it constantly.

16c. By the eyelid. The moment danger threatens, the eyelid automatically closes, shutting out anything harmful. That is what God does for us who entrust ourselves to Him.

17a. ". . . He is the rewarder of those who earnestly and diligently seek Him [out]."

17b. Rewards; recompenses.

17c. A back pay, sort of like Workers' Compensation.

18a. He means that sooner or later He will make everything right. He will see we get everything coming to us.

18b. Pray for our enemies, for those who mistreat us, abuse us, and take advantage of us.

18c. To take care of us.

18d. He determines and solves and settles the cause and the cases of His people.

18e. With Jesus as our Friend, the Holy Spirit as our Advocate, and the heavenly Father as our Judge, we can retire from self-care, knowing that justice will be done — so that we can be anxious for nothing.

Endnotes

Introduction

[1] Romans 8:28.

Chapter 2

[1] *Webster's II New Riverside Desk Dictionary* (Boston: Houghton Mifflin Company, 1988), s.v. "anxiety."

[2] *Webster's New World College Dictionary,* 3rd ed. (New York: Macmillan, 1996), s.v. "anxiety."

Chapter 6

[1] James E. Strong, "Hebrew and Chaldee Dictionary," in *Strong's Exhaustive Concordance of the Bible* (Nashville: Abingdon, 1890), p. 52, entry #3427, s.v. "dwell," Psalm 91:1.

Chapter 7

[1] Based on definitions from W.E. Vine, Merrill F. Unger, William White Jr., *Vine's Complete Expository Dictionary of Old and New Testament Words* (Nashville: Thomas Nelson, Inc., 1984), "New Testament Section," p. 91, s.v. "CAST," A. Verbs.

[2] Vine, p. 89, s.v. "CARE (noun and verb), CAREFUL, CAREFULLY, CAREFULNESS," A. Nouns, 1.

[3] Footnote to 1 Peter 5:8 written by A.S. Worrell in *The Worrell New Testament* (Springfield, MO: Gospel Publishing House, 1980), p. 352.

[4] Footnote to 1 Peter 5:8 written by A.S. Worrell in *The Worrell New Testament* (Springfield, MO: Gospel Publishing House, 1980), p. 352.

[5] Footnote to 1 Peter 5:8 written by A.S. Worrell in *The Worrell New Testament* (Springfield, MO: Gospel Publishing House, 1980), p. 352.

Chapter 8

[1] Tingay and Badcock, *These Were the Romans* (Chester Springs, PA: Dufour Editions, Inc., 1989).

[2] James E. Strong, "Greek Dictionary of the New Testament," in *Strong's Exhaustive Concordance of the Bible* (Nashville: Abingdon, 1890), p. 47, entry #3339, s.v. "change," 2 Corinthians 3:18.

[3] Based on definition in Webster's 3d, s.v. "metamorphosis": "a marked or complete change of character, appearance, condition, etc."; "the physical transformation, more or less sudden, undergone by various animals during development after the embryonic state. . . ."

Do you have a real relationship with Jesus?

God loves you! He created you to be a special, unique, one-of-a-kind individual, and He has a specific purpose and plan for your life. And through a personal relationship with your Creator—God—you can discover a way of life that will truly satisfy your soul.

No matter who you are, what you've done, or where you are in your life right now, God's love and grace are greater than your sin—your mistakes. Jesus willingly gave His life so you can receive forgiveness from God and have new life in Him. He's just waiting for you to invite Him to be your Savior and Lord.

If you are ready to commit your life to Jesus and follow Him, all you have to do is ask Him to forgive your sins and give you a fresh start in the life you are meant to live. Begin by praying this prayer...

> *Lord Jesus, thank You for giving Your life for me and forgiving me of my sins so I can have a personal relationship with You. I am sincerely sorry for the mistakes I've made, and I know I need You to help me live right.*
>
> *Your Word says in Romans 10:9, "If you declare with your mouth, 'Jesus is Lord,' and believe in your heart that God raised him from the dead, you will be saved" (NIV). I believe You are the Son of God and confess You as my Savior and Lord. Take me just as I am, and work in my heart, making me the person You want me to be. I want to live for You, Jesus, and I am so grateful that You are giving me a fresh start in my new life with You today.*
>
> *I love You, Jesus!*

It's so amazing to know that God loves us so much! He wants to have a deep, intimate relationship with us that grows every day as we spend time with Him in prayer and Bible study. And we want to encourage you in your new life in Christ.

Please visit joycemeyer.org/salvation to request Joyce's book *A New Way of Living*, which is our gift to you. We also have other free resources online to help you make progress in pursuing everything God has for you.

Congratulations on your fresh start in your life in Christ! We hope to hear from you soon.

About the Author

JOYCE MEYER is one of the world's leading practical Bible teachers. Her daily broadcast, *Enjoying Everyday Life*, airs on hundreds of television networks and radio stations worldwide.

Joyce has written more than one hundred inspirational books. Her bestsellers include *Power Thoughts*; *The Confident Woman*; *Look Great, Feel Great*; *Starting Your Day Right*; *Ending Your Day Right*; *Approval Addiction*; *How to Hear from God*; *Beauty for Ashes*; and *Battlefield of the Mind*.

Joyce travels extensively, holding conferences throughout the year and speaking to thousands around the world.

JOYCE MEYER MINISTRIES

U.S. & FOREIGN OFFICE ADDRESSES

Joyce Meyer Ministries
P.O. Box 655
Fenton, MO 63026
USA
(636) 349-0303

Joyce Meyer Ministries—Canada
P.O. Box 7700
Vancouver, BC V6B 4E2
Canada
(800) 868-1002

Joyce Meyer Ministries—Australia
Locked Bag 77
Mansfield Delivery Centre
Queensland 4122
Australia
(07) 3349 1200

Joyce Meyer Ministries—England
P.O. Box 1549
Windsor SL4 1GT
United Kingdom
01753 831102

Joyce Meyer Ministries—South Africa
P.O. Box 5
Cape Town 8000
South Africa
(27) 21-701-1056

Other Books by Joyce Meyer

Straight Talk

Teenagers Are People Too!

Trusting God Day by Day

The Word, the Name, the Blood

Woman to Woman

You Can Begin Again

Joyce Meyer Spanish Titles

Belleza en Lugar de Cenizas (Beauty for Ashes)

Buena Salud, Buena Vida (Good Health, Good Life)

Cambia Tus Palabras, Cambia Tu Vida (Change Your Words, Change Your Life)

El Campo de Batalla de la Mente (Battlefield of the Mind)

*Como Formar Buenos Habitos y Romper Malos Habitos
(Making Good Habits, Breaking Bad Habits)*

La Conexión de la Mente (The Mind Connection)

Dios No Está Enojado Contigo (God Is Not Mad at You)

La Dosis de Aprobación (The Approval Fix)

Empezando Tu Día Bien (Starting Your Day Right)

Hazte Un Favor a Ti Mismo ... Perdona (Do Yourself a Favor ... Forgive)

Madre Segura de sí Misma (The Confident Mom)

Palabras de Poder (Power Words)

Pensamientos de Poder (Power Thoughts)

Sobrecarga (Overload)

Termina Bien tu Día (Ending Your Day Right)

Usted Puede Comenzar de Nuevo (You Can Begin Again)

¡Viva con Esperanza! (Get Your Hopes Up!)

Viva Valientemente (Living Courageously)

* Study Guide available for this title

Books by Dave Meyer

Life Lines